GOING
PUBLIC

GOING PUBLIC

HOW SILICON VALLEY REBELS LOOSENED WALL STREET'S GRIP ON THE IPO AND SPARKED A REVOLUTION

■ ■ ■ ■ ■ ■ ■ ■ ■ ■ ■ ■

DAKIN CAMPBELL

TWELVE

NEW YORK   BOSTON

Twelve

Hachette Book Group
1290 Avenue of the Americas,
New York, NY 10104

twelvebooks.com

twitter.com/twelvebooks

First Edition: July 2022

Twelve is an imprint of Grand Central Publishing. The Twelve name and logo are trademarks of Hachette Book Group, Inc.

The publisher is not responsible for websites (or their content) that are not owned by the publisher.

The Hachette Speakers Bureau provides a wide range of authors for speaking events. To find out more, go to www.hachettespeakersbureau.com or call (866) 376-6591.

Library of Congress Control Number: 2021952135

ISBNs: 978-1-5387-0788-3 (hardcover), 978-1-5387-0790-6 (ebook)

Printed in the United States of America

LSC-C

Printing 1, 2022

To my wife and children, for their unwavering love and support

Author's note

I first started thinking critically about IPOs during the summer of 2019 as the real estate startup WeWork prepared to sell shares to the public. A financial writer for more than a decade, I had a passing knowledge of how investment banks worked with private companies entering the public markets for the first time. It wasn't until my editors at Insider scrambled a team of reporters to dig into what was happening at WeWork that I got my first good look at the process.

I soon learned that startup founders, venture capitalists, and even some bankers had been raising questions for years about how IPOs were being handled. By the time of WeWork's planned offering, Spotify and Slack had already chosen an alternative approach to listing their shares. Venture capitalist Bill Gurley was loudly banging his drum for other startups to follow suit. Change was in the air.

That didn't make it any easier to understand what was really happening. IPOs were a world within a world, a corner of Wall Street made up of its own characters, customs, and regulations that was nearly as hard to pull apart as the mortgage bonds that sparked the global financial crisis. As WeWork's listing quickly slid off the rails, I set out to learn as much as I could.

I devoured news reports, perused research papers, and sought out startup executives, investors, bankers, and lawyers. By the time I was done, I'd spoken to roughly 75 people over more than 150 interviews. Some of those agreed to speak on the record, many of them with the belief that their comments would help readers to understand and appreciate their perspective, and their voices are reflected in the text.

Most of them, however, asked for anonymity to describe private conversations. I have tried to verify their accounts from other sources who were in the room, news reports, official documents or government filings, text messages, videos, or PowerPoint slides, to name just some of the resources I relied upon. In a few cases, recollections contradict one another. I have been thoughtful about coming to an accurate version of events. A reader shouldn't assume that someone spoke to me just because I describe that person's thinking. In numerous cases, I reconstructed what an individual thought by speaking to others who spoke to them directly or were otherwise in a position to know.

Throughout the book, I have avoided adding unnecessary analysis to the text. My hope is that the reader will come to his or her own conclusion based on how the narrative unfolds and the specific details of each transaction. I readily acknowledge that there is a fierce debate swirling around the current IPO process and the importance of various actors such as investment banks to the process. This book won't settle that debate, but I hope it can add to the dialogue by bringing readers into the rooms where big decisions are being made.

I hope you leave this book with a richer and more nuanced understanding of IPOs, how Wall Street and Silicon Valley are jockeying for supremacy over the process, and what it would mean to most efficiently funnel capital to the companies doing the most to drive economic innovation.

Last, I hope you like reading the story as much as I enjoyed discovering it. Thanks for reading.

Dakin Campbell
April 2022

GOING
PUBLIC

PROLOGUE

Apple Computer, Cupertino, 1980

On a mild December day in 1980, Steve Jobs made his way across San Francisco to an office building that rose above the city's financial district. Passing through the terra-cotta archways that gave the facade a neo-Gothic look, Jobs sought out the office of Hambrecht & Quist (H&Q), a small investment bank with offices on an upper floor.

Jobs was the CEO of Apple Computer, a leader in what was then the budding business of making desktop computers. Apple's revenue had climbed past $117 million during the fiscal year that had ended in September, more than the entire industry's haul just three years earlier.

For months, Jobs had been preparing Apple for its initial public offering, the first sale of stock to mutual funds and other public investors. The CEO had come to the landmark Russ Building for one of Apple's last acts as a private company: negotiating with his bankers over the price of the shares Apple would sell.

Months earlier, Jobs had selected Morgan Stanley and Hambrecht & Quist to manage Apple's IPO. Hambrecht & Quist was an early investor in Apple. Jobs was showing loyalty to an early backer by insisting on the location even though Morgan Stanley was larger and more powerful.

As a former computer hacker known for wearing ripped denim jeans and tie-dyed t-shirts, Jobs arrived casually dressed. He joined a group of bankers in suits and ties gathered around a couch in a large office that belonged to George Quist, whose name was on the door. The other named partner, William Hambrecht, was also there, alongside the team from Morgan Stanley.

Jobs and his bankers had been holding weeks of meetings in what was known as a roadshow, talking to investors about their interest in Apple shares. The bankers initially thought to sell shares at $14, but as the investor conversations continued and orders poured in, they realized they could increase Apple's share price without sacrificing investor interest. The question was by how much.

The Morgan Stanley bankers walked Jobs through the investor orders, collected in something known as an order book. As they did, Hambrecht later recalled, Morgan Stanley recommended a price of $18.

Jobs sat there silently and listened. He spoke when the bankers were finished.

"Now, you're telling me that you want to sell the stock at eighteen dollars a share?" Jobs said.

"Yes, that's our recommendation," came the answer.

"You know," Jobs said, "some people have told me they think it might open up maybe as high as twenty-seven or twenty-eight."

Jobs was referring to the price that he thought Apple shares would fetch when they began trading on the stock exchange. He knew that Apple wouldn't directly benefit when its stock price rose—the company would have already sold its stock and collected the proceeds. For that reason, he was interested in capturing as much of the price gain as possible in this meeting, when it would mean more money in Apple's accounts.

Morgan Stanley's bankers told Jobs that they would try to minimize any surge in the stock price, but that they couldn't make any guarantees. One of them eventually admitted that the price could rise quickly, or pop, on the first day. "That is a strong possibility," the banker said.

"Tell me, who will you sell this stock to at eighteen dollars?" Jobs asked. "That'll go to your best clients, won't it?"

The comment left the bankers momentarily speechless. Then they rushed to answer Jobs's question. "Yes," one of them said, "our clients will get a chance to own some stock at eighteen."

The Morgan Stanley bankers explained that they were great clients and would hold the stock for a long time, providing Apple with a stable base of loyal shareholders it could rely on as it navigated the home computer industry.

Jobs looked at them. "Won't they be terribly happy that they bought stock at eighteen that's now selling at twenty-eight? And won't they give you a lot more brokerage business?"

The Morgan Stanley bankers were quiet.

"And then you're going to charge me an 8 percent fee to do it?" Jobs asked. The CEO wasn't being confrontational so much as he was asking simple questions.

In a few short minutes, Jobs had exposed the perverse incentives at the heart of the IPO, a centuries-old process used by companies to raise money from public investors by listing their shares on an exchange. Investment banks sat in the middle, and Morgan Stanley and Hambrecht & Quist owed their loyalty not just to Apple but to the investors who would be buying the stock in the IPO.

Apple and the investors both paid the banks, but in different ways. Apple had agreed to pay them a percentage of the IPO proceeds, and the investors paid indirectly, through trading fees or brokerage commissions. It was known as "dual agency" and was frequently discouraged in the real estate market when brokers represented both buyers and sellers.

From the beginning, Jobs had been skeptical of the institutional bearing of the Morgan Stanley bankers, a bunch of suits with divided loyalties. Now that skepticism was boiling over.

At his insistence, Apple's bankers finally decided to price Apple's 4.6 million shares at $22.

"He was the first guy that I ran into that had really figured out what the IPO process was like," Hambrecht said later. "I went out of there thinking, 'Boy, that guy really has figured it out.'"

Apple's stock quickly rose above $29 when it started trading on December 12, before leveling off to finish at $28.75. It represented a 31 percent gain. The *San Francisco Examiner* marked the event with a front-page story in the afternoon edition. Under a headline that read, in part, "Wall St. gets bite of Apple," the newspaper played up the offering's success. "Wall Street gave Apple Computer Inc. a warm—not hot—reception in its first public stock offering today," the story ran. "According to analysts, that was nearly a perfect launch for the stock in the Cupertino-based maker of personal computers."

Apple's IPO heralded its arrival into the scrum of the world's financial markets, where companies go to raise money by selling stocks and bonds to professional, and amateur, investors. Few are as important as the IPO market, where shares are sold for the first time.

For years after Apple's offering, the IPO market stayed largely unchanged. A pattern began to emerge in the technology industry, as hardware and software companies became a larger part of the economy and attracted a broader swath of investors. The shares of the most popular companies, those providing industry-disrupting technology or access to an expanding internet, soared high above the IPO price when they began trading. Investors receiving the shares in the IPO enjoyed near-instant profits. And startup entrepreneurs wondered if they could have gotten a higher price.

Reformers tried repeatedly to fashion something different. Inspired by Jobs's insight from 1980 and a belief that there was a better way to calculate an IPO price, Hambrecht struck out on his own in the late 1990s. He set up a new company called WR Hambrecht + Co. and designed a modified Dutch auction to sell shares. Hambrecht's OpenIPO, as he called it, collected bids in secret and auctioned off shares starting at the highest price and moving lower until the entire offering was sold. Then all buyers paid that lower price. It was used by nearly two dozen relatively small companies to go public over the following few years. Hambrecht struggled to attract widespread acceptance amid skepticism from larger companies and pushback from investment banks that enjoyed handsome fees and wielded immense power within the established system.

When the search giant Google was ready to go public a few years later, cofounders Sergey Brin and Larry Page thought they might try their hand at IPO disruption. They sought out Hambrecht's advice, and though he stayed involved, they forged their own path with a modified auction structure. But when Google had to slash its share price to get the deal done, critics had all the ammunition they needed to bad-mouth the new approach and persuade entrepreneurs to stick with conventional wisdom.

If either Hambrecht or Google had found success, it could have ushered in the largest change to the IPO market in decades, presaging a new era in how technology companies raised money to fund innovation: a radical restructuring of the power dynamics that existed among the venture capitalists that fund startups' early growth, the public investors who later fund it, and the investment banks standing in the middle. Instead, the system remained largely unchanged.

In 2018, a promise of wide-scale innovation again visited the IPO market when Barry McCarthy, the CFO of music streaming service Spotify, succeeded in redesigning the process. Borrowing inspiration from earlier efforts, McCarthy worked with bankers, lawyers, and regulators to list Spotify's shares directly on the exchange, bypassing underwriters and fashioning a new role for investment banks that kept them at arm's length.

Far from being a flash in the pan like OpenIPO or Google's auction, McCarthy's creation caught fire. Nearly a dozen large technology firms have now directly listed their shares on an exchange. Dozens more executives, such as those at video gaming software company Unity and food delivery app DoorDash, considered a direct listing before deciding to disrupt aspects of the traditional IPO process itself.

Unity introduced auction-like features inspired by Google's offering, while DoorDash did away with something called a greenshoe, an agreement that gave banks the option to buy more shares at the IPO price. It acted as insurance for companies but often simply delivered more profits to banks. Other startups challenged the traditional six-month period in which company insiders were forbidden to sell shares.

It didn't stop there. Inspired by the innovation of the direct listing, businessmen and investors dusted off a little-used technique to raise money from investors and use it to buy other companies. Known as blank check companies, their growing acceptance provided firms yet another way of accessing the public markets.

Along the way, innovative entrepreneurs received cover from vocal venture capitalists, such as Benchmark's Bill Gurley, one of the world's most successful technology investors, and independent advisors like Lise Buyer, a veteran of Google's offering who dispenses IPO advice from an independent advisory firm.

In taking on the status quo, this collection of startup executives, investors, and advisors upended a system embedded with powerful financial incentives. In 2020, investment banks earned $1.8 billion in fees for underwriting $38.7 billion in technology IPOs, or almost 5 percent of the money raised, according to Dealogic. The 2021 figures through mid-November for fees and proceeds, the amount brought in by companies selling shares for the first time, were roughly double those amounts.

Finally, the revolution that Bill Hambrecht and others tried to start in the late 1990s appears to be taking hold. As it does, some of the financial markets' most powerful players may see their roles dramatically altered. To understand how the change came about and where things are going, it's important to explore the challenges and choices faced by the pioneers who dared to challenge the status quo.

This is their story.

CHAPTER 1

Ford Motor, Detroit, 1956

WHEN Bill Hambrecht visited a small electronics manufacturer in San Carlos in 1967, Silicon Valley was a very different place than it is today.

An energetic man who played football at Princeton, Hambrecht was head of West Coast corporate finance for Francis I. duPont & Co., one of the country's largest brokerage firms and investment banks. Hambrecht had gotten his job on the West Coast because he was one of the few duPont bankers with technology experience. He had spent three years in central Florida arranging financing for defense technology and missile systems companies around Cape Canaveral.

Silicon Valley's technology industry was then dominated by larger companies. Big government contractors. Lockheed had a big presence out at Moffett Field. Hewlett-Packard Co. started in a Palo Alto garage in 1938 and had grown by selling products to the government during World War II and the Korean War. It was a world in which it was still considered difficult to start a new company. Small players weren't always taken seriously.

So when Hambrecht's boss at duPont asked him to visit Farinon Electric, a small firm that was bringing in several million dollars a year in revenue, Hambrecht was initially resistant. He thought it would be a waste of time. Nonetheless, he drove out to San Carlos and introduced himself to Bill Farinon, the company's founder. Farinon, whose firm manufactured microwave equipment used for voice communications, had successfully discovered how to sell into the notoriously closed Bell System. The collection of concerns led by Bell Telephone Company dominated the continent's telephone networks.

After the two men had spent the better part of a day together, Farinon told Hambrecht that his father-in-law, who had put up most of the capital to get him started, wanted his money back. Farinon was thinking about an IPO. He didn't want to have to sell the company to come up with the money.

"You're really too small," Hambrecht recalled telling Farinon. The banker listed several rules then used by Wall Street to judge whether companies were ready to go public. At the very least, they needed five years of earnings and roughly $1 million in after-tax profit.

"Who made up those rules?" Farinon asked.

"I don't know," Hambrecht answered. "They are the rules."

The founder raised his voice. "Those goddamn rules," Farinon said. "They were set up for you guys! So you could make a lot of money. They have nothing to do with me. How about looking at this from my point of view. I want my company to stay independent. I need some money."

As Hambrecht was leaving, Farinon tried again. "Do you think I have a good company here?"

"Oh yes," Hambrecht answered. "I think you really do."

"Would you put in some of your own money?"

"Absolutely, I would love to buy stock," Hambrecht said. "I don't have very much money," he told Farinon. But Farinon had something good.

"If you're willing to buy stock for yourself, why aren't you willing to sell it to the public?" Farinon demanded.

Hambrecht didn't have a good answer. The following year, Farinon sold shares to the public for the first time in an IPO led by White, Weld & Co., one of duPont's fiercest competitors.

Farinon's parting question nagged at Hambrecht.

■   ■   ■

Not long after his visit to San Carlos, Hambrecht received word that he was in line for a job that would require him to move back east, where duPont was headquartered. It wasn't the kind of opportunity that you turned down. But Hambrecht and his wife had come to enjoy living in California. If they were to stay in California, Hambrecht knew he would have to find a new firm to work for.

The dilemma was fresh in his mind when he heard about a promising technology company down the coast in San Diego. Hambrecht had befriended a banker with an outsized personality named George Quist. Quist ran Bank of America's small business investment company, or SBIC, a fund set up after the 1958 passage of legislation intended to spur investments in startups. Bank of America used its SBIC to buy up stakes in nascent microwave and semiconductor companies. Hambrecht and Quist had already done a couple of deals together, and now Hambrecht asked his friend to join him on a trip to San Diego to visit the technology company. The gregarious banker soon agreed, and the two men booked a flight to Southern California for the sole purpose of looking into the company.

They arrived and visited the technology company, then went to the Kona Kai Club, a resort on a spit of land in San Diego Bay where they were staying before heading back the following day. Over scotch and not much food, Hambrecht told Quist about his opportunity at duPont. Did Quist know any firms that might be hiring?

Quist was looking for something new to do too. A CPA by training, he'd run a company that merged into Ampex, one of the early stars of the emerging technology industry. He followed a college friend to Bank of America and managed a portfolio of more than fifty companies. By the time of the San Diego trip, Quist was restless.

As the two men got deeper into their scotch and the night lengthened, they agreed that there wasn't a firm doing what they wanted to do. Davis & Rock and Sutter Hill, two early venture capital firms, had formed just a few years before to make investments in promising technology companies. But no one was merging venture capital and investment banking—investing in startups and then supporting their public offerings as an underwriter once they'd grown big enough to attract public market investors.

It still seemed like a good idea the next day, and they sketched out a business plan on the flight home. The men thought that if they could find and invest in five new startups, they could establish a strong franchise. They soon raised $1 million from other investors.

"We got together and decided that if we could become not only a venture capital company but an investment bank," Hambrecht later said, "we would be a welcome addition to the other venture capital firms on the peninsula."

In 1968, they formed Hambrecht & Quist, focusing entirely on the technology industry. Farinon's parting comment "really stuck with me," Hambrecht later said. "That became the mantra at Hambrecht & Quist…became the quality screen for us. If we'd put our own money in it, we'd take it public."

◼ ◼ ◼

Hambrecht & Quist stepped into an IPO market steeped in rich history.

Investors had traded stakes in government projects or private enterprises for hundreds, if not thousands, of years. The Romans had *partes*, thought to have been used to finance public projects. The Dutch listed shares of the Dutch East India Company in the early 1600s and used the money to finance trading expeditions to faraway lands. Holland became a formidable center of trade in part because its relatively well-developed financial markets allowed businessmen to raise money for speculative endeavors.

Across the Atlantic, the first American public offering took place soon after the new country gained its independence. In 1781, the Bank of North America set out to sell 1,000 shares for $400 each. More than four months later it had only raised about $70,000. To ensure that the company would sell its shares and open for business, the United States government soaked up a majority of the shares. One early IPO investor was Benjamin Franklin, who purchased a single share to show support for what observers considered to be a critical step in the financial independence of the new nation. After its first year of operation, the bank paid out a dividend of almost 9 percent.

Over the next century, the capital needs of the companies developing the new nation's industrial might only grew. The Civil War brought about an industrial revolution that gained steam in the second half of the nineteenth century. Railroads, oil companies, and steel concerns financed themselves by selling shares. In the early days, the process was often cumbersome and localized to New York or other large cities. Companies would offer stock to individual investors gathered around small brokerage offices. As the companies grew larger, so too did their need for investors with deeper pockets. Investment bankers, who acted as middlemen connecting companies to wealthy investors, took on greater importance.

Bankers took active roles in advising companies and in many cases even sat on their board of directors. Jay Cooke, the Ohio-born financier, is largely credited with founding the nation's first modern investment bank. He helped finance the Union army's operations during the Civil War by selling more than $800 million in bonds to various investors. He did so by recruiting a ragtag sales force made up of insurance agents, real estate brokers, and even tavern owners. He used the new technology of the telegraph to confirm orders, and developed "working men's savings banks," offices that were open late and offered bonds in small increments. Cooke showed that investors across the country could be counted on to buy an offering if it was marketed correctly.

In the following decades, John Pierpont Morgan, the mustachioed banking scion, gained fame for leading a corporate consolidation wave. In 1907, when the Dow Jones Industrial Index slumped 37 percent, Morgan staved off a financial panic by convincing other wealthy financiers to prop up failing financial institutions and brokerage houses. During his career, Morgan played a role in forming and financing such well-known companies as U.S. Steel, International Harvester, and General Electric.

The passage of the Banking Act of 1933, known as the Glass-Steagall Act, prohibited banks that accepted deposits from engaging in the business of buying or selling stocks and bonds. The First National Bank of Boston was forced to spin off a securities arm that became known as First Boston Corp.

By the 1950s, after two world wars had required a prodigious capital-raising effort from the now mature nation, investment banking enjoyed a golden era. Hundreds of retail brokers operated from offices on Main Street in small-town America. Those offices formed a network that the brokerages used to sell stocks and bonds to individual retail investors in the communities where they were located. Their clients were largely businessmen, lawyers, and other wealthy individuals in those communities.

As the middle part of the decade approached, Ford Motor Co. considered selling shares for the first time. One of the largest U.S. companies of the era, Ford was private largely because Henry Ford was notoriously against selling shares to the public, which he saw as a form of indebtedness.

In the 1930s, Ford transitioned much of his family's shareholdings to a newly created nonprofit called the Ford Foundation so that he wouldn't have to pay taxes to the administration of Franklin Delano Roosevelt. Ford felt that FDR was leading the United States into a war that he couldn't support. Funded with nearly 90 percent of the automaker's shares, the foundation was instantly one of the largest philanthropies in the world.

All those shares, however, were largely worthless to the foundation unless it could sell them on the open market for cash that it could use for its philanthropic efforts. So in the 1950s, members of the family began looking for a way to take Ford public.

Goldman Sachs's Sidney Weinberg, known as "Mr. Wall Street" for his work ethic and financial acumen, had been a friend to the Ford family for years. Henry Ford had been a vocal anti-Semite and Weinberg, along with many of Goldman's bankers, was Jewish. But Weinberg grew close to Ford's son, Edsel, Edsel's wife, and Charlie Wilson, a close associate who was by then helping to run the Ford Foundation. After Edsel died, Wilson approached Edsel's son, Henry Ford II, about selling some of the foundation's shares to diversify its holdings. The son soon agreed, insisting that Weinberg and Goldman Sachs work on behalf of the family's automaker rather than for the foundation.

Weinberg planned the IPO in secret for nearly two years. The preparations revolved around a complex negotiation involving the competing demands of the Ford family, the foundation, the New York Stock Exchange, and the Internal Revenue Service. Weinberg ultimately came up with a scheme that satisfied the various parties and allowed the family to keep control of the automaker.

When it came time to sell the deal, Blyth & Co. Inc., a San Francisco–based investment bank, secured the lead banking role. Goldman Sachs was listed third on the company's IPO filing, after First Boston Corp. and before Kuhn, Loeb & Co.; Lehman Brothers; Merrill Lynch, Pierce, Fenner & Beane; and White, Weld & Co. The seven firms each agreed to purchase 308,000 shares and sell them off to their network of clients.

Below those seven, Ford's prospectus, the document that accounts for the bulk of a company's submission to register stock with securities officials, listed more than 200 other investment banks and brokers on the front cover. They were part of a syndicate of 722 investment banks and over 1,000 total firms that were in a group charged with selling small lots of shares to retail investors.

Companies required large syndicates, or groups of banks acting in concert, because most investment banks at the time were structured as private partnerships made up of capital contributed by the firm's senior bankers. That left them with limited funds to buy up large blocks of stock from industry titans like Ford.

Writing about the transaction at the time, the *New York Times* said that "probably never before in the history of the securities business has there been so much curiosity about the price at which a stock was to be placed on the market. And probably never before has the success of a public offering depended so little on the price. The underwriters say that the offering is sure to be oversubscribed by a wide margin."

The Ford IPO was the largest of all time, raising $658 million by offering 10.2 million shares at $64.50. (Ford paid $15 million in fees to the underwriters.) The stock closed at $70.50 that day, representing a modest 9.3 percent increase.

The following year, 1957, Blyth once again led a high-profile offering, managing the IPO for Hewlett-Packard, then a maker of electronic measuring equipment. (It wasn't until 1966 that the company began selling computers.)

"Wall Street in 1956 was a cottage industry," said Bruce Foerster, a former navy officer who joined the Street fifteen years later and struck up friendships with older bankers who worked on Ford's IPO. The industry's private partnerships were mostly small affairs, while some of the larger ones, including Goldman Sachs, didn't have large networks of individual investors that they could tap to buy a large stock or bond issue, Foerster said. "You needed all those firms."

■ ■ ■

By the 1970s, the financial markets had begun to change dramatically. On February 8, 1971, the National Association of Securities Dealers, a self-regulatory organization that came out of the Great Depression to oversee securities markets, activated its National Association of Broker Dealers Automated Quotation (NASDAQ) system.

Initially, NASDAQ focused on stocks of companies too small to qualify for trading on the New York Stock Exchange (NYSE). Those stocks traded in the over-the-counter market, where it was often difficult to learn share prices at a given moment in time. Acting as a central place to collect those prices, the NASDAQ started by offering prices on 2,500 securities. It was the world's first electronic stock market, and soon became the venue of choice for technology companies floating shares for the first time.

In October of that year, Intel listed on the NASDAQ by enlisting sixty-four underwriters to sell less than $10 million of shares. A maker of silicon computer chips, Intel was founded three years earlier by two former Fairfield Semiconductor engineers, Gordon Moore and Robert Noyce. More so than the Ford IPO, or the Hewlett-Packard IPO, which had happened years before the tech revolution took hold in Northern California, Intel's IPO marked the region's arrival on the national stage. Earlier that year, a writer for *Electronic News* christened the region "Silicon Valley."

Investors were also beginning to change. In 1975, 426 mutual funds controlled less than $46 billion in assets. But with the September 1974 passage of the Employee Retirement Income Security Act (ERISA), mutual funds and other asset managers began to control a larger share of investment assets. ERISA set guidelines for pension funds to own dividend-paying stocks, and they scrambled to hire third-party firms like mutual fund companies to invest on their behalf.

As mutual funds proliferated, so too did the ranks of professional investors. And they demanded research about the markets or attractive investment opportunities. At first, smaller specialty firms like H. C. Wainwright and Mitchell Hutchins made a good business providing that research. The full service investment banks, like Goldman Sachs, dragged their feet. But it wasn't long before the larger firms realized that they would need to offer research if they wanted to build deep, and lucrative, relationships with the growing class of professional investors.

"Goldman was a tiny little firm in the 1970s," Foerster recalled. "They prided themselves among other things on being not the first to adopt new policies or new procedures or new gimmicks or new securities but the last, because they didn't want to have any of their clients have something that blew up before people knew how it traded in the secondary market."

That philosophy would be challenged the following decade when the bank set out to improve its standing in the rankings of stock underwriters, in the process redesigning how IPOs got sold.

Chapter 2

British Gas, Detroit, 1956

By the late 1970s, Bill Hambrecht and George Quist had made a name for themselves bringing small companies to the market. Though Hambrecht & Quist was never guaranteed business from the companies the two men invested in, their stakes gave the firm a stable base of potential clients.

Larger companies still chose the larger investment banks like Morgan Stanley and, to a lesser extent, Goldman Sachs. Morgan Stanley had been quicker to see the vast money to be made in the technology industry. In 1975 the bank hired Ben Rosen, an electrical engineer with a degree from Caltech and an MBA from Columbia Business School, to analyze emerging technology companies. Rosen authored a newsletter and held a conference, establishing himself as an enthusiastic electronics analyst focused first on semiconductors and then microcomputers.

But it was a young venture partner at Hambrecht & Quist, Larry Moore, who convinced his bosses to invest in one of the region's early personal computing pioneers. Founded by Steve Jobs and Steve Wozniak, Apple Computer soon generated buzz thanks to a Jobs-led marketing push that established the firm as a designer of handsome machines for educational institutions and creative types. Hambrecht invested for a small stake, joining investors including Arthur Rock, Intel's Andrew Grove, and Sequoia Capital, the venture capital firm founded by semiconductor pioneer Don Valentine.

In 1980, Apple needed money to fuel its growth, and early investors wanted a chance to cash out. The company interviewed investment banks for the job of selling shares to the public, ultimately settling on Morgan Stanley. It was something of a surprise that Jobs also chose Hambrecht & Quist and insisted that the smaller bank be given an equal role to that of Morgan

Stanley. "He was deeply loyal to people that supported him early," Hambrecht said later. "We got our role as co-manager in that offering, I think, primarily because Steve just insisted on it. And not only insisted on us being there, but insisted that we be treated as an equal partner."

The Morgan Stanley/Hambrecht & Quist partnership wasn't as strange as it seemed. As an undergraduate at Princeton, Hambrecht had been friends with Dick Fisher, the Morgan Stanley partner overseeing the firm's equities business at the time of the Apple IPO. Fisher had already gone to Hambrecht a year or so before and asked for help getting Morgan Stanley into the business of underwriting technology firms.

Other large firms, sensing that there was money to be made, also looked at breaking into the burgeoning scene. When those firms approached Hambrecht for his advice, he asked them for a list of the companies that interested them. Almost invariably, they would tick off the top firms by revenue, showing little understanding of or interest in the smaller firms with promising technology that might become future industry titans. But when Hambrecht asked that same question of Fisher, the banker gave him a list that showed real insight. Apple was on it.

"I remember looking at his list, thinking, Okay, he's the smart one. He's the one that's going to win," Hambrecht recalled. The other bankers "were looking for volume, where Dick obviously had people that were looking for the real technology leaders," he added.

At that point Morgan Stanley had so much power that it would refuse to co-manage an offering with another firm. You did it their way, or they wouldn't do it. "They dominated the game," Hambrecht said.

Jobs forced Morgan Stanley to break that rule when he insisted that they work with Hambrecht & Quist on the Apple transaction. In another first, they also agreed to evenly split the fees from the deal. Fisher's colleagues gave him a hard time, because the bank could have demanded a much bigger slice. But what Fisher realized, which Hambrecht would only later come to see, was that there would be a huge amount of wealth creation generated by the Apple transaction. He would split the fees on the IPO underwriting and then clean up when it came to managing the money for the founders and employees, all of whom became wealthy. Those were services that Hambrecht & Quist couldn't even offer. Fisher "said that he looked at a company like Apple and realized that Apple would never be a very good investment banking client for them because it was such a cash generator," Hambrecht said later. "Once they got the IPO done, they really didn't need any more money." In other words, Morgan Stanley couldn't count on being hired again by Apple, because the company didn't have much use for its services.

Before he could sell Apple, Hambrecht needed to wrap up the IPO for Genentech, a four-year-old biotechnology company. Hambrecht & Quist had an investment in that firm too. It would be a busy second half of the year for the bank, now in its twelfth year.

Genentech was a biotechnology startup cofounded by a venture capitalist at Kleiner Perkins, one of the valley's first big-time VCs, and a scientist and pioneer in recombinant DNA technology. Together the two men had led Genentech in 1978 to its first significant breakthrough, synthetically produced human insulin.

In mid-October 1980, Hambrecht & Quist sold Genentech shares for $35. The shares quickly surged by about 150 percent to as much as $88 before settling at $71.25, for a 104 percent gain, in what the *Wall Street Journal* called "one of the most spectacular market debuts in memory."

Despite Genentech's splashy showing, investor attention soon turned to Apple. CEO Steve Jobs had built Apple into a computer maker that captivated the attention of the investor community by focusing on the look of the device and the ease with which it could be used. Jobs later said that he was inspired to strive for perfection by the Beatles' John Lennon. Media outlets debated the merits of the offering throughout the fall. "Not since Eve has an Apple posed such a temptation," the *Wall Street Journal* declared. On the Monday of the week the IPO was scheduled, Jobs and millions of others lost an inspiration when a Beatles fan shot and killed Lennon outside the courtyard of the Dakota, his Upper West Side residence in New York City. The tragedy cast a momentary pall over the offering.

When the company finally settled on the price and completed the offering, it became the largest IPO since the Ford transaction in 1956. Shares began to trade on December 12, a rollicking day at Apple's Cupertino headquarters.

One executive brought in cases of champagne, while other employees debated the construction of a large thermometer that would show the mercury rising as Apple's share price rose.

The offering created dozens of instant millionaires within the company, largely due to the stock options they'd been granted. By one estimate, there were more millionaires created in Apple's IPO than in any other IPO in history to that point. Some percentage of those employees brought their wealth to Morgan Stanley to manage, supporting Fisher's larger plan.

■ ■ ■

With Apple's and Genentech's IPOs putting it on the map, Hambrecht & Quist bred competitors. Soon three regional firms patterned themselves after the early pioneer—Alex. Brown & Sons; L. F. Rothschild, Unterberg, Towbin; and Robertson, Colman & Stephens—and showed the wisdom of catering to the technology industry. The four soon earned the moniker "Four Horsemen."

Much larger investment banks also began to take notice of how Silicon Valley was growing. By then, in the early 1980s, Morgan Stanley and Goldman Sachs had followed the lead of the smaller brokerages and built out large research arms they used to market ideas to institutional investors and collect trading commissions as payment. As the investment banks consolidated power, so too did the institutional investors. Between 1980 and 1995, the number of mutual funds went from 564 managing $135 billion in assets to 5,724 managing $2.81 trillion, according to a later Investment Company Institute report.

The decade would see Morgan Stanley cede its underwriting dominance to Goldman Sachs. In 1984, a forty-one-year-old trader at Goldman Sachs named Eric Dobkin was promoted to oversee a banking unit that underwrote stock issues. At the time, Dobkin's boss, Jim Gorter, was looking for a way to improve Goldman's ninth-place ranking. A confident banker fond of pinstripe suits, Dobkin had been selling large blocks of already public stock to mutual fund clients. He came to an insight in the shower that changed the landscape of Wall Street. Up to that point, trading desks staffed by executives who enjoyed liquid lunches sold IPOs to a largely retail client base by holding a cocktail hour to market the issues. Company management told its story to retail brokers, who went out and sold lots of one hundred to two hundred shares to individual investors.

Dobkin realized that the mechanics of how he was marketing his block trades to large investors could be used to sell IPOs. When a big block came in to sell, Dobkin would turn to the Goldman analyst covering the stock and ask what he thought of it and who might want to buy shares. Couldn't that analyst play a similar role in IPOs, visiting investors and telling the company's story?

Public offerings had other advantages too. The SEC required firms to file a prospectus, which was largely considered a legal document. Dobkin figured he could use the business details contained in it to craft a story about how a company was special. Make it into a marketing document. And if Dobkin could get management teams to visit institutional investors in their offices, or at least their home cities, the investors could hear the company's story straight from the people running it.

The following year, Dobkin created Wall Street's first investment banking unit devoted to underwriting stock issues and began catering to the likes of Fidelity, T. Rowe Price, Capital Group, and Janus. His timing couldn't have been better. Just as he was creating the division, British prime minister Margaret Thatcher began selling off large government-owned gas, petroleum, and telecommunications concerns. Other countries were doing the same, which required their chosen underwriters to cast an increasingly wide net for investors with the cash to buy up the issues. Capital markets were going global and becoming increasingly integrated.

Dobkin traveled to Washington frequently to visit the Securities and Exchange Commission, where he huddled with government officials to discuss possible changes to the regulations. The SEC had been created in 1934 by Franklin Delano Roosevelt to oversee the financial markets after the 1929 crash and the onset of the Great Depression. It was charged with watching out for investors and acting as one of the chief regulators of U.S. financial markets. Its lofty mission made officials wary of bending or rewriting rules that had been laid down over the course of decades.

But regulators were also cognizant of being outmaneuvered by officials in other countries and losing clout, and they were open to Dobkin's entreaties to rationalize U.S. regulations when dealing with these countries. Sometimes that meant translating prospectuses into three or four languages. Other times it meant joining with national securities regulators elsewhere to harmonize rules around pricing and information dissemination.

In those days, Dobkin would often fly the Concorde, the supersonic passenger jetliner, between New York's John F. Kennedy International Airport and Heathrow Airport in London. He could get on the plane at 1:45 p.m. in New York, land at 10:20 p.m. in London, and get a couple more hours of work in before sleep. The following day, he could do breakfast, lunch, and dinner meetings. He could then wake up the next morning, take a 10:30 flight from London, and be back in New York in time for the start of the workday.

"I could spend literally a day away from the office, do a boatload of meetings and dinner and all, and get back to New York in time for business the following day, or I could spend the next day and go for two days," Dobkin said. "It was just extraordinarily helpful."

The travel wasn't luxurious—the seats were narrow and stacked four across, with an aisle in the middle—but it was fast. And that was the idea. The quick trip allowed Dobkin to visit clients in person, the preferred method for investment bankers who felt it was better to develop relationships in person than on the phone. With easy access to London, Dobkin could meet face-to-face with British officials tasked with choosing the investment banks that would help them sell the government's assets.

When Dobkin began his quest to climb up the league tables, which ranked companies by fees, deal volumes, and other yardsticks, Morgan Stanley was a powerful presence at the top of the underwriter rankings. The investment bank, which had been formed by two J.P. Morgan & Co. partners in 1935 after passage of the Glass-Steagall Act, had an early leg up on work with the British government.

In 1984, Morgan Stanley made a series of mistakes that opened the door for Dobkin and his Goldman Sachs colleagues. Morgan Stanley led the first privatization of British Telecom (BT), handling the distribution of shares to U.S. investors. In those days, UK rules required banks to hold on to the shares for more or less two weeks before passing them out to investors, meaning they'd be on the hook for any losses or gains.

In the United States, banks weren't taking much risk. They'd price a deal once they'd built a book of investors and quickly distribute the shares. If they couldn't sell the entire thing, the bank might hang on to a stub of shares. Many bankers considered that a reasonable risk to take. But Morgan Stanley refused to take the risk of holding the BT shares for weeks, and the Bank of England had to step in to backstop the position. British government officials weren't happy.

Goldman's rival made a second mistake. Due to a variety of technical factors, the BT shares were expected to be popular in the UK, and prognosticators believed that the stock would perform well on opening day. When it did, many of the U.S. investors who had received shares from Morgan Stanley turned around and sold them back into the UK market, in a process known as reflow. The result was a more concentrated base of investors than the UK government wanted.

Goldman got its big break two years later. In March 1986, the investment bank underwrote the IPO for Microsoft, the software pioneer founded by Bill Gates and Paul Allen. Goldman and H&Q competitor Alex. Brown & Sons co-managed the sale of 2.8 million Microsoft shares for $21 apiece.

Later that year, Goldman won the job of advising the Thatcher government on the privatization of British Gas. Selected as the lead underwriter for the portion of the deal that would be sold to U.S. investors, Goldman unloaded $8 billion in stock. It was the largest UK privatization and the largest equity offering ever.

In 1987, the investment bank once again outmaneuvered Morgan Stanley for the mandate to help the UK sell off its remaining stake in British Petroleum, a $12.4 billion deal that set a new record for the largest UK privatization. The bank was left with a large underwriting loss when it got stuck with BP shares after the market crashed on October 19, 1987, a day later called Black Monday.

It was UK privatizations more than anything that established Goldman's name and propelled them to the top of the underwriting rankings, Foerster recalls. "In the early eighties, John Whitehead and others at Goldman Sachs would call Bob Baldwin and Fisher at Morgan Stanley" and ask to get onto deals, Foerster said. But as the decade progressed, it became harder to persuade CFOs to hire an underwriter other than Goldman, he recalled.

"They all wanted Goldman because they wanted to be able to go to the CEO and the board and say, 'I got Goldman to run that IPO,'" he said. "When they got the BP business away from Morgan Stanley, and Eric Dobkin was key to that, that was a huge coup for Goldman."

During this time, bankers continued a trend spawned a decade earlier, when ERISA helped give rise to the growth in mutual funds: they moved away from marketing to thousands of retail brokers who held direct relationships with the masses of individual investors scattered across the country and instead largely engaged with a growing class of professional investors.

Such investors had the education and the knowledge to evaluate companies coming to the market for the first time. By focusing on fewer investors with more buying power, bankers were able to better understand each investor's individual style. And they learned how to fashion their pitch based on the preferences of each. Once the bankers spoke to enough investors, they could pool that feedback and use the common attributes to create a specific marketing and pricing strategy.

Dobkin came to believe that IPOs were exercises in psychology as much as they were capital raising. If that was true, a well-orchestrated marketing effort led by an analyst who was an expert in his field and bankers who were familiar with a broad investor base, he thought, could successfully sell new issues.

Goldman established a model that roughly exists in form and function today. The bankers created a research note, effectively an internal memo, that summarized the deal and got distributed to the sales force. The bankers then held a conference call, typically less than an hour, to answer any questions and brief salespeople on the deal.

It was then up to the salespeople to call the mutual funds that were their clients and talk to them about the deal. While Goldman did have wealth managers, those clients would be individuals and families, and that became a smaller part of the process. Retail went from getting 50 percent of Ford's IPO in the mid-1950s to getting 15 percent or less of deals that Goldman would bring public in the 1990s and 2000s. To the bankers, this was simply a reflection of a change in how securities got bought and sold.

As the assets held by mutual funds increased, their managers gained a level of power that they quickly learned how to use. It was common in the 1990s, Foerster recalled, for firms like Fidelity to withdraw from an IPO unless they got a discount to the fair value. If that didn't work, the money manager would threaten to take its trading business elsewhere.

CHAPTER 3

Netscape Communications, Mountain View, 1995

As the power of the money managers rose, so too did the influence of the analysts, the men and women in charge of delivering new investment ideas and the trading revenue that would result. Ben Rosen's influence had helped Morgan Stanley win the Apple IPO. It was just one example of how analysts trusted by investors could have a large influence on whether money managers bought the shares of a particular company.

Wall Street research analysts had to keep pace with the intelligence and training of the portfolio managers, and the investment banks soon turned to business schools to hire analysts. The money and prestige that the banks could offer to promising recruits soon created an advantage over the smaller research shops that had been first to the business model.

"Institutional investors had the ability to vet IPOs, read the prospectuses, do some earnings modeling, compare it to the models of analysts," Foerster said. "As the SEC loosened the restrictions on an analyst to make projections and to do forward modeling, retail brokers on balance had no ability to do that. They didn't have the time to do it, they didn't have the skill sets to do it, and most individual investors had neither the time nor the skill sets to do it either."

That also meant that bankers who were underwriting stock and bond issues for those same companies came to rely on the analysts to help them sell the companies' stories to institutional investors. To sell the stories, though, analysts needed to be bullish on the companies' prospects.

Investors, in turn, would seek out the smartest analyst on a particular stock to help them understand its prospects. If a bank employed that analyst, it would mean more trading business from investors who had read the analyst's research. And it meant investment bankers could offer a more compelling case to potential clients making a decision about which bank to pick for a stock or bond deal. If an analyst had a loyal following among investors, it became that much easier for the bankers to sell the security.

The growing importance of analysts also gave them more power, and placed them between company executives wanting positive spin at the investment bank they'd hired and investment bankers who wanted particular analysts to offer their rosy projections in pitch meetings to win the deal. Once the deal was won, analysts could be discouraged from tarnishing the company their colleagues had just underwritten with a negative opinion.

"Equity research became so powerful," Foerster said, recalling an example to prove his point.

In 1987, PaineWebber's transportation banker, Joseph Steuert, and the firm's top-rated railroad analyst, James Voytko, almost came to blows over the latter's refusal to improve his numbers in order to win underwriting business, Foerster recalls. PaineWebber was pitching to underwrite the IPO for Consolidated Rail Corp. (Conrail), the successor to a number of railroads that went bankrupt in the 1960s and 1970s. To win the deal, Joe Steuert believed that the firm needed to come up with a particular valuation for the railroad. That was the analyst's job. "We had a very headstrong head of the transportation group with PaineWebber, a very talented new business guy, and we had the number one analyst," said Foerster, who was then head of stock underwriting at PaineWebber. "The head of the corporate finance transportation group's putting pressure on the analyst." Foerster recalled Steuert saying, " 'You've got to come up with this multiple or we're not going to get on the cover of the document.' "

"I can't do that," Jim Voytko responded. "I won't do that."

Foerster recommended that the team fly down to Washington early and practice their pitch at a lunch at the Army Navy Country Club in Arlington, Virginia. The idea was that Steuert and Voytko would keep talking and try to find a way to bridge their differences, or at least come up with a number that everyone could agree on. By the end of lunch, the two sides were getting closer as everyone left the dining room for taxis that would take them to the meeting.

Foerster recalled standing at the front desk paying the bill when one of the young bankers came running in.

"Bruce, get out here right away."

"What's going on?" Foerster asked.

"Joe and Jim are ready to square off and have a fistfight in the parking lot over the multiples."

PaineWebber didn't get chosen to underwrite the offering. Conrail chose Goldman Sachs.

Foerster wasn't deterred and he came up with another angle. Under SEC guidelines that sought to prevent underwriters from overhyping a company they were taking public, research analysts at banks involved in a new issue were prevented from publishing research until almost a month after the IPO. Regulators wanted investors to have that time to read and digest the final prospectus before they were influenced by Wall Street research analysts. Foerster turned down Goldman's invitation to join the deal—PaineWebber's roster of individual investors was attractive to the other firms—so that PaineWebber could write a report on Conrail prior to the IPO.

Titled "Guide to the Conrail Prospectus," the pre-IPO research report was a huge success—hundreds of institutional investors asked for a copy. Banks provided research to investors for free in return for an expectation that investors would pay for it if they found it helpful or useful for making an investment. With so many reports going out to investors, Foerster prepared to reap the gains when those firms came to PaineWebber on the day of the IPO to buy shares as payment for the report.

As Foerster was standing on the trading floor waiting for the orders to flow in, the head of block trading came over to him. The word was that the Goldman bankers running the deal were so incensed by PaineWebber's actions that they had issued an ultimatum to their trading accounts: "Nobody's going to do business with PaineWebber today or else," Foerster recalled the trader saying.

His firm didn't do much business that day. "We didn't write a ticket, basically," Foerster recalled. "That's how strong Goldman's power was by then."

Institutional investors' power had also continued to grow. In March 1991, PaineWebber was underwriting a hot biotech deal, Foerster recalled. The deal was well oversubscribed, meaning that Foerster's firm had many more orders to buy than it could fill. Fidelity called asking for a discount and threatening that they would walk away from the deal if they didn't get it. Foerster instructed a colleague to tell Fidelity to take a hike. He had more than enough buyers without them.

Soon after the deal was priced successfully, Foerster was strutting around the trading floor when his secretary came up to him and grabbed his shoulder. Donald Marron, PaineWebber's CEO, wanted to see Foerster in his fourteenth-floor office.

"Don, how are you doing?" Foerster said as he walked in. He noticed Marron wasn't smiling, but then he seldom did.

"I understand we priced a big offering," Marron said.

"Yes, we blew it out the window."

"How much did we give Fidelity?"

"Well, they were trying to run the deal for us and they tried to price it, and I told them to go stick it."

"Yeah, I know you did. I just got a call from Ned Johnson," Marron said, referring to Fidelity's CEO.

Johnson was one of the most powerful men in the investment management industry. In the few minutes between when Foerster's guy had informed Fidelity that they were out of the deal and the time the deal was priced, the news had traveled all the way up in Fidelity to Johnson, who had rung Marron.

The call served to remind Marron, and Foerster, that Fidelity could take its very lucrative trading business elsewhere if PaineWebber ever tried that again. During those years and later, Fidelity also liked to invoke what was known as its "two-for-one" rule, which required banks that wanted to do business with the mutual fund manager to allocate twice as many shares to Fidelity as they allocated to any other investor.

"I don't know what Fidelity's revenues at PaineWebber were, but they were huge," said Foerster. He had no idea how much Fidelity paid his firm in trading commissions. "We couldn't afford to lose that order flow, and so they used that as a club. And if I had been at Fidelity, I would have done the same thing. It was war."

■ ■ ■

In 1991, a research analyst named Lise Buyer joined T. Rowe Price, which, like Fidelity, was growing into one of the most powerful institutional investors.

With wavy hair and a big smile, Buyer was the daughter of a Buffalo, New York, journalist father and educated at the Nichols School, a local private institution. She studied economics and geology at Wellesley College before matriculating at Vanderbilt University's business school.

After her MBA, Buyer moved to New York for a job at Fred Alger Management, a pioneering firm in a type of investing that made wagers on fast-growing stocks like those of the technology industry. Fred Alger emphasized fundamental analysis, the practice of evaluating companies based on economic forecasts, industry trends, and specific financial metrics to determine if they would make a good investment.

Buyer got her start as a retail analyst, visiting stores and local malls to poll workers about what was selling, but it wasn't long before she started covering technology stocks. After a few years, she left Fred Alger for Prudential-Bache Securities Inc., where she covered Tandy, the precursor of RadioShack, which sold an early personal computer called the TRS-80 that competed with Apple.

When T. Rowe Price came calling, she moved to Baltimore and joined the company's Science & Technology Fund. Started in 1987, it was one of the first mutual funds to make focused investments in the rapidly developing technology space. As the use of personal computers and accessing of the World Wide Web became more commonplace, Buyer helped T. Rowe Price place money on the companies leading the wave. By 1995, she was quoted in news articles as a T. Rowe Price analyst willing to explain new technologies.

By then, Hambrecht had handed off the CEO title at Hambrecht & Quiet to Daniel Case and stepped into a chairman's role. The firm still used the same strategy Hambrecht had started with, taking stakes in promising companies as a venture investor and acting as an underwriter when those companies or others wanted to access the public markets.

One of H&Q's investments was the early internet browser Netscape Communications Corp. Founded by Marc Andreessen and Jim Clark in 1994, Netscape was quickly becoming the dominant browser people used to search the internet. The company chose Morgan Stanley and Hambrecht & Quist to underwrite its IPO.

When Lise Buyer heard about the IPO, she explored whether T. Rowe Price should buy Netscape's stock for the Science & Technology Fund. Buyer was a free spirit who often saw through pretense. The internet economy was just so new, she didn't know how she could come up with a valuation for the company's shares. "Everyone is using their own set of growth rates based on current net-related products and a little crystal-ball gazing and fairy dust," she told the *Wall Street Journal*, unafraid to say what others might have been thinking. "I don't know how you put a value on it—you pick a price you're willing to pay and you find a way to rationalize it."

Those limitations didn't imperil the company's IPO. When Netscape went public in August 1995, it sold shares for $28 apiece. The price was already a doubling of the initial level the investment bankers planned to sell at, but when the stock opened the following day, it surged to $74.75. It closed the first day at $58.25, a 108 percent increase over the IPO price.

The internet boom was officially underway.

In anticipation of the Netscape IPO, Hambrecht wanted to know what to do with a stake in the company that H&Q held in one of its venture funds. Should H&Q keep Netscape's shares, or distribute them to the limited partners who had placed money into its funds? Hambrecht wanted a data-driven answer, so he had asked a couple of colleagues in H&Q's venture department to run some numbers. What they learned startled him.

Like many assets, stocks traded based on supply and demand. If there was more demand for the shares than the supply, the price increased. If there was more supply than the demand could soak up, the price could be expected to fall. Investment banks liked to insist on IPO agreements that prevented company management, employees, and early investors from selling their holdings before 180 days had passed. Known as a lockup, it artificially constrained supply until the company and its backers could sort out investor demand.

Hambrecht's analysis uncovered a surprising pattern in how stocks traded in the days and months after an IPO. Time and again, a company sold stock for a certain price, watched the price increase on the first day of trading, and then noticed it hovering at around that number for four or five months. Investors would then begin selling the stock, and its price would drift lower. At six months, underwriting agreements allowed insiders to finally sell their stakes, or distribute them to investors who could now sell them. The sales dumped more stock into the market. Between six months and two years after the IPO, the stock price often underperformed.

Hambrecht brought the Netscape data with him to the Bahamas, for a meeting he had with John Templeton, the American-born British investor then known for an almost forty-year record of putting up 15 percent returns in his mutual fund. Hambrecht had struck up a relationship with Templeton and tried to meet him every so often. When he did, he tried to bring a new idea or insight he could share.

"I took that chart now to Nassau and I showed it to Sir John," Hambrecht said later. "He took one look at it and he said, 'My God, there's a scam going on.'"

Templeton immediately picked up the phone and called in a programmer.

"Write a program to get us out of the IPOs four months after," he said. "Let's look at the ones we really like two years later."

Templeton's reaction stuck in Hambrecht's mind.

Even as technology companies captured the market's attention, the banker worked on other deals for companies in decidedly older industries. The same year as the Netscape IPO, 1995, Hambrecht teamed up with Foerster on the IPO of Boston Beer Company, the maker of Samuel Adams lager. Boston Beer's founder, Jim Koch, had asked Foerster, who by then had left Wall Street and struck out on his own, to serve as an advisor on the IPO. Koch had a novel idea he wanted to try: selling stock directly to the customers who drank his beer.

Foerster thought it was a lousy idea. So did Alex. Brown & Sons. Goldman Sachs, where the cousin of Koch's mother was a partner, didn't want any part of it either.

Hambrecht was by then open to trying something different. H&Q was already an investor in Boston Beer. So Koch asked Hambrecht to figure out how to sell stock to his customers, and at a lower price than he sold it to the professional investors. "Jim just wanted his beer drinkers to have a bargain," Hambrecht recalled. "Give a little edge over the institutions."

SEC rules wouldn't allow companies to have two different prices on an underwriting deal. But with Hambrecht's help, Boston Beer ultimately agreed to conduct two deals. It would sell stock to beer customers and then close the deal. Investors couldn't sell. Then it would open the sale for institutional investors.

After some negotiating, Koch and his bankers decided that they would allocate a third of the offering to retail customers.

Koch came up with the idea of putting neck hangers on the six-packs. They advertised that the company was going public and told customers that if they were interested, they should call a number and order a prospectus. The response was overwhelming. More than one hundred thousand people called in saying they wanted to buy stock and sent in checks to purchase shares.

But no one knew how to allocate shares to so many people. Hambrecht ended up hiring a mutual fund system to do it, ultimately apportioning the shares through something like a lottery, almost like pulling names out of a hat. About thirty thousand people got about five hundred dollars' worth of stock each. That meant that they had to return checks from the more than seventy thousand people who'd sent in money and didn't get shares. "I remember thinking there's something wrong about this system when you're sending all that money back," Hambrecht said later.

When the transaction was complete, Hambrecht recalled, he had a conversation with one of H&Q's board members, who was also a top technology executive at Charles Schwab. Schwab was a leader in the hypercompetitive world of retail brokerage, where many firms competed to offer trading accounts for smaller investors. Acquiring customers was hard. Hambrecht told him the story of the Boston Beer IPO.

The executive just looked at him. "You dope," he said to Hambrecht. "It costs us, in advertising, three to four hundred dollars to open a new account. You had a hundred thousand accounts you just gave away!"

Hambrecht realized it was a missed opportunity.

CHAPTER 4

Ravenswood Winery, Sonoma, 1999

Bill Gurley moved to Silicon Valley in 1996. The six-foot-nine Texan was a Wall Street research analyst who had just been hired by Frank Quattrone, a big-name investment banker and the former leader of Morgan Stanley's technology practice. Quattrone had left to build something similar at Deutsche Morgan Grenfell (DMG).

When Quattrone's offer came, Gurley was working at Credit Suisse First Boston. But the analyst had his sights set on becoming a venture capitalist. He made Quattrone promise him a transfer to Silicon Valley. Quattrone not only agreed but told Gurley he would introduce him to all the venture capitalists he knew if he joined Quattrone's team.

Under the model that Goldman Sachs had designed the previous decade, investment bankers and analysts worked hand in hand to market IPOs. While the bankers worked on crafting the company's story and writing the prospectus, the analysts learned the business model and future prospects and explained those to investors. Having a well-respected analyst could help bankers land IPO mandates, and Gurley was one of the best. He'd already earned recognition from Institutional Investor, which polled investors to come up with analyst rankings.

Gurley was a native of Dickinson, Texas, a suburb roughly forty miles southeast of Houston's city center and just nine miles from NASA's Johnson Space Center, where his father, John, had been an early employee. Also named John, Gurley went by the shortened form of his middle name, William.

At Dickinson High School, Gurley distinguished himself as a very good student. Still known as John by some, he was one of just fourteen to graduate magna cum laude; one of many in the 259-strong class to win the Presidential Academic Fitness Award; and chosen for the Lamar University Scholarships.

He was also painfully aware of his height. A yearbook photo of magna cum laude graduates shows Gurley in the center of the last row, rising several inches over the next-tallest student. Gurley's head is slightly angled. He played on the basketball team all four years.

His older sister went to work for Compaq, the early microcomputer market leader based down the road. She received options that paid off handsomely when the company went public. The younger brother was hooked on the thrill of technology, and credits that exposure to a realization that working in the technology industry could be both interesting and lucrative.

After high school, Gurley spent two years at Millsaps College in Mississippi, before transferring to the University of Florida to play basketball. Wearing No. 52, Gurley stood out not for his athletic prowess (he played as a reserve alongside future NBA players Dwayne Schintzius and Vernon Maxwell) but for his intellect. When the team's depth came into question just before the NCAA tournament in 1988, his coach had this to say: "Bill and I both hope he doesn't play. The only trips he's made since early in the season have been to the science lab." He actually did play—for one minute, during which he missed his only shot. Florida lost the game to Michigan in the second round. The Texan appeared on the Southeastern Conference's Academic Honor Roll with a 3.77 grade point average in computer science.

After Florida, Gurley followed his sister to Compaq for a couple of years before he left to get his MBA from the University of Texas at Austin. By his own admission, Gurley entered UT as a mature student. He threw himself into studying financial concepts for a career on Wall Street. After graduation, he cold-called a number of well-known investment banks before getting a job at Credit Suisse First Boston (CSFB) in 1993.

It wasn't long before Gurley made a splash for Quattrone's DMG technology team. In early 1997, he downgraded Netscape Communications, the internet browser Hambrecht had helped take public. Microsoft was preparing a challenger, and Gurley worried about Netscape's ability to weather the competition. The stock slumped nearly 20 percent on Gurley's report. (The report so angered Marc Andreessen that he still holds a grudge.)

■ ■ ■

Gurley's knowledge of the internet helped Quattrone's team land the assignment to take a small online bookseller called Amazon.com public.

Amazon.com was already a well-known name, and it was a surprise when founder and CEO Jeff Bezos selected Deutsche Morgan to lead the transaction. Many had expected Morgan Stanley or Goldman Sachs to underwrite the company's IPO, but Bezos thought Gurley understood his business model better than most. The analyst spent hours talking to Bezos and began to put together his report.

When it came time to price the shares in the IPO, in the middle of May 1997, Gurley found himself in the New York lobby of the Four Seasons Hotel on the phone with Quattrone. The banker had been talking to Bezos, hashing out a price for Amazon.com's shares.

Deutsche Morgan initially set a range of $12 to $14 for the shares, then increased the price to $16. Bezos thought he could get even more and wanted to raise it by another $2. Did Gurley have an objection? Quattrone wanted to know.

Gurley was comfortable with the higher price. Amazon.com priced its shares at $18 apiece.

The following day, Amazon.com opened near $30 before settling in for the close at $23.50. That represented a 31 percent pop, right in line with where corporate executives liked to see their stock after the first day of trading. Over the following days, Amazon's stock declined, trading as low as $16.

Critics accused Bezos and DMG of pricing the deal too aggressively. They said no one would buy Amazon.com's stock again after getting burned. The stock reversed its decline less than two months later and never again touched its IPO price as Amazon.com's revenue and gross profit surged.

Bezos, Gurley, and Quattrone were proven right.

■ ■ ■

After less than two years working for Quattrone, Gurley was ready to try his hand at the venture capital industry. He lined up a job at Hummer Winblad Venture Partners, a respected firm based in San Francisco, and left Deutsche Morgan in late 1997.

The task of covering the internet had grown too large for any one person and Quattrone hired several analysts to replace Gurley. One of those was Lise Buyer, the T. Rowe Price analyst. Quattrone knew Buyer from his trips to Baltimore showcasing IPO candidates to T. Rowe Price's portfolio managers.

Buyer was the most senior analyst Quattrone hired to cover consumer-facing internet companies, and she moved to California for the job. When Quattrone moved to Credit Suisse First Boston the next year, Buyer moved with him. By then, research analysts were widely quoted in industry and general-interest publications and well paid. Buyer was making more than $1 million a year.

She made the reverse move that Gurley and many others had before him, coming from the buy side and moving to the sell side. And she brought a fresh perspective. Knowing that investors often did the hard work of coming up with their ideas of future prices on potential stock picks, she refused to put price targets on many of her companies; at one point, she didn't have targets on fifteen of the eighteen companies she covered. She felt that the industry was too new and the business prospects too uncertain for precision to be possible.

At Credit Suisse, a former colleague remembered, Buyer had strong opinions and wasn't afraid to stick to them in the face of criticism. As a woman in a male-dominated field, Buyer defended her ideas and her territory, often in a frank, open, and straightforward way. When it came time to talk to investors, Buyer told them she had been in their seat and understood their position. She came across as analytical and confident.

As the internet boom continued in 1998, Buyer's conservatism looked increasingly out of touch with how investors saw the industry. Or how company executives viewed the opportunity to sell shares and cash in on the enthusiasm. In July 1998, Mark Cuban's Broadcast.com surged nearly 250 percent in its first day of trading. Readers of the following day's *New York Times* were told that the stock had enjoyed "the best opening-day gain of any company in Wall Street history." Over the following months, many investors and startup executives came to see first-day pops as a sign of an IPO's success.

In September 1998, the online auction house eBay went public at $18 a share, with backing from Benchmark Capital, a venture capital firm set up in 1994 with the unusual model of sharing profits and investment decisions equally among a small group of partners. Benchmark had a more than 20 percent stake in eBay when it went public. The shares climbed 163 percent by the end of trading on the first day, a surge that annoyed eBay founder Pierre Omidyar because it meant that he could have sold shares at a higher price and collected more proceeds for his company.

Around that time, Credit Suisse bankers and Buyer spoke to theGlobe .com, an early social network, about a potential IPO. As with the rules Hambrecht had laid out to Bill Farinon in 1967, many investment banks still relied on revenue thresholds to guide their decision about a company's readiness for the public markets. Credit Suisse's analysts and bankers had their own threshold: if a company had less than something like $10 million in revenue, it was too immature for an IPO.

Buyer told theGlobe.com executives that they should wait a couple more quarters, till they had more revenue. Then they would look more like an IPO candidate. Bear Stearns, however, was much more cavalier. The bank, in the second tier of IPO underwriters, took theGlobe.com public in November 1998. The stock jumped 600 percent, the biggest one-day gain in history. Many other companies who had heard a similar message from Credit Suisse now flooded the phones and email inboxes of the firm's bankers. Buyer lamented the degradation of underwriting standards when the analysts held their weekly call. Within weeks, Credit Suisse had joined most other investment banks in lowering their underwriting thresholds to match those of Bear Stearns. To resist meant losing out on IPO fees.

When CIBC Oppenheimer analyst Henry Blodget put a $400 price target on Amazon.com in December 1998, Buyer once again reminded readers of the *Wall Street Journal* how hard it was to value an internet stock. "It is not realistic to say that any of us can see out that far with any degree of accuracy....No one should be confused that there's any degree of certainty in a prediction of that kind."

Blodget's target was for one year. Amazon.com reached $400 within a month.

And Gurley joined Benchmark Capital, backers of eBay, in 1999.

■   ■   ■

By this time, Bill Hambrecht had become interested in exploring alternative approaches to bringing companies into the public markets. He set up a modest subsidiary of Hambrecht & Quist to experiment, seeking out smaller companies that were ignored by larger banks and open to new ideas. Hambrecht's first couple of IPOs were successful, but it wasn't long before his colleagues at Hambrecht & Quist clamored to take his deals for their larger, more established franchise.

Hambrecht's desire to reform the IPO system was increasingly at odds with his own colleagues. One time, he allocated shares not to H&Q's best trading clients but to those investors he felt would hold the stock for a long time. A couple of jilted investors put H&Q in the "penalty box," steering their usual trading activity and its related commissions to other firms. "My sales department was ready to lynch me," he recalled.

Hambrecht and CEO Daniel Case, the older brother of America Online CEO Steve Case, decided that it would be best if Hambrecht pursued his ideas on his own. In late 1997, the banker and venture capitalist announced his retirement from the firm he'd founded thirty years before.

The events of the mid-1990s had driven home at least three ideas that would propel Hambrecht into the next phase of his career.

- Price deals closer to the market clearing price so you don't get as much of the pop that leads investors to flip shares.
- Get access to the customer base, because they are the most loyal shareholders a company will ever have.
- Find a way to avoid the conflicts of interest that had become so stark at firms that both underwrote IPOs and catered to trading clients.

Freed from the institutional structures of H&Q, Hambrecht set up his new firm, WR Hambrecht + Co., and set about designing something new. He had seen plenty of IPOs and thought that holding an auction for the shares might make sense.

Hambrecht set out to research auctions and got advice from professors at Stanford University who had designed an auction for the U.S. government to sell off access to broadband spectrum, which was becoming increasingly desirable with the rise of the internet. (Two Stanford faculty members, Robert Wilson and Paul Milgrom, won the 2020 Nobel Prize in economics for their auction studies.) Compared to broadband, a stock offering seemed much simpler, Hambrecht thought.

"The old system made our firm very successful. My partners kept telling me don't fix what ain't broke," Hambrecht said later. "But I couldn't understand why you wouldn't use an auction."

He hired a technology whiz named Alan Katz from Texas Instruments to serve as his chief technology officer; Hambrecht & Quist had done a joint venture with TI. Hambrecht hired four developers to write the code that would become the OpenIPO system, an online auction marketplace designed to sell new shares more equitably.

Hambrecht made a couple of key decisions. The longtime banker knew enough not to try to cut out the large underwriters. He and his team designed the system so that they and their investors could participate in the auctions as well.

Hambrecht also based his technology on an algorithm designed by Canadian-American economist William Vickrey. Vickrey's auction process involved collecting bids and then selling the asset being auctioned to the highest bidder but at the second-highest bid. It was intended to encourage bidders to submit the highest price they were willing to pay. The idea was that if investors knew that their bid was only used to win the auction, and that they would be paying the second-highest price, they would be more inclined to put in a higher bid. Vickrey was a Nobel Prize–winning Columbia University professor considered the godfather of congestion pricing for coming up with a way to balance the supply and demand of public transportation use.

Hambrecht's system used a technique called a Dutch auction, named after the way flower merchants in the Netherlands sold their goods. The process involved offering securities at one price and then moving it lower until there were enough orders to sell the entire lot. It worked like this: If Hambrecht wanted to sell 10 million shares he might start the auction at $10. If investors only wanted to buy 2 million shares at that price, he would lower the price to $9. That might be enough to sell the other 8 milion shares, allowing Hambrecht to sell all 10 million. Those who put in a bid at or above $9 paid that price—regardless of whether their bid was higher, or their coziness with Wall Street. The process involved a new way to price and allocate shares but it still required Hambrecht's firm to buy the shares from the company as an underwriter.

Hambrecht's was the third such effort to try to sell new shares on the internet. Wit Capital, out of New York, was earlier to the idea. But Wit's approach was drastically different from the OpenIPO system. It was geared to sell directly to retail investors. Started in 1996 by a former attorney at Cravath, Swaine & Moore to sell shares in the Spring Street Brewing Company, which made a wheat beer called Wit, the online brokerage partnered with other underwriters on dozens of deals. Wit Capital sold shares electronically to individual investors on a first-come, first-served basis. E-Trade, one of the first brokerages to trade shares online, also owned something called E*Offering.

Nonetheless, establishing the OpenIPO process took Hambrecht a year or so, with much of that spent negotiating with the SEC over the auction system's rule set. Hambrecht, who had put $10 million into the company, found the regulators to be good partners. "They wanted to see it happen," he said, "but we had to get everything approved by them."

Once Hambrecht had the system ready to go, he sent out mailers intended to provoke his old investment banking colleagues and their potential clients. One side of the flyer read, "One for me. None for you. One for me. None for you." The other side was more expansive: "Most investment bankers lead a very hard life. After they take care of each other they have to take care of their friends. And after they do that they have to take care of the people they'd like to have as friends. You can imagine that after all of this hard work there aren't very many IPO shares to go around."

Hambrecht announced the new business by giving a series of interviews. He was an insider now willing to disclose how the process worked. Hambrecht told Reuters that the OpenIPO would disrupt Wall Street's allocation process and that this would mean a higher price for a company's shares: "Most of the allocations go to the big institutions, because they go to a broker's best clients. We're opening up the process for groups currently excluded—small institutions and individual investors who have an affinity for the company."

He added, "You get a more logical, rational price than the discounted one. The Dutch auction process ought to come out with a logical pricing that's closer to where the real market level is going to be."

In 1999, Hambrecht would get his first opportunity to try his new system. He signed up Ravenswood Winery Inc., a Sonoma County winery known for its zinfandels and an irreverent slogan: No Wimpy Wines. Hambrecht aimed to sell a million shares of Ravenswood in the range of $10.50 to $13.50. He charged the winery just 4 percent of the issue price, a healthy discount from the 6–7 percent that was then the typical underwriting fee for a traditional offering.

To bid in the OpenIPO system, investors had to have a brokerage account at Hambrecht's firm or with one of five other small brokers who also signed up to participate in the process. There were other rules: Investors entered bids for how many shares they wanted to buy and at what price. After several weeks of collecting orders, Hambrecht's process would set the price at whatever level was needed to sell all the shares. Anyone willing to pay more than that price would get all the shares they asked for, while those who bid at the price would get a percentage of their order filled.

No individual investor could get more than 10 percent of the entire deal, and the banker also kept the option open to limit sales to investors willing to purchase at least 1 percent of the entire issue.

In the end, Hambrecht was able to sell all one million shares, raising $10.5 million, though the final price was at the low end of the proposed range: $10.50. Shares rose 38 cents on the first day of trading.

It was a subdued opening to what Hambrecht hoped would be a game-changing proposition. About three thousand people put in orders, and roughly 75 percent of them got some shares. But Hambrecht also said he would stick to higher-profile companies in the future as he tried to get some traction for his new auction system.

■ ■ ■

In April 1999, the same month Hambrecht wrapped up his first attempt at reforming the system as an insider, a younger man started his first job in Silicon Valley as an outsider.

Barry McCarthy Jr. was in his late forties, a wiry former investment banker from New England with an itch to take a company public. He would soon get his chance. McCarthy had been on a ski trip with his family weeks earlier when he got a call from a recruiter looking to hire a CFO for an unproven DVD-by-mail business in California named Netflix. Netflix's founders, Reed Hastings and Marc Randolph, needed a CFO who could withstand Hastings's no-nonsense approach.

Hastings flew to meet McCarthy in Colorado, where the two men had dinner together. McCarthy soon accepted the position. His family stayed in Princeton, New Jersey—McCarthy had a child who was finishing school—and he drove west in his Ford Explorer listening to a series of tapes from the Practising Law Institute, a nonprofit that provided ongoing education for lawyers, about how to take a company through an IPO.

Hosted by Alan Austin, a partner at Wilson Sonsini Goodrich & Rosati, one of the first law firms to organize itself around technology clients, the lectures provided an overview of the SEC rules that governed public companies and their IPOs. McCarthy learned, for example, that the Securities Act of 1933 governs IPOs, while the Securities Exchange Act of 1934 governs companies once their stock is trading in the public markets. McCarthy had CFO experience, having worked at Music Choice for the previous six years, but no experience with public companies or IPOs.

Named after his father, an advertising executive, McCarthy grew up in Greenwich, Connecticut, with three siblings. The children's grandfather had been mayor of San Francisco in the early years of the twentieth century. Barry Jr. attended Greenwich Country Day School before boarding at the coed Hill School, in Pottstown, Pennsylvania, where he played high school football, hockey, and lacrosse.

In 1971, McCarthy enrolled at Williams College, where he studied history and played lacrosse.

After Williams and the University of Pennsylvania's Wharton School, McCarthy landed on Wall Street, on the trading floor at a firm, First Boston, that would become Credit Suisse First Boston. Tasked with keeping an eye on public policy issues and other research topics, he read popular newsletters that arrived by fax. One day, the organization governing accounting rules for public companies changed how companies could account for receivables. They could now sell loans and book the gain or loss immediately.

McCarthy noticed the implications almost instantly. The change meant that Ford could make loans to new car buyers and sell them right away instead of relying on a loan from a large bank. McCarthy got $40,000 from his boss to explore the potential of bundling the loans into securities. He hired a lawyer and a PhD to figure out the bond math. The small team borrowed the trust structure that had been created for mortgage-backed securities and called their creation receivables-backed certificates.

Infighting over who would own the new business ultimately prevented First Boston from using the structure. When others at the bank created something similar a few years later, few thought to credit McCarthy with the invention. But the project had a more personal impact. McCarthy discovered he wanted to run something himself, instead of advising others. He left the investment bank in 1990.

Even as he drove west into the glare of the first dot-com boom, McCarthy stuck to his East Coast ways. He arrived for his first day of work, on April 15, 1999, wearing a blazer.

At Netflix, McCarthy would develop an affinity for upsetting the status quo.

CHAPTER 5

Petopia.com, San Francisco, 2000

As 1999 rolled on, the NASDAQ touched new highs. Investors demanded a piece of the Next Big Thing, leading stock prices of many internet companies to surge on the first day of trading. The media hyped those price gains, considering them signs of a successful offering, even as they handed near-instant profits to anyone lucky enough to get stock in the IPO.

The frenzy granted even more power to the Wall Street investment banks underwriting the offerings. The process involved helping company executives to shape the company's story, price the stock being sold and choose the investors to receive the shares.

Largely hidden from the investing public, the final one of those three roles, the allocation process, was one of the most important steps in the entire IPO process. Startups hired bankers to find buyers for their shares at attractive prices, leaving banks empowered to distribute shares as they pleased. Executives may have had some favorite investors, but most of the allocations were based on suggestions made by bankers.

It was the same dual agency conflict of interest that had bothered Jobs back in 1980. Hired by companies to sell their stock, banks also had a duty to the investor clients buying the shares. What made it particularly problematic on Wall Street was the mismatch between the frequency with which investment banks dealt with the two sides of their customer base. Investors—mutual funds, hedge funds, and high-net-worth individuals, predominantly—often dealt with the bank's trading desks day after day, with the best clients paying millions of dollars in trading commissions. Corporate issuers, on the other hand, had needs that were much more episodic—they usually underwent one IPO only, and maybe hired the bank for a bond sale, follow-on equity offering, or merger advice in the years after.

The financial incentives encouraged bankers to give preferential treatment to investors over company issuers. As the millennium ended, investment bankers had come to realize that IPO shares were like currency they could use to reward their best clients, or prospective clients—especially if the shares were discounted in order to deliver immediate gains.

Their lock on the process gave banks the means to engage in a practice that became known as spinning. Bankers took some portion of the shares in an IPO they underwrote and allocated them to corporate executives they had identified as potential clients. Though not illegal at the time, the practice was thought to encourage corporate executives to favor those banks that had handed them shares in previous deals. Even Hambrecht & Quist was the subject of an inquiry into the practice. Hambrecht later said it took place after he'd risen to chairman and given up the CEO's job.

In other cases, banks allocated desirable shares to investors in return for the promise of later trading commissions, sometimes calculated as a percentage of the gains made by the investor when the IPO shares surged. As banks worked for issuers to sell shares and raise corporate funds, they were handing cheap shares to favored clients in order to win future business. Critics were left to wonder, rightfully, if the banks were deliberately underpricing the IPOs.

With technology fees fueling investment bank coffers, some of the industry's biggest players looked to cash in. In May, Wall Street's last major investment banking partnership came to an end when Goldman Sachs sold shares to the public. Unlike the IPOs for many of its clients, Goldman's shares rose just 33 percent on their first day of trading.

Few bankers personified the excesses of the era more than Frank Quattrone. By this time, his technology group, which included investment bankers, research analysts including Lise Buyer, and private bankers, set up retail brokerage accounts for corporate executives and seeded them with hot IPO shares. During Quattrone's time at Credit Suisse, the bank set up more than two hundred brokerage accounts for technology executives and filled them with a few hundred shares each of the most popular IPOs, regulators later alleged. As the stock appreciated in the days and weeks following, the executives found themselves sitting on tidy sums due to Quattrone's generosity. Known as "Friends of Frank," the executives would often select Credit Suisse for future investment banking assignments, netting Quattrone's group millions in fees. If they didn't, according to the allegations, Credit Suisse would later cut the share of IPOs that they awarded to those executives.

The practice was beginning to bother Buyer, who explained how the system worked in a July 1999 email. The "only unpleasant part of all this," she wrote to someone outside the bank, was that allocations were increasingly going to friends and family of the investment bank. "So it becomes something of a 'you scratch my back, I will scratch yours.'"

Credit Suisse also allocated shares to institutional investors in return for trading commissions. Beginning in April 1999 and continuing into 2000, Credit Suisse bankers allocated IPO shares to over one hundred customers, largely hedge funds, willing to send between 33 percent and 65 percent of their profits back to the bank, the SEC later alleged. The bank paid $100 million to settle the allegations.

The link between allocations and trading commissions had devolved into "almost a straightforward financial transaction," Hambrecht recalled. If you gave an investor $1 million in first-day profits from allocations of an underpriced IPO, that investor would repay the favor with $500,000 of commissions within a week. "That was pretty hard to avoid," Hambrecht later said. "That was the primary reason why I finally felt that the only way we could change the system was to do [the IPO] with a new firm that was not dependent on the institutional brokerage business."

Goldman Sachs was also getting into the game. On September 17, 1999, Goldman's David Dechman sent an email to some colleagues asking them to consider how the firm could better use the IPOs they were doing to win business. "The hot deals are obviously a currency, which can be used to please institutions, please high net worth individuals, acquire new customers (perhaps for GS.com), help ECM as per the memo, etc.," he wrote, referring to the bank's equity capital markets business. "How should we allocate between the various Firm businesses to maximize value to GS?"

A senior Goldman Sachs executive, Robert Steel, who was co-head of equity sales, later wrote an email to a senior executive at Putnam Investments, a large Boston-based asset manager that was then one of the firm's biggest clients: "It is my view that we should be rewarded with additional secondary business for offering access to capital markets product."

The same month that Goldman's Dechman sent his email, Chase Manhattan, the second-largest U.S. bank, pledged to purchase Hambrecht & Quist for

$1.35 billion to expand its footprint in securities underwriting. One of the architects of the deal was James B. Lee Jr., a Williams College classmate of McCarthy's who was a senior banker at Chase Manhattan. The transaction made H&Q the last San Francisco–based investment bank to give up its independence. Citigroup Inc. had bought Travelers Corp. the prior year, ushering in a wave of consolidation that witnessed the largest U.S. commercial banks making inroads into the Silicon Valley tech scene. NationsBank Corp. and BankAmerica Corp. had already purchased Montgomery Securities and Robertson Stephens, respectively.

The system of underwriting IPOs had broken down in other places too. The opinion of research analysts and the tailwind they could provide in selling a deal became so important that senior bankers leaned on them to write favorable reports.

But analysts had to walk a fine line. The NYSE and the National Association of Securities Dealers rules required analysts to have a "reasonable basis" for their recommendations and to write reports that gave a balanced picture of a stock's risk and return without exaggerated or unwarranted claims. In November 1999, Citigroup analyst Jack Grubman upgraded AT&T from a longtime rating of "neutral" to a "buy" after Sanford Weill, the co-CEO of Citigroup and a board member at AT&T, asked Grubman to take a "fresh look" at the company. In return, Grubman allegedly asked Weill for help getting his kids into a prestigious nursery school. Just a few months later, in February 2000, AT&T named Citigroup subsidiary Salomon Smith Barney one of the lead managers on the IPO of its wireless business, paying SSB $63 million in fees for its work. The SEC later charged that Grubman had upgraded AT&T to curry favor with Weill and get his kids into the nursery school. Grubman got a lifetime ban from the securities industry and a $15 million fine, which Citigroup settled with regulators. Weill avoided a penalty.

"Grubman was the linchpin for SSB's investment banking efforts in the telecom sector," the SEC later wrote in its complaint. "He was the preeminent telecom analyst in the industry, and telecom was of critical importance to SSB. His approval and favorable view were important for SSB to obtain investment banking business from telecom companies in his sector."

At one point, one of Credit Suisse's bankers asked Buyer to take a look at a company called Petopia.com and prepare an IPO pitch. The request was surprising to Buyer, who felt that she should be able to maintain her independence and endorse only those companies that she honestly felt had a strong future ahead of them. "He didn't ask me if I was interested in covering it—I was told to, because CFSB wanted the banking business," she said. Buyer later refused to cover another company the bankers wanted to take public.

Bankers got even more bold when they engaged in laddering, the practice of allocating underpriced IPO shares with the implicit understanding that investors would buy more shares in the aftermarket at successively higher prices. When securities officials later investigated the practice, more than three hundred companies ultimately were forced to settle lawsuits over it. Why the companies? Securities law holds them to a higher form of liability for misstatements in the securities filings, with the understanding that they have the best idea of what's said in those filings. The law holds other parties to the transaction, such as underwriters, to a lesser standard that requires them to simply prove they conducted a reasonable look into a claim, or did due diligence.

By November 1999, WR Hambrecht + Co. was busy propping up its first OpenIPO transaction. A public filing said Hambrecht and his firm had purchased as many as 6,000 shares a day, most of the 6,400 average trading volume, giving them a 13 percent stake.

When Christmas rolled around, fifty IPOs had been priced in December alone, with an average first-day trading gain of close to 100 percent.

■   ■   ■

On Friday, March 10, 2000, the NASDAQ Composite Index peaked at 5,048.62. The crash began the following week, just as McCarthy was preparing to file documents for Netflix's upcoming IPO. Instead, Netflix shelved its plans. The company would lose almost $58 million in 2000, remaining in business by virtue of a cash cushion McCarthy had raised months before to make the company look good to IPO investors.

On March 20, a *Barron's* story highlighted the fact that many of the most sought-after internet companies were burning through their cash reserves.

The carnage quickly piled up. In the week of April 10, at least sixteen IPOs were withdrawn, including that of internet browser AltaVista. Many of the transactions that went through did so at prices below their offering ranges, including those of Packard BioScience, PEC Solutions, and Embarcadero Technologies. Still, as many as 376 companies were in registration to sell shares totaling $50 billion.

In May, Lise Buyer joined the venture capital industry, becoming a general partner at Palo Alto–based Technology Partners. She arrived in time to help Technology Partners deploy its seventh fund.

In November 2000, with the markets still showing a lukewarm reception to internet companies, Aristotle International Inc. withdrew its planned IPO slated for Hambrecht's OpenIPO system. The NASDAQ Composite Index fell 39 percent for the year.

■ ■ ■

In May 2002, McCarthy tried again at Netflix. This time he was successful, raising $83 million by selling 5.5 million shares for $15 apiece. The stock closed the first day of trading at $16.75, an increase of 12 percent. The IPO valued the company, with 600,000 subscribers, at $330 million.

That month, the public began to get some answers to the question of what lay behind the dot-com boom and bust. Eliot Spitzer, an ambitious New York State attorney general who by then had earned the moniker "Sheriff of Wall Street" for his efforts to clean up the financial industry, reached a settlement with Merrill Lynch over charges that it offered "tainted" analyst research.

Merrill Lynch's Henry Blodget, the analyst who had placed a $400 price target on Amazon.com's shares when he was at Oppenheimer, agreed to be banned from the industry after the SEC charged him with securities fraud for allegedly promoting shares of investment banking clients even as he privately doubted the companies' prospects.

The following year, Quattrone's empire crumbled. The National Association of Securities Dealers alleged in a civil case that Friends of Frank accounts were used to win investment banking business, violating rules against gifts and gratuities. The NASD investigation led the SEC and the Department of Justice to open their own probes.

The DOJ criminally charged Quattrone with obstructing justice over an email he forwarded from a colleague that reminded Credit Suisse employees to "clean up" their files pursuant to the firm's document retention policy. Authorities claimed that Quattrone knew that Credit Suisse was being investigated over an IPO it had underwritten and that his email amounted to encouragement to employees to destroy evidence.

In April 2003, Quattrone turned himself in to U.S. authorities to face the obstruction of justice charges, becoming the first Wall Street executive to be charged in connection with the investigation into the allocation of IPO shares to favored clients. His case became a sensation, captivating the attention of the public when it went to trial. Quattrone testified that he was simply following the firm's document retention policy and knew next to nothing about the investigation into IPOs. He was convicted at trial and sentenced to eighteen months in prison. NASD imposed a lifetime ban from the industry. (Both punishments were later dropped after Quattrone successfully appealed his conviction and the Justice Department agreed to a deferred prosecution agreement under which all charges were dismissed in August 2007, and Quattrone was free to return to the financial industry.)

Analysts were caught up in the investigations as well. Spitzer joined with the SEC, NASD, and the New York Stock Exchange in announcing final terms of the Global Analyst Research Settlement, an agreement intended to eliminate conflicts of interest between investment banking and securities research. At more than one firm, analysts had been paid based on their participation in the investment banking business and the fees the firms brought in from it.

Ten of Wall Street's largest underwriters paid $1.4 billion and agreed to a series of structural reforms to prevent analysts from being influenced by investment bankers or company executives. The underwriters agreed to physically separate research from investment banking, set up separate reporting lines and budgets, remove investment bankers from having a role in choosing which companies analysts covered, discontinue the practice of paying analysts based on investment banking fees, and ban analysts from participating in pitch meetings or roadshows.

A *Frontline* documentary about the worst of the dot-com crash that aired around that time explored alternative approaches to the flawed IPO process.

Both Buyer and Hambrecht, who had continued using his OpenIPO system with some success, were interviewed about how a Dutch auction might be an answer to the excesses of the past. "Dutch auctions make a great deal of sense theoretically, right?" Buyer said. "Everybody pays what they're willing to pay, and that's how you parse out the stocks. But it didn't play well in an environment where people wanted that marketing news, right? There is no headline that says, you know, 'XYZ Corp Trades Up 90 Percent on Its First Day' if there's a Dutch auction."

And yet that's exactly what Google would try.

CHAPTER 6

Google, Mountain View, 2004

The internet was just reaching the masses when Sergey Brin and Larry Page walked onto the palm-lined campus of Stanford University as graduate students in computer science. They developed an algorithm called PageRank to search the rapidly growing internet and released it into the wilds of Stanford's network in 1996. Two years later they incorporated Google to market the search engine they'd developed. By 2003, the company they founded was on the cusp of going public and making them both billionaires.

Google wasn't the first search engine, but five years after its founding, it was quickly becoming what the *Wall Street Journal* dubbed the "front door to the web." It had set out to challenge Yahoo! for search supremacy at a time when many realized that search would grow into a big business. Yahoo! had become one of the first of the era's tech darlings when it sold shares in April 1996.

Google grew rapidly, both in a business sense and in the number of its shareholders of record. The latter was a metric that the SEC focused on, requiring companies with more than five hundred shareholders to file a document—a Form 10—with financial information for public investors. As Google neared that threshold, Brin, Page, and CEO Eric Schmidt began to think about selling shares to the public. To do so, they needed more experts in finance. Former Treasury Department official Sheryl Sandberg had been acting as the company's senior finance official, but as a senior executive in the sales operation she was already spread thin. The company hired George Reyes, a longtime executive at Schmidt's former firm, Sun Microsystems, to be CFO, and looked for other talent.

In March 2003, Sandberg hired a Harvard Business School graduate and Goldman Sachs investment banker named Kim Jabal as finance director in the

online sales department. Raised in a Chicago suburb, Jabal had a round face
framed by a head of tightly coiled blonde hair. She wasn't particularly ambitious, but she was interested in math and engineering. As an undergraduate at
the University of Illinois at Urbana-Champaign, Jabal had distinguished herself by being named an Edmund J. James Scholar, recognition awarded to students with "outstanding academic records, high aptitude, solid reputation, and
self-discipline." She joined Arthur Anderson after graduation and spent much
of the 1990s planning large-scale information technology systems for clients.

When she grew tired of that world, Jabal headed east to Harvard and then
back west for two years in Goldman Sachs's technology, media, and telecommunications (TMT) practice. Older than many of her colleagues at Goldman,
Jabal chafed at the male-dominated hierarchy and the always-on culture of
the investment banking world. After one recruiting dinner in Boston shortly
after Goldman gave BlackBerrys to junior bankers, she hopped into a cab
with her colleagues, only to witness everyone go head-down, staring at their
phones. Jabal was appalled. Goldman thought it was offering a great lifestyle
perk, but she didn't see it.

When Sandberg came calling in late 2002, Google was one of the hottest
companies in town. Jabal had joined Google within months of the arrival of
Buyer, the former Credit Suisse analyst, who had weathered the various investigations into Wall Street's IPO activities with her reputation intact. She was
hired to help Google prepare for the IPO. The two women worked in different parts of the company—Buyer reported to the CFO, while Jabal was in a
business division. But they would overlap during IPO preparations.

Buyer hadn't lost her fondness for evocative language or her aw-shucks
personality. When *Fortune* caught up with her in May 2003, she told the
magazine that she'd been hired to be Google's "official lug-nut checker." The
comment gave cover to her real duties and downplayed her importance. Her
office was on Salado Drive in Mountain View, in one of a collection of low-
slung buildings just east of the Bayshore Freeway that had become Google's
home. Employees ate food prepared in a small mobile-home-type structure
across the street.

The Silicon Valley that Google inhabited when Buyer joined the company was a very different world than the one she had known at Credit Suisse.
The dot-com crash had thrown cold water on the over-the-top marketing and

hype that she had described to *Frontline* the year before. The river of IPOs had dried to a trickle. In 1999, 476 companies had sold shares for the first time, while 380 firms entered the public markets the following year. By 2001, the tally had fallen to just 80, and activity was even lower in 2002, when 66 companies sold shares for the first time.

The dearth of technology competition meant that Google had its pick of talent. The company hired undergraduates out of Stanford to do customer service. Its market position also meant the company could think about doing something different when it came time to sell its shares to the public.

Buyer soon began working on "Project Denny's," so named because a small group of executives had begun holding covert meetings about Google's planned listing at the chain restaurant close to the offices. Regularly in attendance were a core group that also included Reyes and two of Google's lawyers, general counsel David Drummond and a more junior member of the team, Jeff Donovan. By then Brin, Page, and Schmidt had come to a belief that there ought to be a better way of going public.

At the time of Buyer's arrival, the IPO market was quiet, with Silicon Valley still firmly hungover by the dot-com crash of 2000 and 2001. And yet the group was not content to simply restart the IPO market and bring heat back to a technology sector that was still licking its wounds. They set their sights on reimagining the decades-old process, bringing an engineer's mindset to something that had long been the redoubt of Wall Street.

The founders had witnessed the excesses of the dot-com boom and bust, and as they began to think about their own IPO, myriad investigations into investment bankers' allegedly illegal activity would occasionally make their way into the news headlines.

In meetings at Denny's and in closed-door discussions at Google's offices, consensus began to settle on holding some sort of auction. Google was auctioning off thousands of ads every day on its site. There may not have been a company with more auction experience on the planet. If structured right, an auction could also allow Google's users, individual investors scattered across the world, to participate on the same terms as the largest investors.

Google's executives "were engineers and computer scientists," Buyer said much later. "And for engineers and computer scientists you can always architect a better way." As they went looking for experts, the small group of employees found Notre Dame finance professor Ann Sherman, who had done a lot of work on auction theory, and Hal Varian, dean of the University of California–Berkeley's school of information management and systems, who had started working with Google as a consultant in May 2002. They examined a couple of telecom IPOs in Asia that had used an auction process to sell shares. Singapore Telecommunications (Singtel), for example, offered three tranches of shares, including a retail portion that was priced at a discount to encourage small investors to buy into a national asset. Singapore's government made it easy to place orders through automated teller machines.

Google's rumored IPO sparked intense interest. At a May 2003 conference hosted by JPMorgan Chase in San Francisco, Schmidt brushed off IPO talk with a smile. In August, Brin told another conference that Google discussed a possible IPO with its board only once every two or three board meetings and that the company had more pressing issues at hand. Google didn't need the money an IPO would provide, Brin told the audience, due to its profitability and annual revenues. He also cited distractions that he wasn't eager to embrace, such as meetings with Wall Street analysts and investors, or disclosing the company's financials in detail.

In Mountain View, Google executives began thinking about hiring banks. They wrote a request for proposal (RFP), a document that companies sometimes sent to investment banks ahead of a formal pitch process. Several questions in it were about auctions or hinted that Google might be leaning in that direction.

Google was obsessed with secrecy. The writers of the RFP, including Buyer, included slightly different questions in each so that if one of the questions was leaked to the press, they would know which bank had done it.

At Morgan Stanley, the task of responding to the RFP fell to the technology investment banking team, led by Michael Grimes and a capital markets banker in his midthirties named Colin Stewart. Stewart was a Dartmouth College alum who was based in the firm's Menlo Park office, a rising star who had recently returned from a post running equity capital markets in Asia. He reported to Jon Anda. Ted Pick, head of the bank's syndicate desk and known for being surly, was also involved in the deal.

At Credit Suisse, some of the bankers decided to lean into Google's questions, and thought about pitching a modified auction for a retail portion of the offering. The year before, Hambrecht co-managed an offering for Instinet, a trading system then owned by Reuters, using some elements of a Dutch auction. The Credit Suisse team thought it could do something similar.

Google's executives read through the RFPs they'd received. They invited Morgan Stanley, Credit Suisse, Goldman Sachs, JPMorgan, and many other banks to an event that would be held at the Page Mill Road offices of Wilson Sonsini, Google's law firm. The invitation came with a strict set of instructions. Bankers weren't allowed to wear jackets and ties. Bank CEOs weren't allowed, only those who would be working on the deal. When they arrived, the bankers were to avoid signing in under their name or their firm's name to preserve secrecy.

As the date got closer, Goldman CEO Hank Paulson repeatedly called Google angling for a pass to attend. Paulson was an investment banker by training and enjoyed calling on powerful clients. Google executives weren't swayed, and Paulson did not attend. In the years after the deal, Goldman executives would trade a story about Paulson just not being "Googley" enough.

On an autumn weekend in 2003, the bankers made their way to a large room on the second floor of a Wilson Sonsini office in central Palo Alto. John Hodge and Andy Fisher, bankers at Credit Suisse, were there. Eff Martin, Stephen Pierce, and George Lee led Goldman's contingent in Paulson's absence. Paulson's former Goldman colleague Bob Rubin attended on behalf of Citigroup, where he served on the board. Nancy Peretsman, a banker with Allen & Co., brought her dog.

As they listened to the bankers, the Google team looked for substance. This was not a beauty pageant, and no bank was guaranteed a role in the transaction. JPMorgan made a cute video about Google, which failed to impress the Google team because it wasn't substantive.

Goldman took another tack entirely. As the top IPO underwriter at the time, Goldman's bankers arrived at the meeting floating on hubris. They told the assembled Google executives that an auction would be a mistake, and that if they pressed ahead it was going to be a disaster. They should let Goldman do it Goldman's way.

At the conclusion of the pitches, some banks didn't hear anything for many weeks. That didn't stop some of them from talking to reporters, and the media hyped up the prospects for a future Google offering. In an October

2003 article, Reuters quoted an anonymous investment banker: "Search is very hot right now. They have great momentum. It's a weak IPO market and there's tremendous focus on Google."

The upcoming offering, in other words, had done what Silicon Valley hadn't been able to do for at least three years: capture the public's imagination. In a *Wall Street Journal* article from November 4, under the headline "Our savior?," writer Bret Swanson captured the mood:

> The world's expectations of Google, however, are grander still. In an IPO wasteland, where offerings this year hit a 29-year low, some in Silicon Valley view Google's suspected 2004 public debut as a second coming. A $20 billion IPO could reinvigorate the Valley and part the waters for a new round of Internet capital. (Not to mention single-handedly salvage a nearly wiped-out $2 billion venture fund for top-flight Kleiner Perkins.) Still not satisfied, some are hoping Google uses its exalted platform to transform the entire hierarchy of the closed and clubby IPO system.

During the first week of November, Google sent a one-page document with five questions about auctions to Credit Suisse and asked for a meeting. Andy Fisher was playing golf with some East Coast friends to celebrate their birthdays at Pebble Beach. He had no choice but to cut his trip short and drive north.

The search company's executives had asked the bankers to keep their identities secret, so when the Credit Suisse team arrived they signed in as "AF & Co," Fisher's initials. The meeting was held in a nondescript conference room with Brin, Page, Buyer, Reyes, and Drummond.

A month or more later, Buyer called Credit Suisse again. Google was ready to make its selection. But first, Schmidt wanted to meet one of the firm's bankers and look him in the eye. "Eric wants to have this meeting, and we want one person from Credit Suisse to come and meet with him," Buyer said.

Since Credit Suisse figured the discussion was likely to deal with the mechanics of an auction, they chose to send Fisher, one of their ECM bankers, to meet with Schmidt.

Fisher crammed for the meeting. "I prepared like nobody's business, because I figured it was probably the most important meeting of my career." It would be in Mountain View.

Fisher met with Schmidt in a large auditorium. The two men found a couple of chairs in the huge space and sat down for a discussion. It was just the two of them. Fisher was primed to talk about auctions. "Can you please tell me by what the demand for IPOs is overstated in an IPO?" Schmidt asked him. He was referring to percentage or amount: in other words, how much of the demand for IPOs was bullshit.

Fisher hadn't prepared to answer that question. "I teach a class at Stanford, and there was a guy in my class, and he worked for a money manager," Schmidt continued. "He said it was his job just to lie as much as he possibly could about how much demand he had, so he could get as much stock as he possibly could. So how much is the demand overstated by?"

Fisher thought there was no hiding anything from this guy. "Well, these things are twenty times oversubscribed," he answered. And then he walked Schmidt through the math. "It's twenty times oversubscribed because all these people give you orders for 10 percent of the deal. They don't really want 10 percent of the deal—they don't expect to get 10 percent of the deal." By giving a bigger number, the investor expected the bank to factor that into the allocation process. Hopefully, the investor's outsized order would garner it a bigger percentage of the deal.

The meeting went on like that, with Schmidt asking questions about the inner workings of the IPO market and Fisher answering, for about forty-five minutes.

Fisher left thinking he'd performed pretty well. He'd answered Schmidt's questions and given him the sense that Credit Suisse knew what it was doing. The following Friday, he got another call from Buyer. Google had hired Credit Suisse as one of the lead banks for its upcoming IPO. Fisher was elated. Who were the other bookrunners? he asked.

Morgan Stanley and Credit Suisse. That's it, she said. Goldman would not lead the deal.

After hanging up, Fisher did what any self-respecting banker would do after getting a call like that. He screamed.

And then he took the afternoon off. He grabbed a young banker who was a decent golfer and headed to the public course at Crystal Springs, off Route 280.

. . .

With the banks hired, it was time for the organizational meeting to bring everyone up to speed.

It was again held at Wilson Sonsini's offices. Drummond, Google's general counsel, had been a lawyer at Wilson when he helped Page and Brin incorporate the business, and the ties between the two firms were strong.

Morgan Stanley and Credit Suisse hired Simpson Thacher & Bartlett LLP partner William Hinman. Hinman was already a well-respected lawyer, with an honors degree from Michigan State University and a law degree from Cornell University. He had been a member of the editorial board of the *Cornell Law Review* during his graduate schooling.

As bankers and lawyers gathered for the meeting, many of them still didn't know how big Google was by revenue, or how fast it was growing. The Credit Suisse bankers had organized a betting pool among themselves, and its members made a wide range of guesses.

At the meeting, Schmidt got up at the front of the room and began to present Google's financials. In 2003, the company's net revenue was close to $1 billion.

One lawyer in the room was stunned. "Oh," he said.

It was simply orders of magnitude bigger than any other private tech company at the time. To put it in perspective, bankers had been taking companies public with $3 million to $5 million in quarterly revenue at the height of the dot-com boom in 1999 and 2000.

Most of the Credit Suisse bankers had guessed something considerably less. Only one got anywhere close to what Schmidt disclosed.

. . .

Once the organizational meeting was completed, Google and its advisors got down to designing the auction. Morgan Stanley and Credit Suisse were invited to a meeting at headquarters, convened in Google's executive offices, in a glass-walled conference room. Once again, the number of bankers who

were allowed to attend was restricted. Jon Anda, head of corporate finance for
Morgan Stanley and the former equity capital markets chief, was there. Fisher
was there for Credit Suisse, sitting across the table from Schmidt, Page, Brin,
and Reyes.

Anda, Stewart, and others at Morgan Stanley were striving to come
up with an auction process that could handle the huge influx of orders they
expected from retail investors. It wasn't an easy task for Wall Street information systems in 2004.

The bankers also spent a lot of time working through the ways in which
they would accept the orders from other banks that would help underwrite
the offering. Individual investors had never before put in an order with a price
limit, which meant some of the banks that would be accepting those orders
needed to add a field to the order-entry systems. And Morgan Stanley needed
to come up with a way to accept the orders electronically from other banks
and merge them with the other orders. Google wasn't interested in having the
orders sent by fax.

As they worked out the details, the Morgan Stanley bankers had to bring
along the rest of their firm. A new approach meant more risk, and their bosses,
Vikram Pandit and John Havens, wanted to know how the Google IPO could
enhance the firm's franchise, not destroy it.

Another idea would have been to have an auction for institutional inves-
tors and let retail investors tag along but not let them actually set the price.
The bank even submitted a patent for an institutional-only auction. The
Google executives didn't like that idea.

To accomplish what it wanted, the bankers had to make some hard
choices. A good deal of those choices had the effect of stripping elements of an
auction out of the system.

When it came time for Anda to speak, he stood up and approached a
whiteboard at the front of the room, where he scrawled a few of Morgan Stanley's ideas for the structure of the auction. He proposed that investors could
put in a bid and only change it once. When Anda was done walking the room
through some of the bank's suggestions, Schmidt rose and took his place at
the whiteboard. With a marker that might as well have been red, he proceeded
line by line to cross out the items Anda had listed.

Google wouldn't be doing what Morgan Stanley had proposed, and the company wanted its bankers to know quite clearly that it knew it had veto power and intended to use it. Google wanted the auction to be as flexible as possible to encourage individual investors to get involved. The bankers at Morgan Stanley, working with Google engineers, weren't sure their technology could handle it. They worried that they wouldn't be able to sort through the thousands of orders that they were expecting, some in penny increments. Everything that Google wanted to do that would enhance flexibility for retail was something that made the software that much harder to write.

"Google was very much, 'Let's democratize this,'" said one of the lawyers involved. "The banks were like, 'Let's make sure we can make it work.' And there was a little tension between those two ideas."

Morgan Stanley ultimately built an auction system that could accept a billion bids.

*   *   *

With the broad outlines of the auction system coming into focus, Google's team wrote the company's prospectus. At the same time, its lawyers prepared to file a Form 10. Google had breached the threshold of five hundred shareholders. The document, governed by the Securities Exchange Act of 1934, served to register securities for potential trading on an exchange. According to SEC rules, the form needed to be filed no later than 120 days after the end of the fiscal year, meaning it had to be in by April 29. Google planned to surprise the market and release its IPO registration statement at the same time.

To do so, the company needed to submit its paperwork through an intermediary called a financial printer. A holdover from an earlier era when companies didn't have the typesetting capabilities to create their own securities prospectuses, the financial printer played a role in helping them format documents. By 2004, the printer still played a pivotal role, taking the Form 10 or an IPO prospectus from the company, proofreading, formatting, and translating it, if necessary, and then submitting it through its system to the SEC.

As the deadline neared, the lawyers assembled at the offices of the printer, R. R. Donnelley, on California Ave. in Palo Alto, behind Wilson Sonsini's offices. Like many of Palo Alto's buildings, Donnelley's office was clad in stucco, with a red tile roof, a nod to the region's Spanish heritage. Visitors walked through several large arches before reaching an inner courtyard.

They set up a long table in one room. As April wound down, Google's founders and top executives assembled around the table to do something they called page flips. Drafts of the prospectus were printed out from a kiosk and passed out to everyone to read from beginning to end. Then someone would lead the group, a conductor of sorts, through a page-by-page review. If someone had a change, the conductor made it on the master copy, finally handing that over to the customer service desk at Donnelley for the printer to log them in to the official version housed on their systems. At one point, Google sent over some English majors who were on staff to rewrite some of the legal jargon, and their edits had to be inputted in the same way. Because the process was so archaic, what should have taken minutes instead took hours.

Sometime before the countdown to the deadline, Thursday, April 29, a crowd assembled around the customer service desk at Donnelley. Brin, Page, Schmidt, and Drummond were there for Google, as were the company's lawyers from Wilson Sonsini. Some of the investment bankers were there, and at least one of their lawyers.

Everyone was "holding their breath while last-minute changes were being forced through the document before you hit that magic button that says 'Submit' to the SEC," according to one of the people there.

Finally, Donnelley's people submitted the document to the agency.

As people celebrated, some of the lawyers continued to prevail upon the printer until the Form 10 was submitted.

■ ■ ■

Google's prospectus became required reading from Silicon Valley to Wall Street. It was the first time the public was seeing the company's financial results. It was also the first time the public got a look at the structure of its IPO, which the prospectus addressed in at least three sections.

Near the top of the document, Google explained the reasoning behind its choice of an auction-based IPO. "It is important to us to have a fair process for our IPO that is inclusive of both small and large investors," the founders wrote, in a letter to investors they styled after Warren Buffett's investor communications. "It is also crucial that we achieve a good outcome for Google and its current shareholders."

They continued, "Many companies have suffered from unreasonable speculation, small initial share float, and boom-bust cycles that hurt them and their investors in the long run. We believe that an auction-based IPO will minimize these problems.

"An auction is an unusual process for an IPO in the United States," they added. "Our experience with auction-based advertising systems has been surprisingly helpful in the auction design process for the IPO. As in the stock market, if people try to buy more stock than is available, the price will go up. And of course, the price will go down if there aren't enough buyers. This is a simplification, but it captures the basic issues."

The letter said that the founders were encouraging current shareholders to "consider selling some of their shares" as part of the process to ensure there would be enough supply to set a reasonable market. "The more shares current shareholders sell, the more likely it is that they believe the price is not unfairly low.

"We would like you to invest for the long term, and to do so only at or below what you determine to be a fair price. We encourage investors not to invest in Google at IPO or for some time after, if they believe the price is not sustainable over the long term," the founders wrote, before moving on to sections about "Googlers," or employees, and the company motto, Don't Be Evil.

At the end of pages and pages of risk factors, Google listed six specific to its choice of an auction: the stock price could decline quickly; successful buyers might experience a winner's curse, the term used to describe what happened when bidders won an auction, only to find little demand at higher prices than they paid; successful bidders looking to sell quickly by flipping the shares might be disappointed; successful bidders might receive the full amount of the shares they asked for; submitting a bid did not guarantee an allocation; the systems, procedures, and results of the auction might hurt Google's brand.

Then, under the heading "Auction Process," Google outlined five stages: qualification, bidding, closing, pricing, and allocation. The process wasn't simple. Each buyer needed to obtain a unique bidder ID by clicking a hyperlink. This they could do once they'd met an underwriter group's eligibility and suitability requirements—written to include all types of investors.

Bidders would receive their IDs electronically once they'd provided certain information to the underwriter, and if they could show that they had electronically accessed both the prospectus and the transcript of a management presentation.

Once investors received IDs and the bidding started, they were to indicate the number of shares they wanted to buy and the price they were willing to pay. They could submit more than one bid. There would be a minimum bid size, though Google left that blank in the preliminary prospectus.

Bidders could withdraw at any time until the end of the auction process. If they submitted multiple successful bids at different prices, they should expect to buy all of the shares they had ordered. In other words, bids would be considered in total. Google and its underwriters reserved the right to reject bids that the company considered speculative or attempts to disrupt the bidding process.

The instructions continued. The "master order book" would be monitored to gauge demand, the prospectus stated, and the company provided warnings to investors that suggested Google was preparing for a frenzy of demand that might lead it to sell more shares in the offering, depressing the stock price. "We and the selling stockholders may decide to change the number of shares of Class A common stock offered through this prospectus," the document read. "It is very likely that the number of shares offered by the selling stockholders will increase if the price range increases. In an auction process, this could result in downward pressure on the price. You should be aware that we have the ability to make multiple such revisions up until the closing of the auction and pricing of the offering."

Before Google closed the auction, it would ask the SEC to declare the registration statement effective. The company could close the auction within hours of the offering prospectus's being deemed effective. If bidders were asked to confirm their bids and didn't, their bids would be rejected.

When it came time to decide on a value for the shares, Google said it would find the highest dollar figure at which all the shares could be sold, and then set the IPO price "near or equal to" it. The underwriters would then begin the allocation process. If the IPO price was at or close to the clearing price, bidders should expect to get roughly the number of shares they'd bid for. If the winning bids represented more shares than were on offer, Google would allocate them to winning bidders in one of two ways: pro rata, apportioning a percentage arrived at by dividing the number being sold by the total orders, or maximum share, based on an algorithm that favored smaller bids over larger ones. Tables in the document represented two hypothetical auctions to illustrate the two methods.

In either case, Google said that it would set the IPO price at a level at which bidders would receive at least 80 percent of what they'd asked for.

■ ■ ■

Having filed the prospectus with the SEC, Google began negotiations with regulators. The company intended to set up a website, Meet the Management, to inform investors about what it did and who the founders and senior executives were. It would serve as a central hub to keep everyone informed about the deal. The company's lawyers submitted schematics of what each page of the site would say. In some cases, Google had ideas for educating the public that the SEC didn't let them use. In one instance the company wanted to provide a Bidders Handbook that it had written in plain English as an appendix to the prospectus. In another, informed by their belief that investors should know something about Google, the founders wanted to set up a simple four-question test before buyers would be allowed to bid. The answers to the questions would be found in the prospectus or on the website. The SEC rejected both ideas. The agency also required the company to organize a process so that people without internet access could buy shares. The Google team set up a series of analog notifications it could send to people at each stage of the auction process.

The nuances of the auction and the SEC's requirements bogged the process down and required Google's team to submit amendment after amendment. All of their prospectuses were made public—unlike those issued for much later IPOs, which allowed companies to submit a draft registration statement confidentially and work out certain details with the SEC in private. Instead, the company and the agency hashed out the details of the auction over the course of nine amendments between the end of April and the IPO.

■ ■ ■

On May 21, the company put out an updated prospectus showing that it had hired thirty-one underwriters. Brin and Page were adamant that small-time investors have the same opportunities as the mutual funds and hedge funds, leading them to hire a group of minority-owned and regional brokerages for the deal in addition to other, more typical Wall Street underwriters.

Besides Credit Suisse and Morgan Stanley, who had been listed all along, Goldman Sachs, Citigroup, and WR Hambrecht + Co. received mention, as did Allen & Co., JPMorgan, and Thomas Weisel Partners. Farther down the list were Ameritrade Inc., M.R. Beal & Company, William Blair & Company LLC, Blaylock & Partners LP, E*TRADE Securities LLC, Muriel Siebert & Co. Inc., and others.

Thomas Weisel Partners, the last of the independent boutique investment banks focused on the technology sector, was a surprising choice. A successor to the Four Horsemen, Weisel was run by an investment banker who had founded Montgomery Securities. Since then, the firm had been overshadowed by much larger banks.

Its inclusion owed everything to Kleiner Perkins Caufield & Byers' John Doerr, a Google board member who had a soft spot for Weisel as the last of the independent investment banking boutiques not to have been swallowed by larger rivals. He wanted to see Thomas Weisel Partners succeed, and he pushed for its hiring. Google promised the firm a very small fee.

Hambrecht, also on the deal, had used OpenIPO repeatedly by that time—for Andover.net and Peet's Coffee & Tea Company, for instance. Though not all of his efforts had been successful, he was Silicon Valley's foremost voice on using auctions to price IPOs. The Google team had spoken at length to Hambrecht about his process, though in the end Page and Brin decided on a compromise. There were aspects of Hambrecht's system that they didn't like, so they decided to create their own. Google wanted the offering to be accessible to individual investors, and they felt that Hambrecht's OpenIPO didn't do that in a way that they liked.

His presence on the transaction was a tip of the hat, and Google paid him a small fee from the IPO to recognize his pioneering approach.

The same day that Google announced Hambrecht's involvement, an auction he was handling got pulled. Alibris Inc., the owner of a website that sold new and used books, had met with tepid demand for its shares. In a statement, the CEO said that he stood behind the auction process and predicted that it would become more common among big companies selling shares for the first time.

With such a large number of banks involved in the Google transaction, it was inevitable that many would find aspects of the auction design not to their liking. Some of the bankers were upset that Morgan Stanley and Credit Suisse were requiring them to sign nondisclosure agreements. Others didn't know how many shares they would get in the IPO to pass along to clients, or how they would calculate the fees they should expect.

Compensation for typical IPOs is calculated under what's known as fixed economics. The underwriting fee, calculated as a percentage of the deal or gross spread, is divided up into three sub-fees. There is a management fee, an underwriting fee, and a selling commission. The breakdown was often 20 percent, 20 percent, and 60 percent.

So in a traditional deal, the lead bookrunners, like Morgan Stanley and Credit Suisse, placed two-thirds of the stock with their institutional clients, and each could expect to take home 30–35 percent of the total fees. Auctions like those run by Hambrecht worked in much the same way, though Hambrecht charged a smaller fee than was common.

But in the Google deal, if all 60 percent of the selling concession went to other firms, Morgan Stanley and Credit Suisse would end up making very little. They worried that if the deal was as popular with retail investors as they expected, there was the possibility that despite having spent six months or more designing the auction, they wouldn't make much money. So these two underwriters decided to do away with the selling concession and split the fees between just a management fee and an underwriting fee.

For decades, Wall Street salespeople were paid on IPOs by getting a commission based on how many of their clients put in orders for the stock. By the time of the Google offering, some had done away with those but still awarded sales credits that worked in the same way. It was a mechanism to reward salespeople for getting their clients involved in the deal.

By cutting the selling concession fee from Google's deal, the lead underwriters took away any incentive that salespeople at the regional or smaller firms had to market Google's deal or encourage their clients to buy shares. (Merrill Lynch & Co. dropped out of the syndicate, concerned about the fee structure and the large technology investment it would have to make.)

∎ ∎ ∎

By late July 2004, some of the investment banks worried that Morgan Stanley and Credit Suisse's insistence that they guarantee the orders from their clients, even if the clients couldn't pay, might leave them on the hook to buy stock they couldn't sell. The banks did not like the heavy involvement of retail traders.

Morgan Stanley wondered what might happen if one of those smaller brokerages had many clients who all put in high bids for the stock. If those bids helped make the deal frothy and pushed up the price, the bankers knew that a version of the winner's curse might saddle investors with losses and that they might not have the money to pay for the stock.

The worst-case scenario would mean that investors wouldn't be able to make good on orders they'd sent through the smaller brokerages, and Morgan Stanley and Credit Suisse would have to stand behind the deal. So the underwriters persuaded the SEC to agree that if more than 10 percent of the orders defaulted, the deal would be canceled. The default clause was often written into underwriting contracts, but the SEC had ruled in the past that IPOs meeting the default definition were still effective. The agency had insisted that those deals go through.

The lead underwriters also required that other members of the syndicate stand behind their clients' orders, and they reserved the right to require letters of credit or other credit support if they felt they needed it. The duty of communicating the need for letters of credit fell to Credit Suisse's Fisher, who held a call with the underwriters to tell them.

After the call, Goldman's Stephen Pierce called one of the lead bankers. "We're Goldman Sachs," he said. "We've been in business for a hundred and some years, and we've never had to post a letter of credit for a deal like this and we're not doing it."

In the end, the lead underwriters required all bidders to have enough money in their account to cover the bid.

∎ ∎ ∎

On July 26, Google disclosed for the first time the price at which it would sell its shares. After hearing an appeal from the company, the SEC allowed it to publish a wider range than usual. Google's shares would be sold between $108 and $135 apiece. At the high end of the range, the company would raise nearly $4 billion. The high end of the range was higher than many Wall Street investors and analysts expected.

The following day, Clarium Capital's Peter Thiel joined CNBC to talk about the Google IPO. Thiel had taken his payments company PayPal public on Valentine's Day 2002, selling shares at $13, only to see them rise to more than $20. Though PayPal was sold to eBay later that year, the IPO experience led Thiel to believe that the company left too much money on the table. In December 2003, Thiel told *Barron's* that he had considered selling shares directly to investors before giving in to some of his partners' nervousness to go with a traditional offering, underwritten by Salomon Smith Barney. If he got a second opportunity, he said he'd like to try selling shares directly to investors.

Thiel also knew the Google founders, a fact that put him in an awkward position when CNBC hosts Larry Kudlow and Jim Cramer began to criticize the company's offering. As veterans of the financial industry, both television personalities were known for being sympathetic to institutional investors who watched their network.

CNBC had also successfully built an audience with day traders during the internet boom, and both men spent time speaking on radio, giving them a perspective on what Main Street investors thought about Google. After bantering with Thiel about how Google's valuation compared to Yahoo!'s, the hosts got right to the heart of their doubts about the company.

"Peter, let me tell you what I hear a lot of retail people say today," said Cramer. "A hundred and thirty dollars, to heck with it. I'd rather go buy eBay, I'd rather go buy some of the other dot-coms, which then soar." His comment hit on the widely held belief that investors buy IPOs for the first-day pop, the sugar rush of quick profits they had grown conditioned to expect in the go-go years of the late 1990s.

Google's offering wasn't intended to deliver that, Thiel replied. "Google is not going to get investors who are looking for a quick flip," the PayPal founder said, making the additional point that Google was trying to discourage the hot money on Wall Street. "You shouldn't expect a huge one-day pop. It's going to be priced very efficiently."

Kudlow jumped in to say that maybe the Google founders thought they were a little too smart for their own good. The market will make its own decision, he said.

"I think it's absolutely stupid for these kids, whoever they are," Kudlow said, "to think that that's not going to happen." He continued, coming back to Cramer's remark about the expected price of the shares. "It's a lot of money, one hundred to one hundred thirty bucks, or whatever the spread is anticipated. This is a gang that was going to democratize the share purchases. Now why not price the damn thing at fifteen dollars or twenty dollars?"

Thiel said that Google was looking for long-term investors. "They're looking for people who are going to hold it in the long term. Now maybe there's nobody like that left in this whole country, in which case they're going to have a pretty big disaster when their IPO comes up, you're right. But the assumption is that's not the case."

As the interview continued, Cramer got worked up. He could have been talking for any number of institutional investors. "If you had to ruin an IPO deal, I would do exactly what they did," Cramer said. "They, first of all, didn't court any of the institutions." He was referring to large institutional investors. "The institutions are saying the heck with it. Secondly, I would price the deal in April or May, not in the dog days, but that's because they dithered so long. Then finally, a hundred thirty dollars, the only people who really are going to do that are the institutions, but they're already so upset about this that they're going to go and buy eBay. I mean, who was in charge of this thing?"

Thiel tried to move the conversation with the strong-spirited hosts to a different place. "Let's put this in a broader context," he said. "You have to look at this as part of a long-standing struggle between the tech industry and the banking industry, and it goes to who captures the value. When you build a great company, do the people who build the company, the original investors, get it, or do the bankers on Wall Street? And a lot of what was going on here beneath the surface was a decision to try to cut back on Wall Street's enormous profits and so on down the line."

Kudlow softened his stance. The host said he liked the idea of teaching bankers a lesson and was in favor of the Dutch auction. Cramer countered by asking if Thiel had any involvement in the process. He didn't.

As the segment wound to a close, Kudlow asked Thiel if he would buy the stock.

"Well, it depends on where the auction price is," he said. "Probably not at one thirty-five. If it's around a hundred, I might."

In other words, anything higher than $100 was too much for the PayPal veteran to pay.

■ ■ ■

Professional investors were coming to a similar conclusion as Google executives fanned out across the country for a series of meetings to drum up demand for their shares. The roadshow required executives and their bankers to fly to various cities for often large meetings with investors, conducted in an auditorium or ballroom.

In late July, Google executives visited New York's Waldorf Astoria for a luncheon in the hotel's ground-floor ballroom. Only those investors who were clients of Morgan Stanley and Credit Suisse were allowed into the room, and only after showing identification. Hundreds of investors and analysts were there, giving the event a crowded and chaotic feel.

But when it came time for presentations from Brin, Page, Schmidt, and Reyes and a Q&A, the executives came off as less than polished. They spoke off the cuff, answering questions without consulting their presentation. At one point, one of the executives tried to tell a joke and it fell flat. "I certainly don't think it was our best showing," recalled Buyer, who was sitting in the audience. "It was a little more ad-libbed than would have been ideal. That's the way that Sergey, Larry, and Eric wanted to do it."

Google didn't offer many new details about its competitive position to rivals or about how the auction would work, leaving some investors wanting for information. Writing about it at the time, the *Wall Street Journal* said that "when the presentation, and question-and-answer period that followed, failed to give the investors the insight they came for, there was some disenchantment."

On August 2, Brin, Schmidt, Reyes, and Buyer appeared at a hotel on Boston's waterfront for a presentation in front of a smaller crowd of fifty or sixty investors. As the investors found their seats at tables set with silverware and plates, they found a small menu that introduced the Google team. The Google team was dressed informally, without ties, in keeping with a decision to ignore some of Wall Street's long-standing conventions.

"I was in Boston for another reason and conveniently managed to wrangle an invitation," said Barry Randall, then the lead manager of the First American Technology Fund, part of US Bancorp Asset Management, based in the Twin Cities. Randall, used to evaluating thirty to forty IPOs a year in those days, took two pages of notes as he listened to the Google executives speak. "The first thing that stands out about it is nothing stood out about it. I mean, by this time everyone knew about the auction."

Google's management warned investors that the business was seasonal, with the two middle quarters of the year tending to be weaker than the first or the last. The discussion also touched on Google's relatively new email product, Gmail; the fact that Google would have multiple share classes that gave the founders complete control; and traffic acquisition costs and other financial minutiae. Not one investor asked about the auction, according to Randall's recollections and notes.

"It was shockingly tame and uncontroversial," Randall said. His notes from the meeting were shorter than usual.

■ ■ ■

As Google set out to create the auction process, there were hundreds of tiny decisions they had to make. Many of those had to be run by the SEC, which was particularly sensitive about company executives talking up an upcoming offering outside of the filings they submitted to the agency.

From the moment companies filed a prospectus with the SEC, securities laws required them to observe a quiet period that prevented them from communicating publicly about the deal other than through use of the prospectus. Earlier that year, the SEC had slapped the wrists of cloud-computing pioneer Salesforce.com after the *New York Times* published an article that quoted CEO Marc Benioff while the company was going public. Four days later, the

SEC forced the company to delay its offering and enter into a "cooling off" period that would let the effect of the article dissipate. The incident showed that the SEC was prepared to enforce a strict interpretation of what it considered an offer of securities.

During the week of August 9, as Google was preparing to close the bidding registration period, the company's PR team received word from *Playboy* magazine that the publication would be accelerating the release of a piece based on an interview a contributing editor had conducted with the founders in April, before they'd filed their prospectus with the SEC. It would be in the September issue, available to the public that week. Now Google was quite possibly in the same boat as Salesforce.com. An offering that had already been delayed because of regulatory negotiations and trying to create something from scratch was now in danger of being delayed even further. There was a very real chance that the SEC would consider the piece a violation of the Securities Act of 1933, which forbids companies from hyping their offering during the registration period.

One Wilson Sonsini lawyer, after being told by Google executives about the forthcoming article, thought to himself, *I either use my wastepaper basket to throw up in, or just to pack up whatever I could grab in my office, and go home and say, Okay, I'm done with being a lawyer at Wilson Sonsini.* The lawyer called lead partner Larry Sonsini to let him know what was going on.

Before the lawyers could formulate a response, they needed to know what the article said. On Wednesday, August 11, Google and its team got copies of the magazine and someone took a pile over to Donnelley, the printer. By this point, food wrappers and old papers littered the room. As the stack of *Playboy* magazines sat on the table, lawyers and accountants helped themselves to a magazine from the pile and began reading the interview.

The lawyers knew they had to contact the SEC. The Wilson lawyers, including David Segre, one of the lead attorneys, were already connected to officials at the SEC's Division of Corporation Finance, including Paula Dubberly and Barb Jacobs, assistant directors of the division. When the lawyers finally reached the officials by phone, the SEC drew a hard line.

"We can't treat you better, or differently, than we treated Salesforce," one participant remembers an official saying. "So, sorry, guys, we're going to cool you off."

Then Sonsini spoke up. Already an eminence in Silicon Valley thanks to his early embrace of emerging technology companies, he asked that the agency try to keep an open mind. That he was speaking to two female SEC officials about an unauthorized article in a men's magazine wasn't lost on at least one participant in the call. "Can you just let us at least try and convince you," Sonsini said, according to this person's recollection, "that that's not the right remedy for the situation in which we find ourselves?"

Dubberly was noncommittal. "You can try, but we don't see any way out of this."

The team of lawyers got to work drafting a memo that would expand beyond nine pages to explain to the SEC why Google's IPO could move forward. The work would take them late into the night and into the early hours of the next morning. The lawyers made several suggestions to make it easier for the SEC to rule in Google's favor. One was that with most of the world anticipating the IPO, an interview in *Playboy* was effectively white noise. It wasn't adding much hype to an already hyped-up transaction. The founders had already been on the cover of *Newsweek* and no one read *Playboy* for investment advice.

Simpson Thacher attorney William Hinman, who represented the underwriters, made the point that investors planning to participate in the IPO had to be registered by the time the auction started, on Friday, August 13. The magazine wouldn't be on most newsstands by then. If the SEC required Google to enter a cooling-off period, the company would have to reopen the bidding registration, and then, they could be assured, everyone would have read the magazine. It would throw sand in the cogs of an already complex offering and potentially disadvantage some investors.

They scheduled a follow-up call with the SEC for the following morning.

As they were drafting their memo to the SEC, Hinman foresaw an issue. He was scheduled to be on a plane to Oregon to attend an important family commitment. He wouldn't be able to make the call. But things should be in good shape, he told the founders. The SEC was open to innovation and wanted the deal to go well because Google had democratized the offering process and had broken up the old-boy network of allocations. He wasn't too worried.

Brin wasn't having it. "Oh no, you have to be on the call," he said. "We want you on the call."

Hinman didn't think he could change his flight.

"Well, we'll get you a private plane with a phone," Brin answered. He made a call and spoke to someone.

Early Thursday morning, with the sun rising over the Palo Alto office park where they had been furiously drafting, the team of lawyers faxed the memo to the SEC. And Hinman headed to the San Jose airport. When he arrived, the lawyer asked the pilots of the private plane he would be taking if the phone on board worked well. What phone? they said. They hadn't gotten that detail. Hinman asked them if he could rent a satellite phone. Yes, they said. "Two thousand dollars." A satellite phone it would be.

In the end, the SEC checked in early and Hinman was able to take the call in the airport's waiting area. He and the other lawyers explained their case, and the SEC hung up. By the time he took off in Google's private jet, Hinman didn't know if the SEC would let the company go.

In the end, the agency agreed that it wouldn't force Google to delay the IPO, but the company needed to include the entire text of the *Playboy* interview in an amendment to the company's prospectus. Doing so would ensure that investors reading the prospectus would know what the founders had said, and it would also mean that the company and its underwriters were taking legal liability for the article. If investors later found that they were misled by comments made in the interview, they would have grounds to take legal action.

On Friday morning, August 13, Google put out amendment No. 7, with the *Playboy* article listed as Appendix B.

■   ■   ■

By the time the article was widely available on newsstands that weekend, all the bidders had been registered with one of the underwriters or brokerages involved in the IPO. The auction had finally begun. Over the next several days, the bankers running the process realized that something was wrong. The individual investors that Google had worked so hard to court weren't showing up to bid to the degree the company had expected. Many of the large institutions, the mutual funds, weren't putting in bids for prices as high as the low end of the price range that was in the prospectus.

As Cramer and Kudlow had diagnosed, some of those investors didn't like the auction process. It required not just an estimate of Google's value but an understanding of auction bidding strategies. Legg Mason portfolio manager Bill Miller, for example, felt the need to seek out two auction experts for help in thinking through his bidding strategy.

Others were turned off by what they perceived to be the arrogance of the company's founders and executives. At the Waldorf Astoria luncheon, Google's executives had declined to provide details that investors were seeking. To other meetings, Brin wore a t-shirt, blue jeans, and sneakers with a thick heel. It wasn't the kind of attire the professional investing class, most of whom wore suits, expected to see from technology founders trying to impress them.

Google had recently updated its financials to show that growth had decelerated in the second quarter. The company wasn't offering any projections to Wall Street analysts to model their future performance. So as Wall Street tried to get its collective head around Google's business over the next few years, estimates diverged widely. Some even thought that the company's performance had peaked.

Google thought it didn't need to do anything more to help investors. The IPO had been hyped by the financial media, and during months of preparation, the company had meeting after meeting about how to handle the large flood of orders it anticipated. Now that it was time to collect the orders and they weren't coming in as quickly or at as high a price as the company and its bankers had hoped, Google had to take care of yet another headache. It had disclosed in an earlier prospectus that in issuing shares and options to some employees without registering them with securities regulators it may have violated state and federal laws. The infraction might lead it to have to pay $26 million to buy the stock and options back from shareholders. Now the company learned that the SEC had started a probe of its practices. It needed to alert shareholders. On Monday, August 16, Google disclosed that the agency had "initiated an informal inquiry into this matter and certain state regulators, including California, have requested additional information." The company also disclosed that it had asked the SEC to declare its registration statement to be effective by 4:00 p.m. the following day. The offering was likely to close within hours of the statement's being declared effective.

Tuesday came and went without any public word from Google. Brin, Page, and Schmidt were locked in a tense debate with their bankers. They had orders for roughly 20 million shares at around $85. That was more than 5 million shares less than they planned to sell and at a price that was 30 percent below the middle of the range written in the prospectus.

Members of the company's board who were planning to sell shares on behalf of their venture capital firms—Doerr, for Kleiner Perkins, and Michael Moritz, for Sequoia—decided that if Google's shares were going to be auctioned at such a low level, they didn't want to sell. Between them, Kleiner Perkins and Sequoia had planned to sell 4.5 million shares. Now they wouldn't. Google didn't immediately alert other investors, including Ron Conway, a venture capitalist who had originally introduced the Google founders to Sequoia, about Kleiner Perkins' and Sequoia's change in plans.

"We were calling each one and saying…are you in at eighty-five dollars?" recalled one of the members of the Google team. "We were hoping everybody was, and I'm sure that we were pushing people to stay in, but because we needed that number."

The SEC would need to know about Google's lowered range. As its attorneys at Wilson readied another amendment for release on the morning of Wednesday, August 18, Segre prepared to make a case to the SEC that the lowered range wasn't material. If the SEC didn't agree, Google would have to submit another prospectus for review. That would likely delay the offering by twenty-four or forty-eight hours.

Early on the morning of August 18, Segre called a senior SEC official at her home in the Washington, DC, area. The lawyer explained why Google didn't think the lowered price was material—Google didn't need the money it was raising—and begged the official for a favorable ruling. After some back-and-forth, she relented.

In a statement on the web page it had set up for the IPO, Google told shareholders it would soon file an amendment to its securities prospectus stating that the price range had been lowered. In the amendment that came that morning—its ninth—Google said it was now seeking to sell shares in the range of $85 to $95.

The number of shares to be sold in the offering was also reduced. Google would continue to sell the same number of shares, 14.1 million, while the selling shareholders would only sell 5.5 million shares, not the 11.6 million they'd planned to.

Certain they could get the deal done at that size, Google's bankers called investors to finalize their bids. Due to the auction structure, only investors who had already bid could participate in the auction at the lower price— investors who had sat out the first round because the price was too high couldn't now put in bids at the lower price.

As the bankers made their calls, they were subject to Google's restrictions on telling investors what other investors may have bid. It was common practice for bankers to share updates on investor order sizes or bid prices with other investors, but Google had decided it didn't want its bankers influencing bids in any way.

No sooner had the bankers alerted investors to the lower price than one New York investor who had put in an order for a couple million shares at a price higher than $85 lowered his price to around $80. The bankers now had to persuade him to change his mind or find orders to take his place. Credit Suisse bankers called the investor and told him, effectively, that the company hadn't lowered the range for nothing. There was a reason. Wink, wink. In so many words, they tried to tell him that they had enough orders to get the deal done at $85. He was going to miss out if he didn't increase his bid. The investor didn't change his mind.

Later that day, when it came time to price the deal, Credit Suisse's bankers persuaded Brin and Page to leave the now untidy conditions at Donnelley and move to Fisher's office around the corner, on Hanover Street. Others were connected by conference call. The bankers told the Google executives that at $85 they could allocate each investor about two-thirds of what they'd asked for. Increasing the price to $86 meant that Google would lose a few orders from investors unwilling to pay that price, leaving just enough to buy all the stock. Those investors would thus get 100 percent of what they wanted.

Though opinions differed, enough people advocated for setting the price at $85 and leaving some investors unsatisfied that that's what happened. They would, the theory went, buy the stock once it started trading on the NAS-DAQ, putting a floor under the price. The Google executives agreed and the price was set.

Stock was then allocated to those investors who had put in orders at the lower price. Fidelity, Legg Mason's Bill Miller, T. Rowe Price, Jennison Associates. An A-list of investors, although the shares were sold at a lower price than the company initially wanted. At $85, Google raised $1.7 billion, making it the largest internet IPO of all time. Brin and Page became paper billionaires.

Despite the superlatives of the Google offering, the company's executives were angry with their bankers over the way the deal had gone. The bankers understood it was not the outcome anyone had expected. "You had this whole confluence of factors: the design of the auction, the fact that growth was decelerating, the fact that some institutions didn't want to participate in the auction, the fact that the company was arrogant on the roadshow, etcetera," one of them said. "All of which conspired to make the thing less successful."

With the deal done, Page and Schmidt left to take a private plane to New York to celebrate the IPO. The lawyers and accountants stayed behind at Donnelley to proof the final prospectus, effectively cleaning up after the party. Sometime before midnight on the eighteenth, Brin showed up. He wanted to soak up the ambiance and the stale air of the printer's office one last time. They stayed there chatting and watching the Summer Olympics, then taking place in Athens, on a large television until Brin left sometime in the early hours of the morning.

In the end, Morgan Stanley and Credit Suisse each received 5.3 million to allocate to their clients, representing more than half of the shares on offer. Goldman was third in number of shares. The underwriters received a fee of 2.8 percent, with both Morgan Stanley and Credit Suisse earning $23 million.

The next morning, as part of their trip through New York, Page and Schmidt visited Morgan Stanley's Times Square trading floor to watch the stock open.

Fisher had delayed a family vacation to Montana and stayed overnight in an airport hotel so he could catch a flight the next day. Waiting for his connection in the airport, he stared up at one of the televisions hanging from the ceiling that was tuned to CNBC. The anchors were talking about what a disappointment it was for Google to sell at $85 a share. The stock was likely to fall further in price, they suggested.

For a couple of minutes, Fisher watched them drone on and on. Then the banker dismissed the blather. Having seen all the orders, he knew how wrong they were.

When Google's stock opened later that day, the first trade crossed at $100.

By the end of the trading day, Google closed at $100.34. The stock had risen 18 percent, an ideal outcome after all that Google and its team had gone through. And it had done so on a day that the NASDAQ Composite Index fell 0.6 percent. The *Wall Street Journal* put it succinctly: "Investors who went through the cumbersome auction for Google Inc. shares were feeling particularly lucky yesterday. The countdown to Google's initial public offering of stock was filled with confusion, frustration and miscues. The first day of trading was no different. But shares of the Internet search-engine company proved to be big winners, at least for a day."

The stock performance helped to soften any irritation Google executives may have felt earlier in the process. Buyer remembers being happy with the result. "We were thrilled with it," she said.

When the IPO was done, the underwriters got a second bite at the Google apple. The terms of the deal were such that they were permitted to exercise a greenshoe option, by which they could buy an additional 15 percent of the shares at the IPO price within thirty days of the offering. Google's underwriters bought 2.9 million more shares.

Google paid the entire underwriting syndicate $53.7 million in fees. Almost $5 million of that was then used to pay for expenses such as legal and printing costs borne by the underwriters.

■　■　■

Even though Google may have ultimately been satisfied with the result, Wall Street was not. Helped in part by the *Wall Street Journal*, a narrative began to take hold that the offering had been a failure. The newspaper put out an article headlined "How Miscalculations and Hubris Hobbled Celebrated Google IPO." It opened, "Google Inc. may have needed Wall Street after all."

A Columbia University auction expert offered up a quote that the drop in price reflected a reality that an auction introduced too many uncertainties and led investors to back away from participating in the IPO. A hedge fund manager said that the auction "managed to tee off the broader constituency of Wall Street, and it's obviously hurt them," adding, "Wall Street wins again."

The newspaper wrote that "the result yesterday was a far cry from the great expectations, built up over the months and weeks leading up to the IPO, that demand for Google's shares would help reignite demand for new tech stocks and pioneer a way for new companies to do an end run around Wall Street's old cozy ways." The article put a fine point on the already fraught relationship between the investment banks of the East Coast and the innovation economy of the West, and made the case that Google's actions had escalated the hostility between the two subcultures.

"The people at Goldman think we fucked up the deal," one of the people involved in Google's offering said in an interview. "That's what they wanted to think."

Nonetheless, the narrative that the Google offering was a failure would be used as a cudgel over the following years to ensure that other ambitious startup executives didn't make another serious run at reforming the system. While NetSuite and Rackspace resurrected the auction format just before the climax of the 2008 financial crisis, it would be fourteen years from Google's IPO before another company with the consumer recognition and vision of the search giant would try again.

In the months after Google's offering, the firm's stock price moved all over the place. It touched a high of $201.60 on November 3 after reporting better-than-expected results in its first quarter as a public company and fell when Google insiders started selling. By some measures, the volatility exposed Google's continued frostiness with Wall Street. Executives remained secretive and circumspect of professional investors. They still didn't offer financial projections, which analysts and investors had come to rely on to judge corporate growth rates. As Google had prepared to release its first earnings as a public company in October, the lack of projections led to unusually wide estimates in what analysts expected for the earnings report, from a low of $0.22 a share to $0.61. The company reported net income of $125 million, or earnings per share of $0.45, excluding some onetime costs.

In November 2005, Google executives took an initial step in improving their relationship with the financial world by hiring their first head of investor relations, Kim Jabal, the former Goldman Sachs banker who had been hired by Sheryl Sandberg in 2003. The appointment would give Google an executive whose sole job was to focus on telling the company's story to Wall Street and answering questions from analysts and investors about its finances.

Buyer had taken over some of the duties in the months after the IPO, according to some accounts, but it was time to get someone focused on it fully. The *Playboy* interview and its aftermath had made the founders wary of speaking to the press, and Schmidt recognized that the company needed someone devoted to speaking with investors. Jabal had worked in the background of Google's IPO, pulling data on her business for the offering materials, but otherwise playing a minor part, and now she took on a greater role at the company.

Soon after she started, Reyes, Google's CFO, misspoke about the state of the company's advertising business, and the stock tanked. Google had to file a document with the SEC clarifying the remark. Jabal would handle most of the communications with investors from then on.

Jabal took her job seriously, encouraging the CEO and Google's founders to be more considerate of institutional investors. She held a series of investor meetings, including a large one in New York. She persuaded Google's executives to start providing financial projections for the first time. The combined efforts helped earn a place for Google for the first time on a list of shareholder-friendly companies.

In 2006, her primary purpose of designing the IPO complete, Lise Buyer left Google. Inspired by the work she'd done for Google and the experience she'd picked up, the Buffalo native started her own consultancy to advise companies on the IPO process. She called it Class V Group, a nod to whitewater rapids that are so dangerous to navigate that the American Whitewater Association recommended hiring a guide. Buyer thought it was a reasonable analogy for the IPO process.

It wasn't immediately obvious that she would have a lot of work. After 380 companies went public in 2000, only 282 companies went public in the next four years combined. Another 169 went public in 2005.

CHAPTER 7

Facebook, Menlo Park, 2012

At Netflix's Los Gatos headquarters, a twenty-minute drive southeast of Google's offices along California State Route 85, Barry McCarthy and CEO Reed Hastings were busy growing the company into a subscription success story.

McCarthy, a trim executive with closely cropped hair and glasses, oversaw the company's finances from a large corner office. He helped as the company successfully pivoted from mail-order DVDs into streaming technology. He'd finally taken Netflix public, in 2002, selling 5.5 million shares to value the company at $330 million when it had 600,000 subscribers.

By 2006, McCarthy was enjoying a second life with Netflix. He had almost left the company two years before, tempted by the idea of finding a bigger job elsewhere. Hastings and other executives had successfully persuaded him to stick around to help Netflix fight off rivals—Blockbuster mounted a renewed challenge by getting into the online subscription business and Walmart had entered the business too, before conceding to Netflix.

"You don't leave your friends in a knife fight," McCarthy told a conference call of analysts around that time.

The comment hinted at McCarthy's sense of corporate loyalty, a belief that was often out of place in Silicon Valley's meritocracy. He addressed Netflix's cofounder Marc Randolph as "Mr. Founder" even after being told he could call him by his first name. McCarthy was gruff, used blunt language, and was known to explode into a rage from a standing start. If colleagues caught him on a good day, he displayed a dry sense of humor. One Netflix investor who considered him to be thoughtful and smart referred to him by the nickname "Crusty."

Nonetheless, McCarthy was surprisingly open to constructive criticism.

When marketing chief Leslie Kilgore told Hastings that she found McCarthy to be moody, the CEO instructed her to tell McCarthy herself. She did. The CFO took it to heart and asked his team to alert him if they noticed him veering off into moodiness.

The exchange with Kilgore signified a company culture that increasingly flouted traditional norms. Netflix gave employees a choice over how much of their bonus they received in cash or company stock options. The policy, which departed from the common practice of senior executives making such decisions on behalf of employees, meant that employees could decide how closely to tie their fortunes to their employers. Year after year, McCarthy used the policy to load up on stock options.

Netflix's willingness to test the boundaries of what was acceptable rubbed off on McCarthy. The CFO felt free to explore creative approaches to finance the company, which was losing gobs of money in an industry it was still creating. At one point, Netflix sold shares only to buy them back a few months later when McCarthy decided that investors weren't valuing the company appropriately. Another time he persuaded JPMorgan, where his old college classmate James Lee then worked, to help him raise money through a bond sale even though Netflix hadn't turned a profit.

Throughout his Netflix career, McCarthy never lost sight of the drive that had led him out of investment banking to run his own concern. Early on, he had designs on running Netflix, but Hastings made it clear in one meeting that his pick would be someone else. McCarthy knew the score. Patty McCord, Netflix's top human resources executive, was left to smooth things over with the CFO.

McCarthy stayed at Netflix because the work was interesting and challenging. By 2010 he was ready for something else. In November of that year, he sold roughly 230,000 shares, netting about $41 million. The stock had risen more than 6,200 percent since the company's IPO.

On December 7, Netflix announced McCarthy's departure. "Over the last few years, Barry has balanced his affection for Netflix—and the excitement all of us have felt by the tremendous growth of the company—with his personal desire for broader professional opportunities," Hastings said in the press release announcing McCarthy's exit. "Barry concluded that now is the right time to seek out those opportunities, and we will be cheering for him."

The headline at *Business Insider* said it all: "Netflix CFO Leaves Because He Can't Become CEO." The stock declined 2.5 percent after the announcement, suggesting that Wall Street viewed his exit negatively. McCarthy, then fifty-seven years old, told CNET that the November stock sales represented roughly 51 percent of his ownership in Netflix, and that he still had 49 percent "riding on the future success" of Netflix.

Hastings acknowledged McCarthy's exit during Netflix's fourth-quarter earnings call, on January 26, 2011. "I'd just like to acknowledge that Barry McCarthy has been our CFO and my partner for the last eleven years and there's no way we would have gotten to twenty million subscribers as fast as we did without his incredible work."

One of the investors who had benefited from McCarthy's run was Jay Hoag, a venture capitalist who sat on Netflix's board by virtue of an investment his company, Technology Crossover Ventures, had made in Netflix. Hoag cofounded Technology Crossover Ventures with Rick Kimball in 1995. As Netflix grew—thanks, in part, to McCarthy's careful stewardship of its balance sheet—it turned into one of the venture firm's most successful investments.

Three months after McCarthy's exit from Netflix, Hoag and his partners hired him as an executive in residence, someone the company could count on to help it vet potential investments. McCarthy also joined the board of internet streaming radio startup Pandora, heading toward its own IPO.

■ ■ ■

By then, an entire industry had mushroomed around a business model known as social media. Barely a thought when McCarthy led Netflix's 2002 IPO, the industry had grown into one that sought to connect the entirety of the world's more than six billion citizens. As the sites grew, investors who had flocked to the first version of internet companies in the late 1990s saw the makings of a second wave.

In 2003, Reid Hoffman started LinkedIn Corp. from his living room by inviting 350 contacts to set up profiles. By 2011, LinkedIn had grown to 100 million users. In 2004, Mark Zuckerberg, Dustin Moskovitz, and others started TheFacebook out of their Harvard University dorm rooms. By early 2011, Facebook had grown to more than 600 million users. In 2006, Jack Dorsey, Biz

Stone, Evan Williams, and Noah Glass founded Twitter in San Francisco. By 2011, that service had grown to 200 million users, half of them active.

In May 2011, LinkedIn became the first of those companies to go public. In what was the largest internet IPO since Google's 2004 offering, Morgan Stanley, Bank of America, and JPMorgan underwrote the company's shares at $45 apiece. The shares opened at $83 and rocketed higher by as much as 171 percent above the IPO price during the first day of trading, before closing at $94.25, or 109 percent higher than the IPO price. The pop left many shaking their heads, including McCarthy, who saw it as a sign the IPO process had gotten off track by becoming one focused on delivering first-day stock gains.

"I think it worked the way it was intended, and it was broken," McCarthy said later.

Pandora went public at $16 a share the following month, with McCarthy on its board, doubling the price Morgan Stanley bankers set out in their initial range. The shares rose to as high as $26 before giving up most of their gains to end the day at $17.42, an 8.9 percent increase from the IPO price.

Around that time, Kim Jabal left Google, where she had moved on from investor relations to run finance for the company's high profile engineering division. Her exit ended an eight-year career at the search giant.

■ ■ ■

In January 2011, President Barack Obama pledged, in his State of the Union address, "to reduce barriers to growth and investment." Obama ordered a review of government regulations. "When we find rules that put an unnecessary burden on businesses," he said, "we will fix them."

In the wake of Obama's remarks, a group of eighteen experts convened an IPO Task Force to examine the decline in the number of public companies and come up with solutions to reverse the trend. The number of listed companies in the United States peaked at 8,090 in 1996, before declining to roughly half that in 2010. Critics of the decline believed that it prevented public investors from having productive companies in which to invest their retirement funds. Staying private, they also believed, allowed startups to avoid the harsh but often healthy scrutiny from public market investors that could bring needed discipline to their operations and company cultures.

Buyer was a recognized IPO expert by then, and though she wasn't on the task force, she lent a hand with its work. When the group submitted its report in October to the U.S. Department of the Treasury, its members acknowledged Buyer and others "whose input and expertise contributed to the preparation of this report."

The task force recommended a variety of options that regulators could use to make it easier for smaller companies to go public. It also offered some recommendations to the companies themselves, suggesting that they should become smarter about the ways that the landscape had changed. Electronic trading, for example, had caused investor focus to shift toward trading the stocks of larger companies more quickly rather than investing in smaller companies over a longer period of time.

One of the recommendations addressed how companies should handle their investment banks. "Put at least one firm in a leadership position (sole or joint book runner) that will allocate stock to long-term holders of your shares versus traders," it said, in a section that also recommended that companies "understand the implications of different investment banking syndicate structures and align incentives around performance," "increase the issuer's role in the IPO allocation process with the goal to create an optimal mix of investors for the company," and "limit the number of investors to whom the IPO shares get allocated."

If that was all, the report would have gone the way of so many other such reports, gathering dust on a shelf in some government building. But miraculously, thanks in part to the work of venture capitalist Katie Mitchell, the suggestions made their way into the Jumpstart Our Business Startups (JOBS) Act. The law, which President Obama signed in April 2012, implemented several of the report's recommendations.

The JOBS Act created a category of "emerging growth companies" that allowed firms with less than $1 billion in annual revenue to avoid having to comply with some of the most onerous regulations; a company could file initial registration statements, or a draft registration statement, to the SEC confidentially. That would begin a multi-month process during which the agency and the company could iron out some of their differences around the language that would ultimately be presented to investors in the form of the official registration statement, known as an S-1.

Companies were now permitted to hold "test the waters" conversations, an easing of the securities laws around "gun-jumping"—which Google had almost run afoul of. The rule allowed companies to hold meetings and collect non-binding indications of interest from potential investors both before and after filing a registration statement for an IPO. The idea was that it would encourage companies to hold conversations with investors earlier in a company's life cycle and thereby gauge investor interest in a future public offering.

The JOBS Act also expanded the number of shareholders a company could have before hitting the public reporting and registration threshold, from 500 to 2,000. Now companies could stay private if they had 1,999 or fewer shareholders.

■ ■ ■

By the time President Obama signed the JOBS Act, Facebook was well into its IPO process.

Investors had looked forward to the company's IPO for years. Much like Google was to investing theories around internet search companies, Facebook was a validation of an investing thesis that had grown up around social media's massive growth opportunities. LinkedIn had provided one data point, but its user base was one-sixth that of Facebook's.

Earlier that year, Goldman Sachs had raised money for Facebook from wealthy individuals and thought it had found a way to avoid tripping the SEC's rules around having more than 500 shareholders of record. The bankers put together a special-purpose vehicle to consolidate the thousands of smaller investors. The idea was that the SPV would count as just one investor for the SEC's purposes.

Zuckerberg was reluctant to sell shares to the public, but the changes in the JOBS Act had come too late for the social media company. Like Google, Facebook was set to cross the shareholder threshold at the end of the year and would need to disclose financial information to investors by the following April, whether it was public or not. Submitting those financials without being public would mean scrutiny from public investors without the benefit of being able to raise money from them. By November 2011, Facebook was in talks with banks about filing with the SEC.

Facebook had eight hundred million users, making it the largest social media company in the world. It was already profitable. Like Google, the company showed signs of wanting to do the IPO its own way. Its CFO, David Ebersman, told bankers he was skeptical about what role they could play, because investors were already aware of the company and angling for a piece of it. Nonetheless, investment bankers competed to lead the offering. Morgan Stanley eventually won out, led by Michael Grimes, an intense banker who had also worked on Google's IPO and now ran Morgan Stanley's tech practice through force of will and relationships with some of Silicon Valley's most successful entrepreneurs. Kate Claassen, a banker in Grimes's group with an MBA from UC Berkeley, was also part of the team.

Traditional ways of showing support to emerging technology companies did not apply to the new wave of social media companies. So Morgan Stanley's bankers had come up with a novel approach.

The investment banking playbook already addressed enterprise software clients. Bankers introduced a client to bank colleagues in engineering or information technology who could buy the startup's software, forging closer ties between the two companies. That wasn't available for consumer-facing internet companies like Facebook. Instead, Morgan Stanley lent Facebook a small amount of money in the form of a credit facility. It was a "relationship loan," to show their loyalty and hopefully win the lead mandate when it came time for the IPO. Facebook didn't need money.

In February 2012, when Facebook filed its prospectus, the document listed Morgan Stanley as the lead bank and said that the company would seek to sell $5 billion in shares. At that level, it would surpass Google as the largest internet IPO and earn a valuation of somewhere around $100 billion, more than four times Google's valuation when it went public.

In anticipation of a successful offering, Morgan Stanley bankers met with several promising internet companies around that time to pitch their services. They told them that with any luck, Facebook's offering would open an IPO window that the rest of them could step through into the public markets. Among the companies the bankers met with were Pinterest, the photo-sharing website, and Airbnb, which had crossed the $1 billion valuation threshold the previous year.

In early May 2012, Facebook threw a wrench into its offering. As users flocked to mobile phones, the company struggled to move with them. It was slow to serve up the ads that accounted for much of its revenue on the mobile devices. It revised its forecast lower.

Companies try not to revise projections so close to the offering date during an IPO process. And Facebook didn't spell out its revisions in the 170-page prospectus that it amended on May 9. Instead, the company said its daily active users on mobile were increasing faster than the number of ads delivered to them. But it took steps to spell out the implications in simpler language to the Wall Street analysts and investors who were lining up to evaluate the offering. Almost immediately after the document was out, Facebook started briefing analysts.

Morgan Stanley analyst Scott Devitt received the first call from Facebook's treasurer just minutes after Facebook submitted the amended document to regulators, according to Massachusetts' top financial watchdog, William Gavin, who later investigated and fined the bank over the behavior. Devitt had replaced Mary Meeker, the analyst known as "Queen of the Internet" for her role in promoting the technology industry in the 1990s. It was a role that gave Devitt responsibility for briefing the bank's clients, institutional investors thinking about buying into Facebook's IPO. Many likened the chain of communication to the childhood game of telephone—the company whispers into the ear of the analyst, who then turns and whispers into the ear of the investor.

Prior to the calls, the treasurer had rehearsed with a senior Morgan Stanley banker, according to Massachusetts' investigation and subsequent consent order. They role-played, the banker taking the part of the analyst and the treasurer relying on a script handwritten by the banker. The banker later emailed Facebook's CFO to say that the treasurer "was a champ in the hotel tonight."

Galvin alleged that the banker's involvement violated the conflict-of-interest rules set forth in the 2003 Global Analyst Research Settlement. The rules were intended to preserve a separation of investment bankers and research analysts known as a "Chinese wall," a term that gained popularity after the 1929 stock market crash and is thought by some to be a reference to the Great Wall of China.

"Morgan Stanley's senior investment banker did everything but make the phone calls himself," Galvin alleged. The actions violated rules created after the first dot-com crash forbidding investment bankers from communicating with analysts, Galvin said. Morgan Stanley settled the matter, paid a $5 million fine, and didn't admit or deny wrongdoing.

The banker told Massachusetts officials that to avoid the appearance of impropriety, he had left the room when Facebook's treasurer made the calls. Although Massachusetts officials didn't name the banker, media outlets widely reported that it was Grimes.

Facebook's selective disclosure also had the disadvantage of giving institutional investors an unfair advantage over retail investors. As analysts briefed by the company put out research notes lowering their estimates, retail investors reading the prospectus were left to guess at the hidden implications of the amended language.

When it came time to price the IPO the following week, Facebook executives were undeterred. They asked the Morgan Stanley bankers to price the company's stock as high as they possibly could, based on demand from investors. They set them at $38 apiece, valuing the company at more than $100 billion and confirming earlier estimates.

The stock rose on the first trade, opening at $42.05, before the NASDAQ Stock Market broke down. Pre-trading tests failed to expose a glitch around how the exchange's computers handled canceled orders, leading to more than thirty thousand orders getting stuck in the exchange's computer systems. NASDAQ employees removed a few lines of code, and senior executives, thinking they had resolved the problem, went ahead and released the shares for trading. (The NYSE has human traders, who can step in when problems arise, but the NASDAQ is entirely digital.) The decision eventually cost banks and other trading firms an estimated $500 million.

When NASDAQ officials learned that they had failed to trade thousands of orders, they sold them into the market that afternoon, depressing Facebook's stock price. After Morgan Stanley stepped in to support the stock, it ended trading at $38.37.

Over the following weeks and months, the shares slumped, breaking the IPO price, and touched $17.73 in September. On May 13, 2013, the Securities and Exchange Commission announced a $10 million fine for NASDAQ, the largest ever for an exchange. Facebook had yet to trade higher than the opening price it had set twelve months earlier.

"Exchanges have an obligation to ensure that their systems, processes, and contingency planning are robust and adequate to manage an IPO without disruption to the market," the SEC said in a May 2013 press release announcing the penalty. "Despite widespread anticipation that the Facebook IPO would be among the largest in history with huge numbers of investors participating, a design limitation in NASDAQ's system to match IPO buy and sell orders caused disruptions."

NASDAQ agreed to pay $62 million to brokers affected by the mistake. McCarthy viewed that as a light penalty and stewed over the fact that no one at the stock market had been punished for such a colossal failure. "I thought that was unfortunate," he later said.

Facebook's stumbles put a chill on the IPO market and convinced many founders that life as a public company wasn't worth the hassle. Airbnb's CEO and cofounder Brian Chesky, a former bodybuilder who had attended the Rhode Island School of Design, had no interest in facing the scrutiny of the public markets. Other founders didn't either.

Facebook was at the top of its game, captivating institutional investors and attracting the best of the best in Silicon Valley. And yet the offering had gone off the rails. Rival startup executives saw an influx of résumés from disgruntled Facebook employees. If Facebook's IPO could go so wrong, what could happen to less hyped offerings?

That thinking coincided with an influx of cash into the private markets, allowing startup founders and executives who didn't want the scrutiny of the public markets to continue to fund themselves privately.

Those dual factors led startup founders to rethink the virtues of staying private and brought an era when they would try to stay private for as long as possible.

CHAPTER 8

Spotify, Stockholm, 2013

Less than a year before Facebook's IPO, the social media company partnered with Spotify, a Swedish streaming company, to offer users of
Facebook the ability to listen to music through its website. The partnership
was the first step into the United States for Spotify, founded by Daniel Ek and
Martin Lorentzon in 2006.

Spotify was not yet the undisputed market leader, and it faced stiff competition from the likes of French streaming service Deezer, which had designs
on getting into the United States, and Germany's SoundCloud. Spotify initially offered its music services for free through Facebook, supporting the
business with ads, but by 2012 it had launched a premium version that required
a monthly subscription. It needed the revenue from subscriptions if it was ever
going to turn a profit. The music business was notoriously difficult to break
into, run by a triumvirate of record labels that controlled access to the libraries
of most popular artists. In 2010, the music industry, including the Recording
Industry Association of America, successfully persuaded a New York court to
shut down music piracy website LimeWire. (Spotify later hired several senior
engineers and executives from LimeWire for its U.S. expansion.)

Even though Spotify, by paying for the rights to use the music it
streamed, was offering an alternative to piracy, the three labels—Universal
Music Group, Sony Music Entertainment, and Warner Music Group—drove
a hard bargain. Spotify paid out roughly 70 cents of every dollar in royalties
to the companies that owned the music. After taking their own cut, the labels
then paid the artists. Most artists outside of the most popular acts received
just pennies on the dollar.

Yoked to the record labels, Spotify would never be able to improve its
gross margins, a measure of how much revenue a company keeps after paying

for the cost of its product. Spotify's success came down to bringing in money from subscriptions and ads, and then paying as little as possible to the record companies.

The unfavorable economics had proved troublesome for Spotify when it came to raising money from venture capitalists. Investors fretted that the record labels would gain leverage in licensing negotiations that took place every two to three years, slicing into Spotify's margins. And yet Spotify's U.S. launch was beginning to attract attention from venture capitalists who had yet to play a major role in the company's funding. In 2013, Technology Crossover Ventures, where Barry McCarthy was executive in residence, began to look at making an investment. The company had already invested in Netflix and Facebook, and now partners Christopher "Woody" Marshall and others turned to McCarthy to vet Spotify.

McCarthy, who had come to understand the streaming service and content acquisition business during his time at Netflix and now served on the board of internet radio pioneer Pandora, conducted months of due diligence. He traveled to Stockholm to meet with Ek and others on the management team. He obtained access to a data room to pore over financial and subscription information.

McCarthy liked what he saw. He thought he recognized an iconic founder in the mold of Netflix's Hastings, and he could tell that the company had some wind to its back in a difficult industry. "I thought this was pretty interesting— I knew subscription and I knew music," McCarthy said. "It was a natural fit."

When it came time to negotiate with Spotify over the investment, TCV found Spotify to be tough negotiators. Startup fundraising had evolved in the years since Hambrecht & Quist. Promising companies in technology, healthcare, biotechnology or other industries funded themselves across numerous rounds of private financing: initially a seed round, collected from angel investors, friends, and family, and then, as the company grew, more formal investors, such as venture capitalists, for ever-larger checks across rounds denoted by letters of the alphabet. The Series A round came after the seed and was followed by Series B, Series C, and so on.

At each round, investors bought shares at a certain price and in numbers that represented an ownership interest in the company. The price and number of shares outstanding placed a value on the company. Startup employees and founders used this number as a marker of a company's success, and for promising companies it was often written up in press reports and discussed at cocktail parties. Startups hoped to raise more money at successively higher valuations.

A down round, when the company raised more money at a lower valuation than its last fundraising, was to be avoided at all costs. It would signal that something had gone wrong since the last fundraising—that the company's position had weakened.

Negotiations with venture capitalists played out in several ways, depending on the strength of each party's hand. If investors lined up to buy a stake due to a company's promising business model or strong growth prospects, or if there was a lot of money from investors to put to work, the company could lead the talks. If the company's growth was slowing or the larger fundraising environment had cooled, investors would have the upper hand. Investors could demand a greater share of the company or include more investor-friendly terms in the agreement between the two companies.

When investors handed over the check, the story of how the talks went would be exhibited in the number of shares the company passed back. At a higher price, the company would raise the same amount of money by selling a smaller stake. Lower prices, on the other hand, meant that the company would have to sell more shares to raise the same amount of money.

When it came time for Spotify to raise money, cofounder Lorentzon was a formidable sparring partner who showed he was willing to walk away if he didn't get what he wanted. In one presentation, he turned his back on investors to show off Spotify's search feature, only to pull up a long list of offensive song titles. With help from Spotify's CFO, Peter Sterky, Lorentzon liked to set ambitious targets for the price of the private shares it sold to new investors. Then one of two things would typically happen: either investors grew desperate enough that they agreed to pay the price the company had set, or months of delay would allow Spotify's growth metrics to catch up with their ambition. The practice meant that Spotify was good at issuing as few shares as possible—never giving up too much to raise the money it needed. The price of the shares was then used to set the company's top-line valuation, the number that appeared in media reports.

A similar pattern played out in Spotify's negotiation with TCV. But what McCarthy and his colleagues at TCV may not have realized was that they were largely bidding against themselves. When TCV finally did invest, it ponied up $250 million in 2013 at a valuation of $4 billion. McCarthy put in some of his own money as well.

TCV had also negotiated a board seat along with its investment and wanted McCarthy to fill it. Ek, who needed to sign off on the idea, agreed.

In February 2014, Spotify announced McCarthy's appointment, placing the former Netflix CFO on a governing body that also included Lorentzon and Ek; Sean Parker, the founder of Napster, one of the original music streaming services before it was shut down for piracy in 2001; and Klaus Hommels, a German-born, Swiss-based venture capitalist and early backer. Spotify had more than six million paying subscribers and another eighteen million using the free version.

The Spotify board seat allowed McCarthy to rectify a mistake he had made the previous October when he joined Clinkle, a buzzy but secretive mobile payments company founded by Stanford computer science student Lucas Duplan and backed by Silicon Valley royalty like Andreessen Horowitz, Peter Thiel, and Marc Benioff. Though McCarthy had long wanted to graduate out of the finance department and into a more important operating role, Clinkle wasn't what he thought it was when he walked in the door. The company didn't have a product and was struggling under the mismanagement of its twenty-something CEO.

It was a rare blunder for an ambitious executive and could have tarnished his reputation had he not quickly rebounded onto Spotify's board. "[Clinkle] was a mistake," McCarthy said later. "I should've done my own diligence. I didn't. If I had, I'd like to think I wouldn't have joined." A year after he got involved, Clinkle rebranded itself in a last-ditch attempt to turn around the business and attract customers. It failed.

Other than TCV, Spotify's investor base didn't include many Silicon Valley venture capitalists. Over its lifetime, the company had funded itself largely with money from European VCs. The record labels had also invested, throwing in with a streaming music pioneer that provided a new revenue source even as it undercut their sales of compact discs and digital downloads.

That TCV was the only company willing to invest in the last round told Spotify executives that they needed to broaden their base of investors in the United States, home to the deepest capital markets in the world. Little did they know that one investor was about to knock on the doors of their Stockholm office largely unannounced.

CHAPTER 9

Spotify, Stockholm, 2014

I n November 2014, Larry Aschebrook and Spencer McLeod, two venture capitalists from the United States, touched down on the tarmac at Stockholm Arlanda Airport, intent on getting a meeting with executives at Spotify. By then, Spotify was one of the most valuable startups in Europe. Two years earlier, employees had moved into offices on Birger Jarlsgatan, a four-lane thoroughfare that ran south to north from Stockholm's harbor through the city's business district. The company was spread across four floors, and the space offered many of the trappings of a prominent startup—a video game area, a Ping-Pong table, and graffiti art on the walls.

Aschebrook and McLeod worked at a little-known venture capital firm called G Squared. Aschebrook had helped start the firm three years earlier to buy shares in startups on the secondary market, an unlisted market where shares traded hands infrequently and inefficiently. He targeted a still-growing universe of large private technology startups valued at more than $1 billion. The companies had been christened "unicorns" in 2013 by venture capitalist Aileen Lee, in an article in *TechCrunch* that introduced the world to the term with the headline "Welcome to the Unicorn Club: Learning from Billion-Dollar Startups."

Billions of dollars flowing into the private markets had allowed those companies to avoid listing their shares publicly, making it difficult for startup investors and employees who wanted to sell. It was much harder to sell shares in a private company than in a publicly listed one.

Private companies had historically kept tight control over shareholders' ability to sell stakes. Updating a company's list of shareholders could be time-consuming, and many executives didn't like to spend precious resources on what they considered a back-office function. Restricting such sales also kept employees' and executives' interests aligned with the company's—holding an economic stake meant that they were incentivized to maximize the value of those shares. The restrictions often acted as golden handcuffs, yoking employees to the company long after they had lost faith in its vision. Or they prevented employees from taking the money from the stake and putting it into other things, such as buying a house or paying for their kids' education.

If employees needed the money badly enough, they typically found other options. They partnered with investment banks on derivatives deals that allowed them to keep their shares but forced them to give up their economic interest in return for cash in hand. Such deals were made out of the company's sight. Other under-the-table transactions were also conducted. In extreme cases, the company lost track of who should and shouldn't be on that list of shareholders. Each bespoke transaction typically required weeks, if not months, of negotiations between buyer and seller, and ultimately required sign-off from the company to complete the transfer.

Spotify was high on Aschebrook and McLeod's list of targets. They had no contacts there but had heard that a shareholder was looking to sell a small piece of the company worth $4 million. They wanted Spotify's permission to buy it.

McLeod had flown in from San Francisco the night before on Scandinavian Airlines, dining on reindeer for the first time. Aschebrook flew in from Chicago. Meeting up at their hotel, the Nobis Hotel Stockholm, in the city's Östermalm district, the two men hugged. They sat down to enjoy a beer before taking a walk around, McLeod in a pea coat, the two men inhaling the crisp air of the Scandinavian winter. They arrived at Birger Jarlsgatan 61, known by the large block letters that adorned the drab facade: JARLAHUSET, or Jarla House. As pedestrians strolled by the home of one of Europe's first unicorns, the two Americans peered into a ground-floor window etched with the Spotify logo. A circular staircase made of polished stone and dark stained wood and an adjacent elevator bank led to upper floors.

For several days running, Spotify wouldn't see the G Squared executives. Eventually, though, the two venture capitalists secured a meeting with a young company lawyer, Peter Grandelius. Walking into Spotify's offices on an upper floor, Aschebrook and McLeod found a small waiting room with one wall dedicated to a cartoonlike timeline of company milestones—moments connected by arrows that curved up toward the ceiling and then down to the floor: six million paying subscribers, a new logo unveiling, new markets in Argentina, Taiwan, Greece, and Turkey. A wire magazine rack held the latest issue of *Gaffa*, Denmark's largest and oldest music magazine, which gets distributed throughout Scandinavia.

Aschebrook repeatedly made his pitch to successively senior Spotify executives that G Squared could become a trusted partner to Spotify when employees or other insiders wanted to cash out. As luck would have it, Aschebrook and McLeod had found a willing partner. From the beginning, Spotify had been more open than most companies about letting its employees sell shares. Ek and Lorentzon believed that employees should have the freedom to sell shares if they wanted. Years earlier, a notice tacked up in Spotify's break room had provided the contact details of an investor willing to buy shares from employees who wanted to sell.

Grandelius passed Aschebrook and McLeod on to a young executive in Spotify's finance department, Johan Bergqvist, who began the process of transferring the stake the G Squared duo had come to purchase. But the Spotify executives had bigger plans. They had already approved the sale of a much larger stake, of about $150 million, before the buyer had backed out at the last minute. Did Aschebrook and McLeod have the money and wherewithal to buy a bigger stake? More or less on the spot, Aschebrook managed to raise the required money to buy the $150 million stake, lining up limited partners who had already invested in G Squared's funds to co-invest alongside the firm.

After McLeod flew back to San Francisco, Grandelius and Bergqvist treated Aschebrook to a traditional Swedish meal and pints of locally brewed beer at Konstnärsbaren, a restaurant near the Nobis.

■ ■ ■

With G Squared on board, Spotify put up impressive growth. In the final two months of 2014, the company added ten million users, bringing the total customer base to sixty million. Fifteen million paid for the premium, ad-free product. Yet the company continued to face tough competition, including from Apple, which had plunked down $3 billion for Beats Music, a streaming service founded by Dr. Dre and Jimmy Iovine, and Beats Electronics. Deezer had expanded to 182 markets by 2013, while SoundCloud had 40 million users and had reached 200 million listeners through its website and on social media by the middle of the year.

It was once again time for Spotify to go out and raise money to fend off the competition and fund its growth plans. Spotify had already raised more than $500 million over the course of six prior rounds. Executives wanted to double that amount in the next round, and Sterky, the CFO, planned to rely heavily on U.S. investors for the money. The company had historically used the capital-raising services of CODE Advisors, a boutique investment bank cofounded by music industry veteran Fred Davis. CODE had helped Spotify in previous years, such as in a 2011 round when it raised $100 million at a $1 billion valuation.

This time Spotify turned to Goldman Sachs for fundraising help. Senior Goldman partner Gregg Lemkau, attracted by Spotify's growth, had gotten to know Ek several years earlier over a cup of coffee in London and helped lead a $50 million Goldman Sachs investment in Spotify. The men discussed Spotify's vast business potential, a landscape that also saw Deezer competing, and what Ek would do if Facebook offered him $1 billion. Goldman's investment came from what its bankers liked to call the "growth fund," which they used to get closer to startups they hoped to advise in the future. With its bankers alongside him, Sterky went on a global roadshow, visiting New York, Boston, San Francisco, London, and other cities to meet with potential investors. They quickly demanded answers about Spotify's latest negotiations with the big record labels.

Relations were icy. In November 2014, Big Machine, then Taylor Swift's label, caused a stir when it publicly removed her catalog from Spotify's service. The label argued that streaming cut into sales of compact discs and downloads. Fears mounted that other big-name artists would follow suit.

Ek responded quickly, writing a blog post to say that Spotify had paid $2 billion to artists since its beginning. "Taylor Swift is absolutely right: music is art, art has real value, and artists deserve to be paid for it," Ek wrote. "We started Spotify because we love music and piracy was killing it. So all the talk swirling around lately about how Spotify is making money on the backs of artists upsets me big time."

To some extent, Ek was right. The record labels had come to depend on Spotify's checks. In March 2015, the Recording Industry of America announced that for the first time, U.S. revenue from streaming music had surpassed CD sales. It was about to overtake digital downloads as the industry's largest source of revenue. But many artists weren't seeing the benefits, with much of that revenue captured by the largest artists.

Nonetheless, the growing importance of streaming revenue to the largest labels meant that Spotify had more leverage than in previous negotiations. Throughout the spring of 2015, Goldman Sachs shopped the Spotify deal around. The market was increasingly awash in capital and Spotify had little trouble attracting interest.

Around the time that Sterky was talking to investors, Ek and McCarthy were engaging in secret talks for the Netflix veteran to replace the CFO. Spotify had begun to think about going public, and McCarthy would bring a big name recognizable to Wall Street into the company's management team.

Leaders and the senior executives they hire often engage in an elaborate corporate mating ritual. McCarthy and Ek met in New York and Los Angeles. McCarthy had remarried and was living with his second wife in Woodside, California. At first the CFO job wasn't discussed outright. Neither a founder of Ek's success nor an executive of McCarthy's stature wanted to be rejected. The men talked in generalities. Eventually the generalities worked themselves into a specific offer. Contract and compensation negotiations soon followed.

McCarthy agreed, acquiescing to move with his wife to Stockholm to be closer to Spotify's management team. First, Spotify needed to wrap up the funding round.

In April, reports surfaced that Spotify was close to raising $400 million. By June, it had raised more than $500 million at an $8.5 billion valuation, with reports suggesting that the company was planning to use the proceeds to get into video and podcasting. One of the investors was Goldman Sachs Investment Partners, an in-house hedge fund focused on venture and growth equity investing out of the firm's asset management division. It was wrapping up a new fund, called Global Private Opportunities Partners II, filled with money from clients of Goldman's private bank. Other investors in the round included Wellington Partners, Baillie Gifford, the hundred-year-old Scottish investment manager, and investment firms TCV, Northzone, Balyasny Asset Management, and Senvest Capital. Nordic mobile operator TeliaSonera paid $115 million for a 1.4 percent stake.

The round included a contract term called a ratchet, which gave the investors the right to take a larger share of the company if later funding rounds came in at a lower valuation. If all went well, they would never have to use it.

Ek presented as one of the startup industry's most forward-thinking leaders, according to one person who invested in that round. Under his direction, Spotify's engineers had pioneered many aspects of agile software development that would later become commonplace. "What Daniel appreciated that few others did at the time, he appreciated that there was a source of sustainable competitive advantage," the investor said, recalling his investment thesis. "The bear case on Spotify at the time was anyone can get access to this music, so there will be no differentiation. When Apple launches, they are so well funded they will wipe the floor with Spotify. What Daniel understood was his moat was the data effect of the business by having captured millions of listening hours." Spotify compared patterns across millions of listeners, came up with insights, and employed those to help introduce new artists that matched user preferences. In this way, it could keep users engaged and using its service.

By most measures, the round was a complete success. It was by far the most money that Spotify had ever raised at once, and it did so at a valuation more than twice as high as the TCV round just two years earlier. Ek nevertheless pushed ahead with replacing his CFO, and Spotify officially announced the change on June 17. News coverage played up McCarthy's experience taking Netflix public in 2002 and helping usher it from a mail-order DVD business to a streaming video behemoth. The *Wall Street Journal*'s story suggested that McCarthy's hiring was a sign that Spotify was preparing for an IPO.

■ ■ ■

Before there was an IPO there would be summer vacation. Spotify's offices emptied out in August as the company's employees took off to enjoy the good weather. There would be plenty of time to work in the dark, cold winter days of winter.

In the United States, McCarthy had spent the first half of the summer preparing for his move to Stockholm. It would be the first time he or his wife had lived outside the United States. They found an apartment in Östermalm, home of hole-in-the-wall pubs, designer boutiques, a large park designed in the sixteenth century, and the Swedish History Museum, with its displays of Viking artifacts. Their building featured a wooden Otis elevator fit for two.

But when he went to Spotify's Jarla House offices, on August 7, a Friday, he was in for a dose of culture shock. He arrived just after 9:00 a.m.... to a largely empty office. Looking around at rows of open desks, McCarthy could make out just two people on the entire floor. A Spotify IPO would be hard to pull off if he didn't have a team around him that he could trust to work hard, the new CFO thought.

"We'd just arrived, and I thought I was dead," McCarthy later recalled.

He discovered that his team would soon return and work diligently toward his goals. An IPO would be unlikely for another reason entirely. Spotify's accounting system was woefully unprepared to track the royalties from music streaming. Downloading distinct music files was simple by comparison. When Apple sold a song for 99 cents, it could reliably split the proceeds among the parties entitled to a cut. When it sold the same song again one hour later, or two days or three years later, it would repeat the same process.

The mechanics and royalty considerations of streaming were complex. Now platforms like Spotify had to keep track of the minutes that users spent listening to millions of individual songs and figure out how to apportion a static pool of royalties based on that. McCarthy knew that if Spotify was going to have to answer to public market investors, it needed to be able to handle the task flawlessly. He had little patience for mistakes.

Pär-Jörgen Pärson, whose Swedish venture firm Northzone became one of Spotify's earliest outside investors when it led Spotify's Series A round in 2008, and a member of the board, remembered those early days when McCarthy was just getting started. "He couldn't really see himself listing a company where he hadn't 100 percent control over the numbers," Pärson said later.

McCarthy began to design a fitness regimen to get Spotify into shape for the public markets. He went shopping for a new ERP system, the combination of accounting, compliance, risk management, and financial planning software that companies use to track bills and receipts. He settled on one sold by NetSuite, whose 2007 initial stock sale had used an auction.

As McCarthy settled in, he set out to build his team. Sterky stepped down from the CFO position to focus on financial planning and analysis while plotting a graceful exit. McCarthy needed someone to run investor relations, the job of communicating with shareholders on an ongoing basis. He also needed a general counsel. One person he considered for the general counsel's job was

Wilson Sonsini partner Bob Sanchez, who had worked closely with McCarthy when he was at Netflix. Sanchez was listed second only to Larry Sonsini on Netflix's IPO filing, and he'd been one of McCarthy's first calls when he had a legal question. The job would require Sanchez to leave Big Law, develop a different skill set, and probably take a pay cut. McCarthy thought of it as a good opportunity for Sanchez. Trust was a factor, too. McCarthy and Sanchez could lean on each other in a new environment, working in tandem to take Spotify public.

■ ■ ■

Perhaps more than anything in his first twelve months, McCarthy would obsess over the company's cash position. He had learned, with Netflix's aborted 2000 IPO, that it never hurt to have company coffers stocked full of cash just in case something unexpected happened. He liked to cite one of his favorite blunt maxims (which he first heard from Andy Rachleff, the cofounder and former general partner of Benchmark Capital) that "cash is oxygen to a business, and oxygen is life."

And he wanted Spotify to be on a stable financial footing when it came time to negotiate with the record labels. "I didn't want the record labels to ever believe that they could slow-roll us in the negotiations and prevent us from going public because we were thinly capitalized," he said later.

By January 2016, he had once again gone out to investors to raise more money. Stock markets were not cooperating. The NASDAQ slumped 8 percent in January, its worst monthly showing since May 2010. He realized that if he was going to raise another pile of cash by selling stock, it would likely be at a lower valuation than what Sterky had commanded in June 2015. In Silicon Valley lexicon, the event would be a down round, a sign to the outside world that Spotify's position was weakened.

McCarthy decided instead to sell a convertible bond. Convertibles are debt instruments that pay interest and can be exchanged for equity at some predetermined point in the future. The conversion feature gives buyers upside they wouldn't get with a regular bond, an option that lowers their risk and results in a lower interest rate for the company than it would otherwise pay.

Uber Technologies, a ride-hailing app that had gotten an early investment from Bill Gurley, had already issued convertible bonds, removing a barrier to technology startups that often had no profits to speak of and were used to raising equity from venture capitalists. Investors had come to view convertibles as a less risky way of getting into the world of startups, acquiring a piece of a high-flying tech company with downside protection.

One similarity between convertible bonds and venture financing was that companies still issued new stock; but for the bonds, it was at the time of the conversion from debt to equity. That wouldn't come until later, meaning McCarthy could raise money without having to suffer the embarrassment of a down round.

With Goldman Sachs's help once again, McCarthy held a series of talks with investors, flying back and forth to the United States. It was his first fundraising effort since leaving Netflix almost six years before. He found a small group of willing investors in San Francisco. David Trujillo, a portfolio manager at TPG Capital who had also led the company's investment in Uber, helmed the negotiations. Two others joined in—Sixth Street, which was TPG's credit investing arm, and Dragoneer Investment Group, founded by Marc Stad. Clients of Goldman Sachs also participated.

Over the course of several weeks in February, McCarthy hammered out a financing package that would dwarf anything he'd ever done. In return for $1 billion, he agreed to allow investors to convert their debt into shares at a 20 percent discount to the IPO price if Spotify went public within the next twelve months. If the IPO took longer, the discount would increase. The interest rate on the debt faced a similarly laddered approach.

The terms meant that Spotify would be required to issue a certain amount of shares at the IPO. The bet was that the amount would be less than if Spotify had used the fundraising round to raise equity.

Some insiders worried that the company was raising too much money at too high a price, recalled Pärson, the Spotify board member. "There was a lot of internal discussion," Pärson said. McCarthy felt that if Spotify could succeed in offering an attractive product, the terms were acceptable, Pärson said, while those who came down on the conservative side of the debate "thought he was just racing far too much to expensive terms."

On February 19, the board of directors voted to allow McCarthy and his team to proceed with the financing. TPG and Dragoneer emailed signed copies of the term sheets and exclusivity letters the same day. Over the following few days, Spotify collected approvals from existing shareholders. On February 22, McCarthy signed a letter of exclusivity on behalf of the company. A twenty-one-day due diligence period began.

In past rounds, the company had set an outlandish valuation and waited either until venture capitalists came calling or the company's performance caught up to it. This time McCarthy had accepted the terms imposed on him in his haste to get a deal done. He was making a bet on the company's future and the ability of the employees to make it perform. It was a risk he was willing to take. For the first time, the company was starting to bring in more cash than it was paying out, a positive sign that would look good to potential public market investors. The clock had started ticking on Spotify's IPO.

On the evening of March 29, news of the convertible bond transaction hit the *Wall Street Journal*, in a piece that highlighted, in the first sentence, the "strict guarantees" that Spotify had agreed to. When the article appeared in the print version of the newspaper the following day, it was the first time many employees had heard about the fundraising. It elicited a company-wide email from McCarthy to explain senior management's thinking at the time.

"As some of you have read in the press this morning, we've signed a deal to raise $1B from institutional investors," McCarthy wrote from Stockholm. The money, he suggested, might allow the company to host a secondary share sale when it came time for the IPO. In other words, if Spotify didn't need more money, it wouldn't issue new shares in an IPO.

When the deal was done, McCarthy had raised twice the amount he'd sought. He added $1 billion to Spotify's coffers. The cash suddenly gave the company some leverage it hadn't had. "Having a war chest, turning cash-positive, all of a sudden the company started to see that they could actually dictate their future in a way that they didn't think was possible just a year prior," Pärson said.

The size and speed of the round left a deep impression on McCarthy. For twelve years at Netflix, he'd had the capital markets wrapped around his finger. He knew how to appease investors and was skilled enough to experiment with raising various types of funding. Something had changed in the intervening years. The relationship between startups needing money and the investors willing to provide it had been dramatically altered. There were now mind-boggling amounts of capital available to private companies, provided by venture capitalists like G Squared, who raised it from pensions, endowments, and wealthy individuals and invested it in promising technology startups.

In covering the news of Spotify's fundraising, the *Financial Times* quoted an investment banker on the implications of the trend. "We are going to see an increasing number of companies delaying their IPOs as long as they can raise private money so easily."

McCarthy put it much more succinctly. "The rules had changed."

CHAPTER 10

Spotify, Stockholm, 2016

McCarthy was ready to change other rules too. He began to think about ways that Spotify could get better at telling its story to investors. The company already gave briefings to shareholders, but McCarthy wanted to do more. At Netflix, he'd developed a reputation for being transparent and doing more than the minimum in his communications with investors. He eschewed the traditional practice of reading a dry, prewritten statement at the beginning of earnings calls in favor of going straight into live question-and-answer sessions with analysts.

He wanted to bring a similar approach to Spotify. During talks with the convertible bond investors, McCarthy reached out to the company's lawyers at Skadden, Arps, Slate, Meagher & Flom to ask them about the possibility, under securities laws, of reporting earnings and holding an investor day even though Spotify was still private. The SEC didn't allow companies to speak to investors once they had begun the process of going public, but there were fewer restraints before the process began. While most private companies chose not to share detailed financial information with investors, McCarthy thought Spotify could.

"There would have been a period of time when we could have communicated with investors openly, and educated them about the company and the strategy, and exposed the management team," McCarthy said later. "I was thinking that there were some advantages to pursuing that best practice sooner rather than later."

And he began to wonder if he could reimagine the act of going public.

McCarthy believed that there were aspects of the process that had stopped working. Since LinkedIn's in 2011, McCarthy had watched dozens of IPOs pop on their first day of trading. While the press liked to cheer such

performances, the three-time CFO knew that underpricing deprived companies of valuable proceeds they could use to invest in the business.

Many in the industry agreed with McCarthy that the model had been
broken for years. The investment banks, for example, used to buy stock
from companies and accept the risk of distributing the shares. In modern
practice, investment banks held the shares for a split-second before electronically passing them from the company to institutional investors. The
bankers simply lowered the price if there was a risk that investors were not
going to buy.

The banks did face some risk, particularly around legal liability, and
could be sued by investors for material misrepresentations in the prospectus.
But critics argued that the underwriting model was an anachronism.

IPOs are risky. They are stock issues from companies that haven't faced
the rigor of the public markets or are less proven than established firms. Many
technology firms are trying to create entirely new industries. Most aren't
making money when they come to market.

Bankers liked to lower that risk by selling shares at a discount to encourage investors to participate. The size of the discount was a matter of debate,
but 25 to 30 percent was often considered a reasonable compromise. Investors
hoped to get rewarded for taking that risk by seeing their investment increase
in value during the first few days of trading. Companies got to raise money
by selling the shares at a lofty enough price that the proceeds supported their
business.

All too often, McCarthy thought, the investment banks applied too large
a discount on highly anticipated IPOs. Or they failed to accurately price the
shares. The first-day performance for particularly popular deals seemed to
increasingly feature a large price increase. The pop left money on the table for
the company.

McCarthy surmised that the root of the problem was that the process
didn't do a good enough job of judging investor demand. It didn't reflect any
interest from individual investors, since the IPO was only sold to clients of
the investment banks, which were largely institutions. And even the investors
who were allowed into the process had an incentive to underbid for the shares,
if they knew they'd get something in the deal.

Some may have wanted to blame the bankers for the mispricing, but

McCarthy didn't hold the same opinion. He didn't view them as rent-seekers looking out for themselves but rather as generally honest people working within a flawed system. "I think they do their best, honestly," he said. "I just think because the process is flawed, it doesn't often achieve the desired outcome."

McCarthy was predisposed to believe that the work of investment bankers was important. He was, after all, a product of East Coast financial institutions, a former investment banker by training. He also had a healthy understanding of how much control the bankers exerted over the process. One need look no further than Google's IPO.

As he thought about whether he could design something new, he considered how the incumbents would perceive it. "I thought the greatest risk here to the transaction, or one of the risks, principal risks, would be organ rejection by the Street generally," he said later. "They're busy. They've got a lot going on. There are a lot of companies to invest in. Nobody's got a lot of time to learn about some new, crazy idea that you've dreamed up that's so far out of the mainstream nobody cares about it. They just can't be bothered. Or there's something about it that so antagonizes the mainstream that they just flip you off and turn their back on you. And organ rejection was one of the afflictions of Google's failed auction." McCarthy worried that if he didn't include Wall Street's most powerful players, they would turn against his deal, as some of them had done for Google, and work to undercut its success.

Spotify now had $1.7 billion in the bank. It didn't need money, and McCarthy was loath to issue the 12 to 15 percent more shares that he felt it would take to get Spotify trading publicly, because that additional stock would reduce his and other investors' stake in the company. And yet it was important to McCarthy and his boss, Ek, that employees and insiders get an easier way to cash out their holdings—Spotify had been more open than many other startups to allowing employees to sell shares privately, but the process was still cumbersome. And the terms of the convertible deal made it clear that Spotify couldn't stay private forever.

McCarthy began to think that if it was that easy to raise money in the private markets, maybe there was an opening to curate Spotify's public debut in a way that better met the needs of the company. That would mean eschewing the traditional IPO process that had just been written into the company's securities filings.

. . .

The week after the convertible transaction closed, on April 4, 2016, Spotify welcomed its new general counsel, Horacio Gutierrez. Sanchez had decided against taking the position, leading McCarthy to poach from Microsoft, where Gutierrez had spent more than seventeen years.

Around that time, Paul Vogel, an internet analyst at Barclays PLC, was having lunch with Facebook's vice president of investor relations, Deborah Tuerk Crawford. Crawford had worked for McCarthy as head of investor relations for Netflix. "I've left Wall Street once and I'm ready to do it again," Vogel recalls telling Crawford. In 2000, he had given up an analyst's job at Donaldson, Lufkin & Jenrette to join an investment firm. He returned to the world of banks when he joined Barclays in 2013. "I just need to figure out what the right move is."

"Would you like to be introduced to Barry McCarthy?" Crawford said. "I know he's looking for someone to run investor relations at Spotify."

Vogel noted that he'd met McCarthy once or twice when he was at Netflix but didn't know him well. "That'd be great," he told Crawford.

Crawford later emailed McCarthy to introduce Vogel. When the two men met, McCarthy made it clear that he was looking for a thought partner. "Barry and I had some conversations about doing an investor day and doing different types of things to really tell the story ahead of going public," Vogel said. "Neither of us had an exact idea of what we wanted to do—it was more like, 'What are things in the process that we would want to do differently if we could? How can we make this better? How can we make it more Spotify like?'"

Vogel, too, had noticed that the IPO process wasn't working. "This notion of creating an artificial first-day pop in the stock is actually not really great for the company, it's not great for shareholders who've been with you for a long period of time," Vogel said later. "We both had come to that agreement pretty early on. And I think we both felt like we wanted to be able to tell the story to the widest group of investors and not just those that the banks chose or who were accredited investors allowed to listen to the information behind the walls that are set up."

Before he could hire Vogel, McCarthy needed to start talking to exchange officials. In May, McCarthy met with Tom Farley, the president of the New York Stock Exchange, known for his boyish looks and nice suits, for what McCarthy later described as "a happy talk, meet and greet." Stock exchanges compete vigorously to host IPOs. And their wooing of startups begins years earlier.

■ ■ ■

McCarthy officially hired Vogel as head of investor relations in June. By then, Sterky had announced his intention to leave Spotify, so Vogel quickly added oversight of financial planning and analysis to his portfolio. Vogel joined McCarthy, to whom he reported directly, as the core of a team that would rethink ways to get the company's message out to the broadest group of investors. "It didn't start out as broad as reinventing the IPO and going public with the direct listing," Vogel said. "It was more, 'What can we do differently?'"

That month, the *Financial Times* wrote about the fundraising environment that McCarthy had run into months before. Silicon Valley's venture capitalists, the newspaper said, had shifted from a focus on growth at all costs to profits matter most. Investors were responding, in part, to a market for initial public offerings that had suddenly disappeared. The article was headlined "Death of the Unicorn?"

Over the course of the summer, McCarthy, Gutierrez, and Vogel set out to learn as much as they could about the IPO process and how they might adapt it to Spotify's needs. McCarthy contracted the legal work to Wilson Sonsini, and over a series of phone calls and email exchanges, the CFO sounded out his old lawyer, Sanchez, on what was possible. One of McCarthy's early questions: Could Spotify go public without issuing new shares?

Wilson Sonsini had helped Google design its nontraditional offering and worked with Netflix when McCarthy was there to design the compensation scheme that allowed employees to choose whether they received their bonus in stock, cash, or whatever mix of the two they wanted.

Sanchez and colleague Michael Labriola did some quick work. They found that there was a category of company that had directly listed their shares on an exchange without undergoing a traditionally underwritten IPO. Most had either been emerging from bankruptcy or were business units being spun out of a corporate parent. The process had allowed those companies to make shares available to public investors. Since they were already established companies, or business units, and presumably known to investors already, the SEC applied an easier regulatory regime and used the Securities Exchange Act of 1934 to govern the transaction.

But when Sanchez pulled in a colleague named Jeffrey Saper, a longtime securities attorney who did a lot of work with investment banks, disagreement broke out within Wilson Sonsini. Saper, who had spent time with the SEC and believed in traditional IPOs, was largely against the idea from the beginning. "Nobody does it this way," one person recalled Saper saying. "This is not the way to take it."

Wilson Sonsini, like many corporate lawyers, was used to guiding clients through existing laws and precedent, not coming up with new creations that then needed to be stress-tested with securities regulators. Saper fit the mold. The Wilson Sonsini partners didn't think that what Spotify had in mind could work, in part because McCarthy wanted to stay away from having to file a registration statement.

It was in some respects an unsettling time at Wilson Sonsini, one of Silicon Valley's oldest law firms, now facing some internal conflicts. A number of partners had grown frustrated with Larry Sonsini and other senior lawyers at the firm who seemed to them to be focused on profit over growth. They felt that they were at times left without the resources, in terms of both manpower and time, to pay proper attention to the business they'd already won or that they hoped to win.

That certainly seemed true in Spotify's case. McCarthy wanted Sanchez to act in the same role as he had done at Netflix, but Wilson didn't have enough people on the East Coast to meet Spotify's demands. The problem was made worse by the fact that McCarthy had squeezed Wilson Sonsini to do the work for a smaller than normal fee.

Sanchez and Labriola conceded that if the transaction involved simply having shareholders list their stock on an exchange, and didn't involve Spotify issuing new shares, the SEC might allow the company to list under the provisions of the Securities Exchange Act of 1934.

By September, McCarthy and Sanchez knew that it was probably technically possible to get Spotify's shares trading publicly without raising capital. "We embarked down a path of imaging that the transaction would be governed by the 34 Act," McCarthy said later. But should they pursue a trans-action to get Spotify's shares trading without raising capital? McCarthy had his regular check-in with Ek coming up and decided that he would finally broach the idea with his boss.

Spotify was designing a gleaming new Stockholm headquarters. It had run out of room in Jarla House; McCarthy now worked out of a different space. On the eighth floor of Jakobsbergsgatan 31, about half a mile south of Jarla House and around the corner from the Nobis Hotel, McCarthy and his team watched over the company's finances. On Tuesday, September 20, McCarthy walked north to Jarla House to meet with Ek. It was a walk he often took, bundled up against rain, sleet, and snow. More than once he grumbled about the dark skies and bitter cold of his adopted home.

McCarthy knew a direct listing would be a nonstarter if he couldn't get his CEO on board. The framing was critical. Sticking it to Wall Street wouldn't have much emotional relevance for Ek, though it did to Lorentzon. But doing something different to better solve Spotify's particular situation might appeal more to Ek's sensibilities. "I had thought long and hard about how I wanted to introduce the idea to him," McCarthy said later.

Arriving at Jarla House, McCarthy made his way to Ek's office. When the two men sat down for their regular catch-up, McCarthy made his pitch. "I have this crazy idea to do something that's never been done before," he recalls saying. Ek leaned in. McCarthy had his attention. McCarthy went on to describe the idea in detail. He said he expected to hear back from Sanchez sometime soon, at which point he'd have a better idea of whether it was doable. Ek liked what he heard. "He wasn't at all dissuaded by the risk of being first," McCarthy said. "Being innovative, being different for a purpose, has great appeal for him."

Meanwhile, Vogel was trying to schedule an investor day, but Spotify was in the midst of another round of negotiations with the music companies, and the talks were dragging out. McCarthy described the basis of the terms that were under discussion. "The bulk of the chunk of money is percent of revenue, independent of plays, and then the money gets divided up based on percent of plays. There are also some guarantees—think of it as schmuck insurance—that protect them on the downside," he said later. "So you're kind of dancing between those two raindrops."

Spotify didn't want to host an investor day until the negotiations were complete. It would give investors another opening to pick at Spotify's business model.

With Ek on board, McCarthy began to think about the role of the bankers in his transaction. He wanted to be thoughtful about how the banks might help him. "Let's think fundamentally about the nature of the advice that their value added," he said later. "What exactly did they do for companies when they took them public? They provide advice, and they provide underwriting. Well, the underwriting risk exists for what, a fraction of a second? There's no real risk, right? The deal is pre-sold. The bank buys it. They want it for a second. They sell it to Fidelity, T. Rowe, everybody else. So all the value-added really is in the advice. And we're going to be public like every other company was going to be public. We were going to present ourselves to the investment committee, just like every other company who's in the process of going public. And so I wanted their advice."

He would have to come up with answers sometime soon.

■ ■ ■

A week later, Paul Kwan headed to the San Jose airport for an overnight flight to Stockholm. The head of Morgan Stanley's West Coast tech practice and the former head of internet and software banking, Kwan had worked with many of the world's largest internet companies. He had known McCarthy for years. The two men worked closely together when McCarthy was at Netflix and used Morgan Stanley's services. Kwan was on his way to see him.

Kwan thought that this meeting would be like dozens of others he would do that year—it would give him a chance to touch base with the client and find out if there was anything he could do to help. Often there wasn't, but bankers were used to calling on clients for years before a big transaction would deliver millions of dollars in fees. Kwan understood that the clock had started ticking on Spotify's public offering, and he wanted to make sure he would be in line to lead it.

The morning of his arrival was cold, and he bundled up for the trip to McCarthy's office. Their meeting was scheduled for 11:30.

Kwan was ushered in, and the two men sat down in a conference room. "I've been thinking about nontraditional ways of going public," McCarthy said. The CFO explained that he needed to give insiders a way to buy and sell shares easily, and that he didn't need any of the money an IPO could provide. He posed a question of whether there was utility in using the traditional IPO process to solve Spotify's unique set of objectives. "We're thinking about doing a direct listing."

Kwan hid his surprise. An expression of skepticism could hurt his chances of getting hired for the transaction. Earning the mandate of being one of Spotify's lead banks, even in a direct listing, would likely deliver tens of millions of dollars in fees. "That's interesting," he told McCarthy. "I understand why you are asking the question. They are the same issues we have been trying to solve for years."

Kwan recognized, in what McCarthy was describing, some of the elements of a corporate spinoff. In 2007, he recalled, EMC, the world's biggest manufacturer of data storage hardware, had directly listed a division that made software for corporations to use that storage more efficiently. It was a successful transaction—EMC received an $11 billion windfall, and the division, named VMWare, became one of the world's largest software firms by value.

McCarthy was planning for only existing shareholders to sell stock. Spotify wouldn't sell anything, but he figured that the company would be in charge of settling on a price for the shares others were selling. "Help me answer these three questions," McCarthy said. "How will I figure out the offering price when I'm not selling anything? How will public investors behave—will they buy it or ignore it? Do we lose any PR or marketing benefits of a traditional offering?"

The two men discussed those questions for some time before it was time for Kwan to go.

"Go do some work on it," McCarthy said.

Kwan walked out of the meeting thinking that he might have an interesting transaction on his hands. And that the deal might solve some of the issues with the traditional IPO.

On October 18, McCarthy traveled to Morgan Stanley's Menlo Park office to meet with Kwan and others on his team. Since Kwan had visited McCarthy, he'd had his fellow bankers work on answers to the CFO's questions. Morgan Stanley had concluded that McCarthy wanted to do something different, and that they wanted to be part of whatever that was. They looked for ways to get to yes.

■ ■ ■

In late October, McCarthy moved back to the United States. He settled professionally at Spotify's Sixth Avenue headquarters in Manhattan, in a seven-story Beaux-Arts building located in the heart of the Flatiron district that was home to many of the city's tech startups.

In December, as the streets of New York began to fill with the sounds of holiday shoppers and the bells of the Salvation Army Santas, McCarthy prepared to show his cards to Farley and his colleagues at the New York Stock Exchange. He was beginning to assemble a cast of characters who could help him pull off a new type of direct listing, and he needed to find an exchange willing to entertain his idea.

When Farley heard that McCarthy wanted a meeting, he had brainstormed with his colleague John Tuttle about what Spotify might want to discuss. On December 16, a chilly and clear day in New York, Farley boarded the subway for the trip north from the NYSE's marble-columned building on Wall Street to Spotify's offices. The meeting was small, just McCarthy, Vogel, and Farley, but critical in terms of bringing another important player on board.

McCarthy had kept Farley in the dark. He'd grown accustomed to having his idea met with skepticism but found that most people eventually came around. He preferred to explain his reasoning in person. When Farley arrived and the three men gathered in a meeting room, McCarthy broke the news.

"I have an idea," McCarthy said. "You're sworn to secrecy."

Farley was intrigued. He agreed to be discreet.

"I want to take Spotify public," McCarthy said, "but I don't want to raise stock, and I just want to list it."

For a second, Farley didn't know what to say. "The banks won't be too happy with that," he finally said.

"Why would I need a bank? I'm not going to use a bank," McCarthy said. "Why does that matter if the banks are happy or they're not happy?"

Farley tried to process this. It wasn't what he'd expected.

"There is some precedent for this, because when companies emerge from bankruptcy, often they just list the stock," Farley told him. "Similarly, when foreign companies list in the U.S. as a dual listing, they just list the stock, and the opening auction mechanism on the stock exchange is what sets the opening price."

"I'm aware of that," McCarthy said. "There's actually been a lot, and I don't understand why companies don't look at this particular avenue."

"I'm trying to understand why you're interested in this," Farley said.

"Well, a lot of reasons. I think I can have a more fulsome dialogue with my investors if it's not governed by a typical IPO quiet period," McCarthy said. He meant one governed by the Securities Act of 1933. "We don't need the cash, so why go raise a whole bunch of cash. The typical IPO process doesn't make a ton of sense to me."

By the end of the meeting, Farley told the Spotify executives that the exchange would like to be involved.

"I love it, I'm in," Farley said. "I want to help. Let me go back, work with the team. Figure out what rules would need to change, if any."

Farley may not have realized it, but he'd already won the competition against NASDAQ. For most of its forty-five years in business, NASDAQ had been the exchange of choice for America's fast-growing internet companies; Apple, Microsoft, and Amazon.com chose the venue for their listings. But by 2016, McCarthy and other tech executives had soured on it because of its system error during Facebook's IPO.

The instant he was off the elevator and out on the street, Farley called his boss, Jeff Sprecher, CEO of the Intercontinental Exchange, which owned the NYSE. As Farley walked down Sixth Avenue, he told Sprecher about the conversation he'd just had with the Spotify executives.

"I've got to tell you about the meeting I just had," Farley said. "I think there's a better way to do an IPO, and Spotify might take the leap."

As the two men talked, Sprecher offered some advice, grounded in his years of experience. "I think they're going to use the banks."

"What do you mean?" Farley asked.

"You know, the banks help you in other ways, and Barry's a smart guy," Sprecher said. "You're not going to want to alienate the top guys. They're going to bring you deals and maybe later on you raise some debt, or you do a convert. You're going to want the research."

He went on. "I like this, but I think the banks will be involved."

. . .

McCarthy also began sharing his idea with board members. Pärson, one of the company's first backers, said that directors discussed it for a couple of months. "It was almost presented initially as a crazy idea." Pärson explored the idea with Farley at NYSE as well. "The thing with Tom was that he loved that idea," Pärson said, "whereas, the NASDAQ people were initially very, very skeptical."

One month after the Farley meeting, McCarthy began to seek out people whose opinion he respected. He reached out to TCV's Jay Hoag and to Andy Rachleff, who had named McCarthy to the board of his digital investment advice company years earlier. He also sought out Mary Meeker, now a venture capitalist, who reminded McCarthy of the importance of having the banks involved. Another person McCarthy contacted was Herb Allen, the patriarch of boutique investment bank Allen & Co. and the host of a star-studded summer conference that McCarthy liked to attend. McCarthy also sought out Ken Broad, a hedge fund investor at Jackson Square Partners who'd been managing a small/mid cap growth fund when McCarthy was Netflix's CFO.

On February 10, 2017, at 1:00 p.m., McCarthy walked into a small conference room named Barracuda on the seventh floor of Spotify's New York offices for a call with Broad. The offices were utilitarian, with concrete floors and white bench-like desks identical to those in the Birger Jarlsgatan 61 offices. The conference room was in the back corner of one floor, adjacent to the desks of McCarthy and Vogel, which faced each other.

McCarthy dialed into the call with Broad, and the two men chatted for a while.

"Hey, what do you think about this as an idea?" McCarthy said, and proceeded to outline his vision for a direct listing.

Broad was open to it. Back in the late 1990s he'd become a student of the IPO process, interested in understanding whether it was worthwhile for small investors to spend time evaluating companies going public through an IPO if there was no guarantee of a large allocation. He shared some of what he'd learned with McCarthy.

One topic the two men talked about was how to think about the traditional IPO and its inherent problems. Broad suggested that McCarthy look into the degree of underpricing in the market, and referred him to a University of Florida professor named Jay Ritter. Call Ritter, Broad said, "if you're trying to frame why this might be better in terms of the degree of underpricing. This guy's the godfather of IPO stats."

CHAPTER 11

Spotify, Stockholm, 2018

By March 2017, McCarthy had done enough research and spoken to enough people both inside and outside Spotify that it was time to officially run his direct listing idea by the board and hear official pitches from investment banks. Company executives and directors convened in a boardroom in the New York office to hear investment banking pitches from Goldman Sachs, Morgan Stanley, and Allen & Co.

Though McCarthy had already briefed Spotify's directors on his plans, he now gave a presentation titled "Why do a direct listing?," and walked the board through his thought process. Most importantly, he showed the board that he had full command of the issues and planned to stick to his convictions. "I'd been pretty clear about my preferences," McCarthy said later. "If they had thrown up roadblocks, the conversation would have gone the other way."

Both Morgan Stanley and Goldman Sachs had done work stress-testing Spotify's plans. Kwan and Grimes presented for Morgan Stanley. Representing Goldman were Lemkau; Nick Giovanni, head of technology banking; and David Ludwig, co-head of equity capital markets. Allen & Co.'s Harry Wagner and Ketan Mehta were there, as were bankers from JPMorgan.

When it came time for Goldman to present, the firm's bankers showed McCarthy and the board that Spotify could get what McCarthy wanted within the traditional IPO structure—that they could reduce the friction of the IPO enough to meet the company's objectives. On one slide, the bankers compared the direct listing as it was taking shape with a traditional IPO, and showed how one could be made to look more like the other. There and elsewhere, they listed a number of options. If Spotify wanted to pursue a traditional IPO, the company or its investors could sell a small amount of stock—not enough to dramatically shrink the holdings of existing investors.

The company could introduce a flexible lockup structure, giving employees and shareholders a way to sell their shares before the customary 180 days enshrined in the language of every IPO prospectus. And McCarthy could be thoughtful and transparent about how he provided guidance.

The Goldman bankers admitted that it would likely be impossible to get away from the "discount on discount" theater that so annoyed McCarthy—giving watered-down projections to analysts who watered them down even more before showing them to investors. The bankers acknowledged that what McCarthy had in mind could work, but that the bank leaned against advising it. If Spotify chose to go the direct listing route, there would be a number of risks that would need to be mitigated. Their message: A company only gets one shot to go public. Don't risk it.

The Morgan Stanley and Allen & Co. bankers also presented, offering their own take on the process then taking shape.

The board debated the idea. Those who still had a significant investment in the company didn't want to be forced to sell in an IPO. They thought that there was still a lot of growth left in the company's model and liked the fact that they wouldn't be diluted by new investors in an IPO. While other board members without a significant investment came from a different place, few felt the need for the company to sell new shares or raise more capital.

"Why should we then have an artificially constructed event that only serves to give the twenty largest institutions that always get allocations some benefit just because they are the twenty biggest institutions," Pärson said of the board's thinking. Nonetheless, the board did have concerns. "It was controversial, because the only direct listings that had been done had been former Chapter 11 companies coming back to the market," Pärson said. "It was seen as not a particularly kosher way of doing things."

Directors also considered two other outstanding questions. First, how would the market go about finding a price for Spotify's shares if it didn't have the traditional IPO process to sound out investors? "The price discovery process was a very, very well-known process in the IPO, but in a direct listing, you had to basically invent that," Pärson said. If that didn't go well, the stock price could whip around dangerously. The board questioned "whether the volatility would be massively problematic for the company, for instance, that the shares would pop far too much," he said.

Second, would Wall Street punish Spotify for its act of defiance? "That was the worry, that we would have the establishment against ourselves... which would create a bad name for the stock in the minds of the investors," Pärson said. "That was the biggest concern I think we had."

At least one board member didn't care too much about that: Lorentzon, the tough-talking negotiator who enjoyed taking a stand. "Martin really liked the idea to screw the banks, early on," Pärson said. "I think he was instantaneously supportive of the idea."

Ek, too, liked the idea of doing something different. "Since Daniel was so positive and Martin was so positive, it was more about how," Pärson said. "And the hows were, of course, they were a lot of different things: How should we work with Goldman, how should we go work with Morgan Stanley? What should the advisors be doing?"

At one point during the session, a small stack of pitchbooks sat piled on the table in front of Ek. At the very top rested a pair of handmade blue sneakers, a gift from Kwan, who had given Ek a similar pair of baby shoes years earlier when he was trying to get close to the founder.

With the sneakers overlooking the proceedings, the founders' support ultimately swayed the rest of the room. Spotify's board signed off on going forward with the direct listing. McCarthy would get his wish.

"There was probably a little bit of the innovator's ego on behalf of Barry," Pärson said. "He wanted to be the innovator. And I think he pushed this and, using his enormous credibility with the financial market then and his past with Netflix, [which] was just soaring at the time, to say that this is the way we should do it. He had so much brand equity that he got away with it."

Spotify chose Goldman Sachs, Morgan Stanley, and Allen & Co. for its bankers.

■ ■ ■

Around that time, McCarthy and Spotify's general counsel Horacio Gutierrez began sounding out law firms as well.

Sanchez and Saper pitched the Spotify team. By then, McCarthy and Gutierrez had grown frustrated with Wilson Sonsini's performance. They weren't getting enough attention from the firm or from Sanchez himself. McCarthy went behind Sanchez's back and sent an email to another Wilson

Sonsini partner. The legal team is frustrated, he suggested, and Wilson Sonsini might need to get some more help.

That email was the last straw for Sanchez. Fed up with an inability to get the resources his clients were expecting, he left for Cooley LLP. Shocked colleagues got notice of his exit in a surprise late-night email. (Over the next two years or so, nearly four dozen Wilson Sonsini lawyers would join Cooley.)

Gutierrez also heard pitches from other law firms, including Latham & Watkins. Dagmara Jastrzebska, a Spotify attorney who joined the firm in January 2016 from Latham, had worked for Latham partner Greg Rodgers. Jastrzebska had wanted Latham to get a chance at winning the earlier work that Wilson Sonsini did, but she wasn't established at Spotify long enough to bring the company in for the work that Wilson ultimately won with their pitch. This time, Jastrzebska got her wish when Gutierrez hired Latham.

With the banks and the lawyers on board, it was time to hold the organizational meeting to get everyone on the same page. On May 3, bankers from Morgan Stanley, Goldman Sachs, Allen & Co., and Rodgers's team at Latham returned to Spotify's offices for the "Project Polaris" startup meeting. Grimes and Giovanni presented the timeline and some high-level thoughts about how they expected the transaction to come together. Though there were half a dozen or so workstreams that came out of that meeting, there was a lot resting on how securities regulators received the proposal. Rodgers spoke up. "We should request an in-person meeting with the staff and go down and engage with them so that we don't spin our wheels on a structure that ultimately ends up not working," he said, according to a person who was in the meeting.

Walking out of that meeting, everyone knew that the reception at the SEC would be critical.

■ ■ ■

Spotify would have to persuade senior officials at the agency who were just starting their positions.

One was William Hinman, the attorney who had worked for Morgan Stanley and Credit Suisse on the Google transaction and had since worked on some of the largest IPOs in history, including Facebook's and the 2014 offering from Chinese e-commerce company Alibaba. Most importantly, Hinman was the incoming director of the SEC's Division of Corporation Finance, one of two offices at the agency involved in IPOs. Hinman was well known to the bankers and lawyers working on Spotify's transaction.

Hinman had been appointed by the incoming chair of the SEC, Jay Clayton, a longtime mergers and acquisitions lawyer at Sullivan & Cromwell with clients like Goldman Sachs. On May 9, the SEC put out a press release announcing Hinman's appointment. "He has spent the last 37 years working in our public and private markets, and he understands the SEC's mission to promote capital formation while ensuring that investors have the information necessary to make informed decisions," Clayton was quoted as saying in the release.

The presence of Clayton and Hinman meant that Spotify's innovative approach would be reviewed by two attorneys with decades of experience in transactions like IPOs. Under SEC rules, only wealthy individuals were allowed to participate in the private markets. And both men were eager to encourage more companies to enter the public markets, where their stock could be purchased by Main Street citizens seeking attractive investment returns. In the five years prior to Spotify's proposed listing, due to the trend of technology companies staying private for longer, it had been wealthy investors and institutions who had benefited from the massive growth in technology companies.

In his first speech as SEC chair, at the Economic Club of New York on July 12, 2017, Clayton told a crowd of bankers and corporate executives that he was focused on fostering capital formation in the public markets. "Evidence shows that a large number of companies, including many of our country's most innovative businesses, are opting to remain privately held," Clayton told the assembled crowd. "I believe we need to increase the attractiveness of our public capital markets without adversely affecting the availability of capital from our private markets."

It would become a key theme of his three-and-a-half-year tenure.

■ ■ ■

As Clayton and Hinman settled in at the SEC, Spotify executives and their bankers and lawyers prepared for their first meeting with the agency. In advance of the meeting, Grimes called Hinman to brief him on the upcoming meeting and Spotify's plans in what one member of Spotify's deal group called "back-channel talks."

On the appointed day in July, McCarthy and Gutierrez awoke early to board an Amtrak train to Washington, DC, for their first meeting with the SEC. McCarthy ditched the jeans and Robert Barakett t-shirt that had become his professional wardrobe at Spotify for a more formal look. He put on a pressed white shirt, a blue suit, black shoes, and a tie. Since his days in boarding school, where he wore a coat and tie six days a week, McCarthy had been particular about how he presented himself. "It wasn't a big reach," he said later. "I'd grown up in that world on the East Coast."

The Spotify executives had spent hours with Latham & Watkins and Morgan Stanley's lawyers going over the script for the meeting—what they were going to say and who was going to say it. The meeting would be a high-wire act—there was no room for misstatement with securities officials in the room. This was showtime.

When the train reached Washington's Union Station, McCarthy and Gutierrez made the ten-minute trip across town to Latham's office, at 555 Eleventh Street NW, where their lawyers had assembled for a pre-meeting briefing. Then they headed back to Station Place, where the SEC's imposing glass and granite home was attached to the train station.

McCarthy, Gutierrez, Rodgers, additional Latham lawyers, and Morgan Stanley lawyers Steven Brown and John Faulkner filed into a nondescript conference room to meet with Hinman and his colleagues at the agency. The meeting began with Spotify's side introducing itself. McCarthy gave a high-level overview of the plan, but it wasn't long before he was relegated to listening to lawyers talk about the nuances of securities law.

Spotify told the SEC that it intended to conduct a transaction governed by the 1934 Act. Doing so would mean that the company would not file an IPO registration statement required under the 1933 Securities Act for companies issuing new shares. Such a filing would subject a company to liability if investors who think they have been misled want to later sue.

The lawyers ran down a list of reasons why they thought their plan was the right way to go. It would be a non-event from an offering perspective, because Spotify wasn't selling new shares. As they imagined it, they said, it would be very similar to a spinoff or a company emerging from bankruptcy.

McCarthy emphasized his desire to hold an investor day, broadcast on the internet, and to issue guidance, the practice of telling investors what they should expect in the next few quarters. Both ideas were central to his idea of bringing radical transparency into the process.

It wasn't long before Hinman put a stop to that talk. "We don't think this is like a spinoff," he said, according to the recollection of one of the attendees.

Hinman knew that there was a lot of money available to tech companies in the private markets. If the SEC allowed Spotify to completely bypass the due diligence, investor education, and legal responsibility associated with having to file an IPO prospectus, he worried that there would be a rush of companies using the process to avoid SEC investor-protection rules.

Hinman also believed that what Spotify was doing looked enough like an offering that the company might be subject to later legal issues even if it hadn't put out a prospectus. The SEC's point was that the investor education piece looked an awful lot like the company encouraging investors to buy the stock, even if it wasn't Spotify's to sell. It looked enough like an offer, in other words, that Spotify should submit a 33 Act filing. The agency's insistence was strong enough that Spotify somewhat quickly acceded to the demands of Hinman and his team and agreed to register its shares under the Securities Act of 1933. McCarthy preferred the 34 Act because it would allow him to release guidance and educate investors using the best practices of public companies, but he wasn't going to fall on his sword in the face of SEC opposition.

The SEC ultimately allowed Spotify to issue financial guidance outside the confines of its registration statement.

■ ■ ■

Over the back half of 2017, Spotify and its advisors worked with the SEC to iron out other mechanics of the transaction. With the chief concern of the Division of Corporation Finance out of the way, the company and its lawyers pivoted to working with the Division of Trading and Markets.

That division is more focused on exchange rules and the regulations that govern how companies can behave regarding their public stock. The division oversees Regulation M, which is intended to prevent market manipulation in the trading of shares. Over several months, Spotify worked with the agency to ensure that it wouldn't violate the regulation.

As the lawyers hashed things out with the SEC, the NYSE, Morgan Stanley, and Goldman Sachs talked through how Spotify's shares would begin trading. One option was to simply let it happen as soon as stocks started trading at 9:30 a.m. Another was to treat the direct listing more like an IPO, whereby the shares are held back from being released for trading until there is a suitable number of orders built up that will serve as a dramatic pricing event to set the stage for a smoother trading experience.

Goldman Sachs's Benny Adler, a senior trader with decades of experience, felt strongly that the direct listing should use the latter approach. Adler had seen stocks in the over-the-counter market move to exchange trading on NASDAQ. They just started trading in the morning, regardless of the size of the trade, and often struggled to find a rhythm.

" 'Let's not do that,' " Adler later recalled telling exchange officials. " 'Let's halt the stock and not allow any trading until that first trade. Let's run an auction.' " The exchange, he said, "agreed that creating a big liquidity event was: a) going to be beneficial to new investors and b) was going to create a much, much more stable stock coming out. And ultimately make the product more attractive to issuers."

Adler's counterpart at Morgan Stanley, John Paci, also contributed to the discussion.

With the transaction coming into focus that December, Spotify asked Goldman Sachs to broker the sale of a large block of stock. The company wanted a sale to set the price in the private market—which it could use to guide public market investors when it came time to list the shares.

Separately, Spotify had long wanted a strategy for expanding into China so that it could participate in streaming music's rise in the world's second-largest economy.

In December, Goldman Sachs delivered on both initiatives, arranging for a share swap with China's Tencent Music Entertainment Group. Tencent would receive a 7.5 percent stake in Spotify, which would take a 9 percent stake in Tencent in return. Spotify also used the transaction to renegotiate the convertible bond terms. They were tied to an IPO that wasn't going to happen and represented a potential legal headache that could hang over the direct listing.

On December 18, having worked out most of the mechanics of the offering, Spotify confidentially filed its draft registration statement with the SEC.

■ ■ ■

On January 8, 2018, two executives at trading firm Citadel Securities braved the freezing temperatures and fifteen-mile-an-hour winds whipping around the Freedom Tower in lower Manhattan as they made their way to Spotify's relatively new offices. The company had outgrown the Sixth Avenue location and signed a lease for three hundred seventy-eight thousand square feet at 4 World Trade Center the previous February. McCarthy had been surprised to find a good deal downtown.

Spotify hadn't yet expanded into all the space McCarthy had signed. The floor felt cavernous as he and Vogel hosted a series of meetings to try to select the companies that could open Spotify's shares for trading on the NYSE. With the company eschewing a traditional IPO, the choice of what was known as a designated market maker (DMM) was an important step in completing a successful offering.

Designated market makers are the trading firms and their employees who work on the floor of the exchange and manually open and close the trading of company stocks. Citadel Securities was owned by billionaire hedge fund manager Ken Griffin, whose own fund was also named Citadel. The two separate businesses often got confused with each other. Citadel Securities was somewhat new to the designated market maker function, having gotten into the business in late 2016 with the acquisition of another firm that had a large presence on the floor of the NYSE. They were looking for ways to advance on the leader, GTS.

There to pitch Spotify was Citadel Securities' Joe Mecane, Peter Giacchi, and two colleagues. McCarthy and Vogel represented Spotify. Over the course of the meeting, Mecane and Giacchi explained how winning the right to open Spotify's direct listing was incredibly important to the growth of their business. The Citadel Securities executives had researched what they could about the direct listing rules as recently put in place by the NYSE and approved by the SEC. The two men told the executives that what they were doing brought risk, and that to avoid embarrassing themselves they should be looking for a partner who could provide the right kind of support. They impressed upon McCarthy and Vogel the fact that they were committed to making the opening of shares work and that they would use their balance sheet to whatever extent was necessary in order to ensure that it went smoothly.

McCarthy and Vogel asked the executives what they should be thinking about around the direct listing. What would still need to be figured out over the next three months? Citadel Securities brought up one question: "Will there be an ability for people to short the direct listing right out of the gate?" a member of the team asked. In other words, could traders bet on the price of Spotify's shares declining the moment they started trading, or would there be some delay?

The question was a new one to the Spotify executives, and they were impressed that Citadel Securities had raised it. "That's a really good question," McCarthy answered. "How come no one else has asked us that question yet?"

The meeting continued until it was time for the Citadel Securities team to leave. When the executives arrived on the ground floor, they saw their competitors at GTS across the lobby waiting to go up. They knew now that this was a real competition. In the days following the meeting, Ken Griffin himself reached out to McCarthy to drive home the point that this was a transaction that Citadel Securities wanted to win.

In the end, Spotify selected Citadel Securities, believing that because the latter wanted the business badly, they would give it the highest level of attention. Over the following months, Spotify and Citadel Securities worked out the details of how the stock would start trading on the exchange. The stock would open just as it did with the release of an IPO, but it would be more difficult to find an equilibrium price since there wouldn't be a price from the night before.

McCarthy met with Griffin, and the two men had several subsequent conversations, including some that took place on Saturday nights. "That guy is a workaholic," McCarthy said later. "There is no detail that escapes him."

■ ■ ■

By then, Goldman Sachs and Morgan Stanley had been working on the transaction for more than six months. But Goldman's longer relationship with Spotify—tracing back to the London meeting between Lemkau and Ek several years before the 2015 fundraising—earned Goldman the lead mandate.

McCarthy broke the news to Kwan and Grimes. Morgan Stanley, which had taken Spotify rival Pandora public, was the relative newcomer, but it had dug deep on what McCarthy wanted to accomplish. The CFO said simply,

"Look, Goldman's been here for a lot longer. There's a longer relationship—we're going to have them involved."

He added, "We want you involved. What do you want in this transaction?"

Morgan Stanley had come to believe that advising the designated market maker was a critical role for the success of the transaction. "We think the most important role is the advisor" to the DMM, the bankers told McCarthy. "We'll take that role."

If Spotify wanted to pay Goldman a little bit more, Morgan Stanley said it wouldn't fight it. "We understand we're not Daniel's...banker that's been there for them in the trenches," they told him.

Adler had argued that both banks should have a say in advising Citadel Securities, but he was eventually overruled by exchange officials who didn't want too many voices to complicate the opening trade. "There were three banks that put a lot of analytical power behind this," Pärson, who left the board the previous summer, said. "I think they realized that they needed to have their fingerprints on this landmark event in order to at least have some way of describing it. I thought that they would be much more passive than they were, but they saw how committed, I think, the company was to this idea. Then they decided, though, that we can't beat them, [so] let's join them."

Spotify filed its registration statement with the SEC on February 28, 2018, making its direct listing plans official. The bank named Goldman Sachs first and said that Morgan Stanley would advise the designated market maker.

■　■　■

On March 15, hedge fund traders, portfolio managers, and Wall Street analysts lined up outside the steel-and-glass entryway of Spring Place, a trendy performance space in New York's Tribeca neighborhood. Many had come from as far away as continental Europe and Los Angeles.

Besides the clothing of the people in line—many dark vests over dress shirts—there wasn't much to distinguish the event from a fashion show or an art fair other than a roughly three-foot-high sign made of white letters. It read "Spotify."

Spotify's investor day had finally arrived, and the music company had pulled out all the stops. There was a palpable energy in the line as the analysts and investors waited to show their identification and have their name checked against a list. Excitement for the event had turned it into an exclusive affair—Spotify had to turn down requests to attend.

The guest list was a who's who of influential technology analysts and investors: Goldman's star internet analyst, Heath Terry; Scott Devitt, the former Facebook analyst at Morgan Stanley; and Justin Post, Bank of America Merrill Lynch's internet analyst. Chase Coleman, the founder of Tiger Global Management, which had invested more than $600 million into Spotify, and Lee Fixel, one of his top technology investors, attended with two analysts. Tiger Global's initial investment came from working alongside G Squared to scrounge up shares in the secondary market.

McLeod attended for G Squared, as Aschebrook was out of the country, and sat beside the contingent from Tiger Global.

After passing through security, the attendees helped themselves to coffee or sparkling water as carefully curated Spotify playlists played through hidden speakers and trays of hors d'oeuvres were passed around. Beyond the lobby, a large room with plate-glass windows offered a commanding view of the surrounding city. Modern white chairs lined up in rows. A small half-moon-shaped stage stood at the foot of a massive screen.

Spotify had been planning this event for months. Its executives—as befitted a music streaming company—wanted to do something more than a typical investor day hosted in one of Manhattan's midtown hotels, like the Mandarin Oriental, where Snapchat had held its IPO roadshow the year before. In a significant departure from the norm, the presentation would be livestreamed on Spotify's website so that any member of the public—not just institutional investors with an inside track—could learn more about the company's business and financial condition.

Once everyone was seated, Paul Vogel, Spotify's investor relations chief, opened the event. Casually dressed in jeans and an untucked dress shirt with sleeves just a touch too long, Vogel elicited polite clapping. Someone hooted. Vogel welcomed the crowd to the company's investor day, reading from a teleprompter as the screen behind him shone with the distinctive green shade of Spotify's logo and his title in white. As he rocked from one foot to the other, he explained why the company had chosen to do a direct listing: they wanted to be more transparent and accessible to a broad swath of investors.

"We believe hosting an investor day prior to our public listing," he said, "will do just that."

Vogel shared two dates with the audience: Spotify would announce financial guidance on March 26, and its stock would start trading on April 3. As he wrapped up, he made a joke about the SEC's safe harbor provision, which protects a company from being sued by investors if it meets certain conditions. For several moments, soft string music played as Vogel gave investors a few moments to read over the lengthy disclosure.

Once Vogel had left the stage, CEO Daniel Ek bounded onto the stage to electronic music and greeted the crowd with a big smile. Ek, bald, with a thin beard, wore a black blazer over a white t-shirt, black jeans, and bright white sneakers.

The founder began with a modest opening, his voice toned down despite the event at hand. In English accented by his upbringing in his native Sweden, Ek, like Vogel, read from a teleprompter. He warned the crowd that it shouldn't expect any parties or figure on seeing executives ringing an exchange bell. The reason, he said, was that going public was never about pomp and circumstance.

"The traditional model for taking a company public just isn't a good fit for us," Ek explained. Spotify didn't agree with the lockups that most IPOs require, because people were its most valuable asset. They should be able to sell their shares when they wanted, he said. So the most important day for Spotify, he said, was not the listing day but "the day after that, and the day after that."

Ek then explained that while he was more a fan of soccer than baseball, Spotify was in just the second inning of its business life cycle. The baseball analogy is one often used in the financial industry. As Ek moved into a brief history of Spotify and how he had come to invent the company, a photo of Stockholm's harbor flashed on the screen behind him.

Nineteen minutes after the program began, Ek handed off to Spotify's chief R&D officer, Gustav Söderström. He was followed by Seth Farbman, chief marketing officer. A short intermission followed Farbman's presentation. The crowd was buzzy, impressed by Spotify's music industry credentials and the cultural hipness that accompanied it. When Ek returned to the stage after the intermission, he did so without his blazer. Charlie Hellman, head of creator marketplace; Troy Carter, global head of creator services; Alex Norström, chief premium business officer; Danielle Lee, global head of partner solutions; and Brian Benedik, the global head of ad sales, followed him in their talks.

"It was impressive," one investor in the audience said later. "They are clearly a very strong team." He continued: "There was a lot of excitement in the air…a lot of energy. They tell a very good story about the music in people's lives.… This was not a quarterly story; this was a change-the-world story."

■ ■ ■

One hundred nine minutes into the recorded event, it was time for McCarthy to speak. The CFO was nervous. This would be the first time he'd spoken publicly since leaving Netflix nearly eight years earlier. Appearing in front of employees or another friendly crowd was easy. He could relax, crack jokes, and act spontaneous. But speaking in front of a large crowd of investors was something else.

McCarthy hadn't had time to practice his presentation, and he hadn't had time to iron out the kinks. Ordinarily, he liked to practice. When he was preparing to take Netflix public in 2002, he and CEO Reed Hastings had visited multiple cities making presentations. They had started in New York, where it was clear to those in the audience that their presentation needed help. McCarthy was so nervous at one point that one of the Merrill Lynch analysts had asked him if he needed a moment alone. By the time the Netflix executives returned to New York, they were able to give a seamless presentation in the ballroom of the Pierre, a hotel across the street from Central Park.

Now, as upbeat music played over the speakers, McCarthy walked onstage to a packed house. He knew many of the people sitting in the white chairs in front of him—big investors and analysts from Tiger Global, Goldman Sachs, and elsewhere.

McCarthy wore a pink dress shirt and a dark suit jacket over jeans and loafers, the buttoned-up CFO presenting a contrast with Ek, the hip founder. Whereas Ek could have been the star of the show at a music event, this, after all, was a day for investors. Their star was McCarthy.

"Good afternoon. I'm going to bring it home here for us," McCarthy said, sounding slightly breathless. He smiled to scattered laughs from the audience. "I know you're all disappointed to hear that." As he previewed what he would cover, he mentioned that since he'd left his last company, Netflix, its stock had risen nearly ten times. So, he joked to those in the room, they should ask themselves if they should buy Spotify's stock the following month when it became available or wait until he retired. McCarthy received more laughs from the audience and appeared to relax a little.

Launching into his slides, he told the audience that they should expect the company to continue spending more than it brought in to fuel growth. It was a characteristic admission from McCarthy—he wasn't going to sugarcoat the company's cash needs.

Spotify's gross margin, though, had improved for three straight years since McCarthy had taken over. In 2016 and 2017, he'd helped negotiate new deals with the record labels that were more favorable to Spotify. It wasn't a "magic trick," he said, it was the record labels acting in their own self-interest to support Spotify's economic model because of its growing importance to the music industry.

McCarthy likened Spotify's improved results to those from his first ten years at Netflix, when the company went from a negative gross margin to a strongly positive one as it grew larger. Scale, as he called it, coupled with data insights and a better user experience, propelled Netflix's growth. What Netflix did, he explained, was come to own demand creation—which kept users coming back to the service, because it continued to serve up new and interesting content. Spotify was beginning to do the same, he suggested.

Investors had come to depend on McCarthy's straightforward approach, and he didn't disappoint. "Becoming the world's largest global music streaming subscription service has been expensive, costing more than a *billion* euros"—he emphasized the *B*—"in cumulative losses," he said. "But the trend toward profitability is clearly apparent."

After a slide heavy in technical finance, McCarthy explained that while he had joined Spotify as an investor and then sat on the board, it wasn't until he got into the CFO's chair that he realized the power of the company's ad-supported tier. Known across the industry as freemium, Spotify used it to attract a large and engaged user base with free services. The company then hoped to persuade those users to pay for the premium subscription product.

By then, many internet businesses had embraced the model to acquire paying subscribers, and most of Wall Street was aware of its value. McCarthy addressed that point quickly. "So now some of you are looking at me like, *Okay, dude, are you kidding me?*" McCarthy joked, briefly stumbling over his words, "which in New York–speak roughly means 'Are you stupid?' And the answer is yes and nope, it just took me a while before I realized the ad-supported service is also a subsidy program that offsets the cost of new subscriber acquisition."

When he got to a slide with a lot of acronyms, he slowed down. On another slide with a confusing chart, he explained the takeaways by listing them, by number, for investors. He gave the audience a clinic on how scale mattered in the industry, using an example of a fully developed company competing with one that was younger in its life cycle. To help explain it, he gave himself the role of the younger company. In the language of financial metrics that so many of the audience understood, McCarthy patiently explained why the more mature company should win every time. To accentuate the point, he said bluntly that the mature company should "beat me like a drum." He came back to the joke after another example. "Not only can you beat me like a drum, but your drumsticks cost less than mine." The audience laughed.

McCarthy wrapped up the presentation by welcoming Ek back to the stage for a few minutes of Q&A.

If the analysts and investors in the audience thought that the event was over when Ek ended his Q&A, they were mistaken. Charlie Puth, the singer-songwriter who had gotten his break as a Berklee College of Music student by uploading song videos to YouTube and had gone on to pop stardom, was there to play for the assembled crowd. When Puth walked onstage, he congratulated Spotify on its "IPO." Kwan, the Morgan Stanley banker, yelled out, "No! It's a direct listing." Some of the crowd got up and danced.

At the end of Puth's set, Spotify's executives mingled with the crowd. Ek and McCarthy spoke to McLeod and thanked him for G Squared's early support of the company.

Another member of Spotify's team roamed around and asked various individuals what they thought. He was surprised to find that people who were usually cynics, hard-nosed analysts and investors, had been won over by the production.

"That," said one, "was a great show."

■   ■   ■

It was just a few weeks later, and Peter Giacchi was fired up. As he walked to the NYSE with one of his senior Citadel Securities traders on the morning of April 3, he saw a black banner draped across the marble facade overlooking Broad Street. In green letters, "Spotify" towered over the street below.

Giacchi, who had attended the January pitch meeting at 4 World Trade Center, was Citadel Securities' most senior floor trader on the NYSE. He was friendly and talkative, a bespectacled twenty-year veteran. This was his Super Bowl, one of the biggest moments in his two-decade career. All eyes would be on him as he stood on the NYSE floor and collected buy and sell orders and settled on a price that wouldn't leave Spotify's shares changing rapidly or unpredictably when they started trading.

Giacchi wore a blue jacket with a castle parapet and his firm's name on the back. He made his way to Post 5, one of a series of large round booths that dotted the floor of the NYSE. He peered at four screens connected to the square keyboard that he relied on every day to open the trading for specific stocks. A crude graphic on one of the screens showed buy and sell orders accumulating at specific prices. It was early, and there weren't many orders yet.

To commemorate the occasion, Giacchi had brought a good luck charm to the pits—his mother, Rachelle, who made the trip from Florida. Rachelle was also a veteran of New York's trading floors, having joined broker Herzog Heine Geduld as an assistant before working her way up to stockbroker.

Giacchi's task would be tougher than usual this morning because of the nature of the direct listing. Ordinarily, investors only had to look at a stock's previous day's close to know the rough price at which it might start trading. Buying into a company that had gone public the night before was made easier by the IPO price, which acted as a rough gauge. But Spotify didn't have any public trading history, and its shares hadn't changed hands the night before in a deal with institutional investors brokered by investment banks. All Spotify had was its $132 reference price, a somewhat made-up figure based loosely on where its shares traded in the private markets. Under terms hammered out the year before, the SEC required the NYSE to come up with the reference price and furnish it to investors. Agency officials couldn't stomach the idea of investors bidding for Spotify's shares without something to guide them.

At 10:30 or so, Giacchi sent a message through the data feeds that connected the NYSE to the global financial markets. Known as an indication, the message gave traders Giacchi's best guess for the price at which Spotify shares would open for trading. He updated it throughout the morning. Orders had started coming into his systems, and he sent out a wide range of $145 to $155.

Buying interest picked up. At 11:03, he sent another message; this time Spotify's price was in a range of $150 to $160. He raised the next indication to $155 to $165. The price was marching higher as demand for the shares outstripped supply.

■ ■ ■

Four miles north of Giacchi's trading booth, Morgan Stanley trader John Paci presided over a portion of Morgan Stanley's trading floor on the fifth level of the bank's corporate headquarters above Times Square. Paci was the senior trader at Morgan Stanley charged with helping to open the shares of popular companies entering the public markets for the first time, a job that often required hours of juggling phone calls and electronic messages in order to match supply and demand. As the advisor to the designated market maker, Morgan Stanley would play an outsized role in helping to set the price of Spotify's shares.

Paci was well suited to the job. He was a former National Football League quarterback with the New York Jets who had multiple phone lines and a group of traders lined up along three rows of desks that ran perpendicular to his in a formation that looked like a capital *E* turned on its side.

For Spotify's direct listing, Paci's task was to collect the sell orders coming from the company's employees, venture capital backers, and other shareholders and match them with the orders he received from mutual funds and hedge funds wanting to buy in for the first time. The task wasn't easy—every time a large buy order came in at a particular price, he would have to call selling shareholders to see if they wanted to sell at that price. Every time the price moved, Paci would have to alert both sides. Once he collected the orders, Paci communicated those to Giacchi on the floor of the exchange, where the Citadel Securities executive used them to arrive at a price that roughly matched the two sides of the market. The two men would engage in a tense act that morning to arrive at a price for which many buyers and sellers would agree to exchange Spotify shares.

That morning, Kwan also received a text from TCV partner Woody Marshall, a member of the Spotify board. Marshall wanted to know where the stock might open and close; the folks at TCV had a friendly wager going about Spotify's stock performance. What did Kwan think?

Kwan knew enough to know he wasn't the expert. He turned to Ashley MacNeill, Morgan Stanley's head of the technology equity syndicate for the Americas. Where is this going to open and close? he asked her. MacNeill had been talking to Spotify investors for weeks, judging their interest in selling the stock. She'd also been talking to other investors and felt confident that she had a handle on the forces of supply and demand.

"One sixty-five and one fifty," she answered.

Kwan shared MacNeill's prediction with Marshall. Colin Stewart, the banker who worked on Google's IPO and was now a vice chairman in capital markets, guessed $162 and $160.

For weeks, Spotify had said that it wasn't going to make a big deal of the direct listing. Ek had said at the investor day that executives wouldn't ring the NYSE's opening bell. A plan to hire a choir, recommended by NYSE officials, fell through. Spotify wanted employees to think that this was just one day on a long journey, not a destination. There was still a lot of work to do.

McCarthy and Vogel made plans to visit Morgan Stanley's trading floor instead. Late that morning they left their World Trade Center headquarters for the subway ride uptown to Morgan Stanley. The executives arrived and joined about a dozen Morgan Stanley bankers gathered around Paci's desk.

Both executives were nervous. McCarthy had been working on the transaction for two years, putting his reputation on the line at critical moments to move it along. An opening trade featuring wild price swings would play into his board's doubts and cast a pall over his creation.

The group around Paci's desk could hear him talking to investors wanting to buy stock and shareholders looking to unload it. He and his traders shouted orders back and forth. Paci propped a phone cradle on his shoulder as he typed commands into his computer.

At 11:32, Paci received a new notification from Giacchi, who had noticed a stabilization in price and narrowed the range to $5. The next indication went out at $160 to $165. A surge in demand to buy shares came in, forcing Giacchi to raise the next indication to $165 to $170.

Giacchi tightened the next indication, narrowing the range to $167 to $170.

As the range narrowed, the energy on Morgan Stanley's trading floor picked up. The crowd around Paci's desk pressed in.

And then more shareholders offered to sell their shares. Giacchi lowered his next indication to $165 to $168. The tension fell.

More buyers came in. And then sellers. Giacchi sent a couple more indications, bumping the price between $170 and $165.

■ ■ ■

For fifteen or twenty minutes on the floor of the NYSE, Giacchi didn't update the range. He prepared to open the stock. As he hunched over his screens, a crowd built up. A photographer directly in front of him prepared to take a shot.

NYSE president Tom Farley was right behind Giacchi, wearing a bright red tie. "We're ready to go. Here we go," Farley said. Stacey Cunningham, the NYSE's chief operating officer, was there too.

But this was Giacchi's show. "Guys, sixty-five." He had to shout to be heard above the chatter of brokers as camera shutters clicked. Giacchi peered in close at his screen to make sure he had the number right. "Guys, sixty-five ninety. Guys, sixty-five ninety."

He stood. "Guys, the book is frozen," he hollered into the crowd, chopping his hand in the air. He would take no more orders. The price was fixed. He called out the stats: "Five point six million opens here at one sixty-five ninety." Five point six million shares traded hands at $165.90. A person in the background whispered, "One sixty-five ninety." "Yay!" someone else yelled.

Those closest to Giacchi could see the all-important light blue key in the bottom right of his keyboard. The one with the four simple letters: "D-O-N-E."

Another Citadel Securities trader hit it. Forty-three minutes after noon, Spotify started trading in the public markets at $165.90 a share.

■ ■ ■

Applause erupted on Morgan Stanley's trading floor. McCarthy and Vogel shook hands, relieved to have the stock launched into the public markets. The bankers around Paci's desk slapped backs and shook hands.

A light mist had begun to soak New York City as McCarthy, Vogel, and a group of Morgan Stanley bankers emerged from the bank's grand lobby. As the Spotify logo rotated with several others on the gigantic video screen on the building's facade, the group posed for a photo before McCarthy and Vogel walked to the subway. Michael Grimes wore the equivalent of a Spotify letterman jacket, with white sleeves, a dark front and back, and the company logo.

Sometime after 2:00 p.m., the two men found themselves back at their desks in Spotify's World Trade Center headquarters. There was no celebration for employees. The adrenaline rush of Morgan Stanley's trading floor had faded.

Over the course of the day, Spotify's stock price never went higher than the opening trade price, and drifted lower to close at $149.01. It was within $1 of MacNeill's prediction.

It was also enough to give the streaming music company a market capitalization of $27 billion, seventh on the list of the biggest companies going public.

More than 30.5 million shares changed hands, or about 17 percent of Spotify's 178 million shares outstanding. Morgan Stanley, in its role as advisor to the designated market maker, handled more than 18 million of those shares, or three out of every five traded that day. Goldman Sachs traded less than 3 million shares.

At one point that afternoon, Vogel looked at McCarthy. "What am I supposed to do now?" he asked. The two men laughed.

"I have no idea," McCarthy answered.

CHAPTER 12

Slack, San Francisco, 2018

With Spotify trading publicly, McCarthy prepared for his annual trip to the Allen & Co. conference. In July, he traveled to Sun Valley, Idaho, for the splashy affair. Hosted by the investment bank since 1983, it was an exclusive ticket available to only the most powerful in the media, technology, entertainment, and sports industries. It was also a way for Allen & Co. to reward corporate clients who chose them for lucrative engagements like advising on mergers, acquisitions, and direct listings.

Held in the rarefied air of a ski resort, the conference allowed business leaders to come together over panels, impromptu meetings, and recreational activities like white water rafting. Conference lore had it that multibillion-dollar transactions were clinched by handshake.

On this July day, McCarthy made his way past the Sun Valley Inn, where the panels and presentations took place, to the waters of the Duck Pond and a grouping of tables and chairs set up nearby for a buffet lunch. Here executives often sat down with institutional investors so they could get to know one other, or met with senior executives at other companies, and this time was no different.

Stewart Butterfield and Sarah Friar, two leaders of the multibillion-dollar messaging app Slack, had arranged to meet with McCarthy to talk through the details of Spotify's recent direct listing. Butterfield's attendance had rated a one-sentence mention in a July 11 *New York Times* article headlined "As Moguls Gather in Sun Valley, Here's Who Might Be in the Mood for Deals."

Butterfield launched Slack in 2013, after Glitch, the online cooperative game he was developing at a company called Tiny Speck, failed to gain commercial traction. The founder shifted the company's focus to the internal messaging app his engineers had designed to communicate on game development and changed the firm's name.

The Slack founder was cut from a different cloth than McCarthy. Unlike the Connecticut native, who, anticipating being drafted, trained with marines during one summer of college before the end of the Vietnam War, Butterfield was born in British Columbia to an American father who had moved north to dodge the conflict. The family settled on a commune and named their son Dharma. They didn't have electricity until Butterfield was five years old.

Butterfield had an early entrepreneurial bug, selling lemonade and 7-Eleven hot dogs on the beach and working at his father's movie theater. If his upbringing didn't give Butterfield an unusual perspective, his schooling certainly did. After attending the University of Victoria, he studied philosophy and the history of science at Cambridge. He didn't have an engineering degree or an MBA. As Slack grew, he took coaching lessons to improve his management style.

Slack was the second company Butterfield had built out of a failed gaming experiment. When *Game Neverending*, which he created with Caterina Fake, then his wife, failed to gain traction in 2004, the two spun out a photo-sharing tool they built. The company became Flickr, an early attempt to seize on social media and user-generated content themes. They sold it the next year to Yahoo! for around $25 million.

Friar was on Slack's board, where she served as the head of the audit committee. She was also the CFO at Square, the app for small businesses known for its white cube that plugged into the headphone jack of an iPhone and allowed merchants to accept credit card payments. Friar ran Square's finance department in 2015 when the company went public, giving her some familiarity with the IPO process.

As the three executives settled in under the mountain sun, the Slack executives asked McCarthy for details about Spotify's direct listing and what he learned during it that he hadn't known beforehand. Over the course of the next hour or so, McCarthy walked the Slack representatives through the direct listing. He stressed the importance of choosing a financial advisor they trusted. In a direct listing, he explained, the SEC forbids company executives from comparing notes with their bankers about investor interest and who might be willing to sell stock. Once it started the formal process, Slack would be dependent on its bankers to determine the supply and demand for shares. Managing those competing forces would have a lot to do with setting the share price and managing its swings when the stock started trading.

The Spotify CFO also warned Butterfield and Friar to mind the plumbing of the financial markets. Spotify struggled with the stock transfer agents, the back-office administrators who registered investor shares so that they could be bought and sold on an exchange. The firms doing that tended to use clunky decades-old technology. Calls to the customer service line sometimes went unanswered.

Spotify left its investors and employees to interact with the transfer agents individually, McCarthy said. If given a second chance, he told them that he would have asked for power of attorney and assigned a dedicated Spotify team to interface with the transfer agents. McCarthy urged the Slack executives to carefully consider their choice.

McCarthy also encouraged the Slack executives to hold an investor day to educate the investing public about the company's prospects. He wasn't convinced that Slack had the right combination of attributes to pull off a direct listing, but he patiently answered Butterfield and Friar's questions. Slack would have to overcome a series of hurdles that were different from the ones Spotify had faced and potentially insurmountable.

One of those was that the secondary market for Slack's shares wasn't as developed as that for Spotify, which McCarthy feared might make it more difficult to come up with an accurate reference price for Slack's shares. Slack didn't have the brand recognition of Spotify—the music streaming company had more than seventy million subscribers when it hit the public markets. Slack wasn't nearly as well known among consumers and the investing public.

Looking for alternatives to email, Slack had grown quickly by partnering with tech startups like Brian Chesky's Airbnb, which had helped pioneer the sharing economy. At one point, Slack went through a period during which it doubled its number of users every three months, making it "one of the fastest-growing business applications in history."

By the time of the Sun Valley conversation, its number of daily active users had reached eight million. Seventy thousand organizations used it. But growth had started to slow. Its user base had grown 45 percent between May 2017 and May 2018, compared to 83 percent in the previous twelve-month period.

One attribute that Slack shared with Spotify was access to almost unlimited capital. Over the years, Slack's success had given it almost unfettered access to capital that would allow it to pursue a direct listing if Butterfield, Friar, and the rest of the board settled on that option.

Slack's fundraising history matched the influx of cash that had flooded Silicon Valley during the years of its existence, fueled by mutual funds and other public market investors who had begun to "cross over" into private funding rounds. In October 2014, investors valued Slack at $1.1 billion, making it one of about forty companies globally with a $1 billion or larger valuation. That was double the amount from the prior year, the *Wall Street Journal* reported, when the term "unicorn" was first used to refer to companies worth more than $1 billion. "In short, 2014 was the year the tech sector went into hyper-drive," the newspaper said.

Slack more than doubled its valuation the following year, to $2.8 billion, when it raised another $160 million in April, leading Butterfield to gush to the *New York Times* about the money available in the private markets. "I've been in this industry for 20 years," he said. "This is the best time to raise money ever. It might be the best time for any kind of business in any industry to raise money for all of history, like since the time of the ancient Egyptians."

In early 2016, Slack raised another $200 million at a $3.8 billion valuation. The round was led by Thrive Capital, the venture firm run by Josh Kushner, the brother of Jared Kushner, son-in-law of then Republican presidential candidate Donald Trump.

Slack's growth was so explosive that it soon attracted competitors. Facebook had its own challenger, Workplace by Facebook, and then in November 2016 Microsoft unveiled its long-awaited Microsoft Teams. The latter was a broadside against Slack—free for existing Microsoft customers, which included an installed Office 365 user base of 85 million people, and available in 180 countries. Microsoft pitched it as a "digital forum" that could be customized for each company, or even among teams within the same company.

Slack showed a plucky side. On November 1, 2016, one day before Microsoft CEO Satya Nadella was scheduled to show off Teams at a Microsoft launch event, Slack emailed a number of reporters with updated usage numbers, saying it was now being used by 4 million individuals daily, and by 28 of the largest 100 companies in the United States.

The following morning, Slack took out a full-page ad in the *New York*

Times that it addressed to Microsoft—an open letter that offered 796 words of advice, modeled on a famous 1981 Apple Computer ad that taunted IBM. It mimicked the Apple ad's large, bold introduction ("Welcome, IBM. Seriously.") in its salutation:

> Dear Microsoft,
>
> Wow. Big news! Congratulations on today's announcements. We're genuinely excited to have some competition.
>
> We realized a few years ago that the value of switching to Slack was so obvious and the advantages so overwhelming that every business would be using Slack, or "something just like it," within the decade. It's validating to see you've come around to the same way of thinking. And even though—being honest here—it's a little scary, we know it will bring a better future forward faster.
>
> However, all this is harder than it looks. So, as you set out to build "something just like it," we want to give you some friendly advice.

Slack said a product's features weren't as important as its design and appeal to humanity. Microsoft representatives told media outlets that the company thought there was room for more than one player in the space.

In an interview with the *Wall Street Journal* after the Microsoft Teams launch published in an article two weeks later entitled "Slack Girds for Battle with Messaging Rivals," Butterfield said, "I've been paranoid about this for a long time."

■ ■ ■

By the time of the Sun Valley conversation, Butterfield had already fielded other ideas about how to enter the public markets. Less than a year earlier, in September of 2017, early Slack investor and board member Chamath Palihapitiya had sponsored something called a special purpose acquisition company, or SPAC. Known colloquially as a blank check company, it was structured as a shell corporation that raised money to buy another company. Palihapitiya's SPAC raised $690 million by selling shares to investors with the stated intention of looking to buy a company "operating in the technology industries."

Blank check firms had been around since the early 2000s and were

considered a financial backwater populated by shady characters prone to mal-
feasance, hardly the province of blue chip corporations or hot Silicon Valley
startups. They were often lampooned for enriching their sponsors and giving
unproven companies a side door to the public markets if they couldn't meet
the high bar of doing a traditional IPO.

Like all blank check firms, Palihapitiya's raised money by selling shares
in an IPO. It didn't have an operating business or assets other than the cash
raised in the IPO, which it held in a trust until its sponsor—Palihapitiya and
his business partner, Ian Osborne—found a company to buy. Then, the cash
raised in the IPO would be used for the acquisition.

The brash Palihapitiya was a six-year-old when he emigrated to Canada
from Sri Lanka with his family. He got into engineering and secured a job at
Facebook in the early days, rising to manage many aspects of the company's
growth. When he left in 2011, he'd amassed enough wealth to become
part owner of the Golden State Warriors, San Francisco's hometown NBA
team.

While the prospectus for Palihapitiya's SPAC didn't identify a target, one
person briefed on his thinking said the investor aspired to take Slack public.
He approached Slack and proposed the idea.

Slack's board wasn't interested. Board members including Butterfield,
Friar, and venture capitalists Andrew Braccia of Accel and John O'Farrell of
Andreessen Horowitz briefly considered the option before ultimately dismiss-
ing it. (In November 2019, Palihapitiya would complete a merger between his
blank check firm and Virgin Galactic, Richard Branson's space company. In
December 2019, Palihapitiya stepped down from Slack's board.)

That was in the past as McCarthy, Butterfield and Friar concluded their
conversation and returned to the conference.

■ ■ ■

One month after the Sun Valley conversation, Slack announced yet another
fundraising, bringing its total haul to $1.26 billion over the course of its rela-
tively short corporate life.

The company raised $427 million from existing investors and new growth
equity investors like Dragoneer Investment Group and General Atlantic, who
led the round, and T. Rowe Price, Wellington Management, Baillie Gifford,

and Sands Capital. The round, which saw investors purchasing shares for $11.91, valued the company at $7.1 billion.

In September, reports began to surface that the company was considering a stock market listing for the first half of 2019. The *Wall Street Journal* said that Slack was in active preparations for a listing it had been informally preparing for since 2017. In an October interview with the *Journal*, Butterfield told the newspaper that Slack had yet to sell shares to the public because it didn't need the money.

"If this was 15 years ago, we would have been public by now for sure, with many times more revenue than companies would typically go public with," Butterfield said. "But companies in that era didn't grow as quickly as we did. And companies of that era didn't have this completely, historically, unprecedented private market."

CHAPTER 13

Slack, San Francisco, 2019

With its coffers full, Slack enjoyed the financial flexibility to pursue a direct listing. As it worked with its bankers to prepare documents for the SEC, one of the things it needed to figure out was who was going to work with the trader on the floor of the exchange to collate the buy and sell orders it expected on the morning of the listing.

For Spotify, Morgan Stanley had been the only financial advisor assigned the role of advising the designated market maker, due to McCarthy's long-standing relationship with Kwan and Grimes. Spotify's prospectus left no room for ambiguity and gave Morgan Stanley a role that put it in position to see most of the trading flow in shares—61 percent of the volume on the first day and then still large percentages in the following days.

When it came time for banks to pitch for Slack's business, Goldman Sachs and Morgan Stanley recommended that there be only one advisor to the designated market maker. One entity should consolidate most of the trading interest—which would make coming up with the clearing price smoother, they said. The role was analogous to an IPO's stabilization agent, a prestigious position that gave an underwriter a loud voice in the decision to exercise the over-allotment option, or greenshoe, and responsibility for stabilizing the stock in the aftermarket. There was only ever one stabilization agent.

Slack executives had been friendly with well-known Goldman banker George Lee, who helped earn Goldman the lead position on the direct listing by telling Slack's executives he wanted the deal to be his "swan song" before moving into Goldman's C-suite. Morgan Stanley once again acknowledged that they were sitting behind Goldman. The bankers argued that they'd developed expertise around advising the designated market maker, knew the objectives, and should run that process.

Slack leaned toward selecting Morgan Stanley for that role, in part because of its experience handling Spotify's opening trade, whereupon Goldman changed its mind and pushed for more than one firm to be named in the prospectus. Goldman had realized that it now needed to fight for the lucrative mandate. It saw that advising the designated market maker—like serving as the stabilization agent in a traditional IPO—could be a very lucrative role. The title encouraged investors to go to the designated bank if they wanted to buy and sell the company's shares; and the more volume that passed through its doors, the more information the bank would have about who owned the shares at any given time. If someone wanted to buy, the bank's traders would know who wanted to sell. If someone else wanted to sell, the bank's traders would know who wanted to buy. There was also ancillary business that the information conferred, such as administering the brokerage accounts for the employees or handling wealth management services for VCs or company executives. Put simply, the bank that controlled the opening trade controlled more information. And on Wall Street information was money.

As the bankers began to put together the company's prospectus, they each pushed Slack's executives to list them as the first-named advisor. As the drafts came together, both of the banks were listed first at various points as advising the NYSE floor trader. That wasn't good enough for Goldman's bankers, and they kept pushing the company to list them first.

Goldman's insistence led Slack CFO Allen Shim to dig into the topic some more. He spoke to executives at Spotify and Citadel Securities. Shim began to believe that Goldman's explanations leaned toward preserving its reputation and status, as opposed to the mechanics or eventual success of the transaction, according to someone familiar with his thinking.

When Slack submitted its draft registration statement to the SEC months later, the language had changed. "Morgan Stanley and our other financial advisors" would advise the designated market maker. Goldman Sachs, however, commanded the coveted position of leading the overall transaction.

The task of ushering Slack into the public markets would once again fall to the same three banks that had run Spotify's direct listing: Goldman Sachs, Morgan Stanley, and Allen & Co. They had earned $36 million for that work.

As Slack's direct listing plans took shape, two of Silicon Valley's buzziest startups also prepared to go public. In December 2018, Uber Technologies and Lyft filed paperwork with the SEC to list through traditional IPOs, leading the *Wall Street Journal* to proclaim that 2019's crop of IPOs could surpass the record set during 1999, when the dot-com boom led companies to raise $108 billion.

Already in 2018, thirty-eight tech companies valued at more than $1 billion sold shares to the public, the most since 2000. Companies raised $61 billion by the end of the year. The *Wall Street Journal* put it colorfully: "The parade of unicorns entering the stock market turned into a stampede in 2018 as tech companies listed shares at the fastest pace since the dot-com boom."

The companies would have to overcome a somewhat novel challenge. With President Donald Trump and the Democrat-controlled House at loggerheads over Trump's proposed border wall, the two sides had allowed the government to run out of spending authority. A government shutdown began on December 22.

Officials at the SEC, responsible for reviewing IPO prospectuses, among other filings, were among thousands of government employees to be furloughed. That meant they couldn't review companies' registration statements. The website for SEC filings, nicknamed EDGAR, also went quiet. IPO plans were in flux until the agency could get back to work.

In January, news reports suggested for the first time that Slack was considering a direct listing, though some of those same reports questioned whether the company had what it took to complete a successful offering. Slack was an enterprise software company, one that sold its services to corporate employers looking for tools to help their employees work more efficiently. Spotify dealt directly with consumers. The two companies' customer bases told the story: Spotify had seventy-one million subscribers when it went public; Slack had around ten million using its product.

As rumors about Slack's listing picked up steam, columnists and tech pundits began scrutinizing the company's valuation and competitive positioning. A January 17, 2019, Reuters Breakingviews column did some back-of-the-envelope math to suggest that Slack's true valuation was potentially 41 percent below that of its last private round, and below that of half a dozen of its publicly traded peers. Nearly every article mentioned that Slack competed against

Microsoft, Google, and Cisco in the increasingly crowded workplace collaboration industry.

One article in the *Financial Times* ran with the headline "Slack Faces Challenge from Big Tech." The newspaper suggested that the proportion of companies using Teams had jumped to 21 percent, outpacing Slack's 15 percent, and that by the end of 2020, 41 percent of companies would be using Teams, as opposed to 18 percent using Slack.

The criticism wasn't new to Butterfield, who gave a quote to the *FT* that he'd been offering for some time, to the effect that there was enough room for a small, focused company to compete against large incumbents with multiple business lines. Butterfield's analogy often cited Microsoft itself in its early fight against International Business Machines. "We think the switch from inbox-based communication to channel-based communication is more or less inevitable," Butterfield said.

As Slack's board dug in on the direct listing, they strived to understand what elements they could borrow from the Spotify transaction and which parts of their direct listing they would have to design themselves. One of the key differences was the concentrated nature of Slack's investor base. Venture firms Accel, Andreessen Horowitz, and Social Capital together owned roughly 45 percent of Slack, which could make having enough shares to trade on the first day an issue.

Unlike Spotify, which made it relatively easy for employees to sell their shares and had a more diverse shareholder base that it had counted on to sell shares in the direct listing, Slack hadn't embraced the secondary market. Spotify had also relied on record labels owning roughly 17 percent of its stock to sell some shares during its early hours as a public company. Slack wouldn't have that luxury. Venture capitalists would have to sell some of their shares on the day of the direct listing. The idea was relatively foreign to them, for two main reasons.

A traditional IPO was typically a very passive transaction for venture capitalists. One or two may have sat on the company's board and perhaps even on the committee that made the final determination of the IPO price. But VCs were usually prevented from selling shares or distributing them for six months because of an underwriter-imposed lockup.

Once they were free to trade, venture capitalists preferred to distribute the shares to limited partners, passing on the responsibility of deciding how and when to exit the position to the pension funds or sovereign wealth funds that had given the VCs the investment funds in the first place. Distributing the shares offered several other advantages. It was tax-efficient. There weren't transaction costs like commissions. And VCs could distribute the shares at a high price.

Venture capitalists didn't have trading desks or the expertise to know when or how they should trade the shares in the aftermarket in a way that would maximize their returns. They also couldn't distribute the shares prior to the listing. The agreements with their limited partners prohibited them from making a distribution until the shares could be declared a liquid asset. A liquid asset was usually defined as one that was quoted or traded on one of the primary exchanges.

The confluence of factors presented a problem for Slack's direct listing. The company's venture capital backers would have to figure out how to sell their shares in the direct listing.

Slack's three largest VC investors—Accel, Andreessen Horowitz, and Social Capital—agreed to jointly hire Cooley LLP to advise them on what they could or could not say to one another. The three firms had struck a gentleman's agreement that they would each agree to sell up to 15 percent of their holdings on the first day. It wasn't a legal or contractual agreement, but rather an understanding that if Slack was going to go ahead with a direct listing, its investors would provide some shares to sell.

The government shutdown finally ended on January 25, setting the mark for the longest in history. With government officials back to work, the SEC began to process the backlog of filings.

On February 4, Slack said it had filed confidentially with the SEC to list shares to the public. That month, Peloton, the maker of internet-connected stationary bikes, started interviewing banks for its own IPO, joining a charge of unicorns that now included Slack, Uber, Lyft, and Pinterest preparing for the public markets. Palantir and Airbnb waited in the wings, though neither company filed with the SEC.

As the months went by, Slack's investors huddled with Morgan Stanley to gain an understanding of how they were going to sell shares in the direct listing.

On Friday, April 26, the company released its much-anticipated listing prospectus, publishing its financial results for the first time. Annual revenue in the twelve months through January had risen 82 percent to $400.6 million, up from just $105 million in 2017. Losses remained elevated, $140.7 million during the twelve months through January because of continued investments in marketing and sales, but better than the $181 million the prior year. Daily active users surpassed ten million at the end of January. Paying customers grew by 50 percent, to 88,000.

Slack also said it still had $841 million of its $1.2 billion in venture funding in the bank.

The filing gave a rundown of the company's largest shareholders. Accel owned 24 percent, while Andreessen Horowitz held another 13.3 percent.

Butterfield and Cal Henderson, a cofounder and the company's chief technology officer, owned 8.6 percent and 3.4 percent of the company, respectively. According to calculations conducted by the *Financial Times*, Accel's stake was worth $3.1 billion, while Butterfield's was worth $1.1 billion.

Slack said that it would list on the New York Stock Exchange with two classes of stock, a setup that was becoming more popular because it locks in the supermajority voting rights for the founders. The Class B shares had been trading in the secondary market within a range of $8.37 to $23.41 in the year ended January 31. The shares had traded privately at $23.50 in March. They were trading even higher on some secondary exchanges.

The following Monday, the We Company, owner of WeWork, joined the rush to enter the public markets, announcing a confidential filing it had submitted to the SEC the previous December. (The document would only become public later, in August, when media outlets and institutional investors questioned the sustainability of its business model. WeWork later pulled its IPO.)

On May 13, Slack held its investor day from San Francisco, putting on a presentation it streamed to the internet for anyone to see. Butterfield opened with a similar joke to the one made by Vogel about the SEC's safe harbor provision. The Slack executive said it was one of his favorites, and then read the first couple of lines as fast as he could before stopping to let the audience look at it.

Once Butterfield got into the meat of the presentation, his pitch was simple. Slack or other corporate messaging apps would eventually replace email. "This shift is inevitable," Butterfield said. "We believe every organization will switch to Slack or something like it."

Slack also posted financial estimates for the three months through April. The company brought in revenue of about $134 million, an increase of 63 percent over the previous year's period. Slack also shared some worrying figures, however. The company's paid subscription base grew just 8.6 percent in the fiscal fourth quarter from the prior quarter, below the average of 11.2 percent over the last seven quarters.

As Slack readied for its public debut, other high-flying tech startups were struggling to navigate the public markets. Shares in Lyft and Uber traded below their IPO price. Pinterest plunged by 15 percent in after-hours trading on Thursday, May 17, after the company reported a first-quarter loss of $41.4 million. Its shares were still above their IPO price, as were Zoom Video Communications Inc.'s, though shares in the videoconferencing company had given up many of their gains.

Nonetheless, May became the busiest month for IPOs since September 2015, with companies raising $15 billion. Another ninety-seven private companies in the United States had a value of $1 billion or more.

■ ■ ■

On Tuesday, June 11, 2019, Slack provided guidance to investors that it expected its revenue to surge as much as 50 percent—to $600 million—in the current fiscal year. It also said it would begin trading the following week under the ticker symbol WORK.

The following Wednesday, June 19, the New York Stock Exchange published its reference price for Slack—$26—valuing the company at $15.7 billion.

The next morning, Butterfield rang the bell at the New York Stock Exchange.

He also sat down for an interview with CNBC's Andrew Ross Sorkin before the stock started trading. Wearing a buttoned-up slate-blue suit over a white t-shirt, he sat on an outdoor stage that the network had set up across Wall Street from the NYSE, at Federal Hall.

Butterfield spoke rapidly as he answered Sorkin's questions about why Slack had chosen a direct listing. Behind the Slack founder, the marble facade of the NYSE building was draped in a purple flag bearing his company's logo. Butterfield was minutes away from becoming a billionaire.

"The big thing for us was—in a traditional IPO, it's the company that's offering shares and you might raise, you know, a billion dollars, or something like that," Butterfield said. "When you raise a billion dollars you dilute existing shareholders by issuing new shares. So we're not doing that, we are just opening it up for trading."

Sorkin pointed out that the chief reason Slack could do this was because it had about $800 million in the bank. "So this is unusual, not a lot of companies can actually pull this off," he said, adding, "but also, you're rewriting the model to some degree. Wall Street, I imagine, did not like this."

Butterfield, his voice rising in pitch, pushed back.

"Everyone says they like it. We'll see...I don't know how much they really like it," he said, smiling softly before going on.

"I think there are a lot of investors who are used to a model where they get this small allocation and they wanted a big one," he said. "In a direct listing, at least they have the opportunity. I mean, I think you saw that with Spotify, some early institutional investors taking huge positions on Day 1, whereas in a traditional IPO they might have only got $25 or $50 million."

Sorkin moved the conversation to fees, asking Butterfield how other companies considering something like this—and he name checked Airbnb—should think about the fee savings.

"The savings weren't that great, to be honest, and that's certainly not the motivator," the founder said. (The company would pay its advisors $22 million, compared to the $85 million that Snapchat paid its advisors when it went public in a traditional IPO in 2017.) Butterfield explained that the company liked the direct listing because it didn't require issuing new shares to raise money it didn't need. The stakes of existing investors weren't diluted. "The big one for us was not having to raise the capital."

Butterfield stared off-screen for a couple of moments before continuing his answer. "One of the hopes for a company like us is that there is not too much volatility. And we are hoping that with this model, where there are many sellers and many buyers, supply and demand, we reach a market clearing price a lot earlier."

Sorkin mentioned the fact that there is no lockup in a direct listing. Butterfield, for example, could sell shares if he wanted to. The founder said that SEC rules forbade him from buying and selling at whim, and acknowledged that he was selling a small stake in the direct listing. Sorkin then asked whether the direct listing—the fact that Slack was soon to be public—would change the company.

Butterfield demurred, shaking his head. "It's a big day. It's a nice moment, especially a nice moment for the team to show some appreciation and recognition from one another for all the hard work.

"We spent the last couple weeks writing thank-you notes to customers and sending them out so that they hopefully would arrive around today. But we're low-single-digit-percentage penetrated into what we think is an enormous market. There are ten million daily active users, but there are a couple hundred million whose working lives are mediated by email and they would all be better off with Slack or something like it. So that's the focus."

Sorkin wrapped the segment by asking Butterfield about valuation, and how investors should think about the company's slowing growth.

"I'm not going to give them advice on that—we're still in the quiet period—but I would say this. In fiscal 2017, $105 million in revenue, '18 was 220, last year was a little over 400. We've guided to 590, 600 for this year. So those are big numbers, and these are numbers that wouldn't have been private companies' numbers before. We are beginning to get to scale, so the percentage growth, you have to balance that with the absolute number of dollars coming in."

At just past midday in New York City, Slack's shares began trading at $38.50. The opening price indicated a 22 percent gain from its highest private market price, a modest premium. Later that afternoon they hit $42, giving Slack a market capitalization of more than $24 billion once all shares and options were counted. One hundred thirty-seven million shares changed hands that day, with the share price closing $38.62.

The listing made Butterfield's shares worth an estimated $1.6 billion.

CHAPTER 14

Unity, San Francisco, April 2019

By the time of Slack's listing, Bill Gurley was a wise man of Silicon Valley: a Benchmark partner since 1999 and an investor behind such well-known consumer-facing names as restaurant reservation app OpenTable, real estate website Zillow, and Uber. His investments earned him repeat mention on the *Forbes* Midas List of top VCs.

By June 2019, Gurley had lost his faith in the traditional IPO process. The venture capitalist had worked in Silicon Valley for more than twenty-five years and had seen or participated in dozens of offerings. He was getting prepared to step back from his day-to-day role at Benchmark, giving him more freedom to speak his mind about the inherent conflicts of interest.

His wariness had set in years earlier, when he was still working on Wall Street. "It started a long time ago," he said later. "I worked on Wall Street from ninety-three to ninety-seven, and the notion that you should match supply and demand and get at a fair price…I'm not the first person who came up with that."

But his immediate frustration had been growing for at least eighteen months. In November 2017, he was on the board of Stitch Fix, the personalized fashion app, when Goldman Sachs and JPMorgan underwrote the company's IPO. During the run-up to that deal, he had a conversation with one of the company's lead bankers that dramatically changed his perception of the traditional IPO process. In a later interview, the venture capitalist shared the anecdote. The banker had called Gurley on the phone. "Bill, this deal is only three times oversubscribed," the banker had said.

Gurley thought that sounded just fine. Any number over one meant there would be a buyer for every share. "Great," the venture capitalist said. "Let's stop the process, print the tape, and move on."

"No," the banker said. "That's the problem. We usually have ten times more supply and demand. We want to get to thirty times."

Stitch Fix had a lot of retail customers who might want to buy the stock. Gurley asked the banker how much of the deal they planned to allocate to those retail investors.

"Five percent," the banker said.

How about 20 percent? Gurley suggested.

The banker declined.

The answer suggested to Gurley that the banker had no interest in considering other ways to stimulate demand for an IPO. "Telling us we have a supply-demand problem," Gurley said, "but being unwilling to consider alternate solutions that would improve that, versus just simply dropping the price."

A day before the transaction was supposed to close, another issue arose. The bank refused to move forward unless T. Rowe Price was in the deal, but the investor was making demands.

That didn't feel right to him. "I was rooting for the process," Gurley said later. "The thing that caused me to pick up the baton was this IPO."

Stitch Fix ultimately priced its shares at $15, below its range of $18 to $20. The company raised $120 million after deciding to sell fewer shares at the lower price. CEO Katrina Lake was the only woman to lead a technology company to go public that year. The shares, which started trading on the NASDAQ stock exchange, opened at $16.90 before closing the day at $15.15.

The disappointing performance was captured by the *Wall Street Journal*, which cited the decision to price at $15 as "another setback for a hot startup looking to cash in on its private-market success." Stitch Fix "stumbled in its stock-market debut," another article in the paper said.

■ ■ ■

Months after the Stitch Fix IPO and Spotify's direct listing, Gurley hosted a retinue of Morgan Stanley bankers including Grimes, Stewart, and Rizvan Dhalla at Benchmark's offices in Woodside, California. They were there explicitly to discuss the subject of direct listings. Gurley had assembled Benchmark's team to hear from them.

As Grimes began his presentation, he told the venture capitalists that he would prove to them that he knew why they liked the direct listing approach. He ran down a list of reasons and suggested that he and the other bankers in the room felt as they did. His ability to put himself in the venture capitalists' shoes showed Gurley that the bank was at least willing to think through the topic.

"They were at least cognizant of the issues," Gurley said later.

One of the issues that venture capitalists and company executives had with the traditional public offering was of course the large fees they often had to pay to underwriters. Typically set at 7 percent of the offering, the fee hadn't moved much lower in years, though large issuers such as Google or Facebook could occasionally negotiate for it to be lower.

When it came time to reward its advisors, Spotify paid about $36 million to its bankers at Goldman Sachs, Morgan Stanley, and Allen & Co. That was roughly 3.8 percent of the company's opening trade. If Spotify had instead agreed to pay underwriters 7 percent in a traditional IPO that sold 5.6 million shares at $165.90, it would have had to fork over as much as $65 million to its bankers.

In October 2018, Gurley had another run-in with Wall Street investment bankers over their handling of an IPO. Elastic was another Benchmark investment in the enterprise software industry that was preparing for an IPO led by Goldman Sachs. Gurley's colleague Peter Fenton sat on the board. Benchmark believed the company had a bright future and could price the shares at around $80 apiece.

When it came time to price the deal, Elastic sold shares at less than half that amount, or $36. Gurley laid the blame at the feet of Goldman Sachs. Benchmark didn't agree with the pricing and told the bank that if it was going with $36, they wanted an allocation of between $10 million and $20 million in the IPO. Goldman wouldn't give it to them. By the time the markets closed on Elastic's first day of trading, the stock had risen 94 percent, to $70. The underpricing cost Benchmark $60 million, the venture firm reckoned.

The Elastic experience left Gurley sour, even though it may not have been as clear cut as he thought. CEO Shay Banon spoke to *Business Insider* the day after the IPO and took responsibility. "As for the pricing, I decided that $36 per share was a fair price for our company."

Gurley said Banon's quote didn't surprise him. "I will tell you that every single time this kind of discounting situation takes place and the press asks the CEO in the heat of the moment, 'Did you just fuck up?' they always say no, and I don't know of a world where that wouldn't happen," he said. "You're sitting there on the biggest day of this company's life, everyone else is throwing confetti around."

Gurley's big trade, Uber Technologies, stumbled out of the gate six months later. Uber sold shares to the public on May 9, 2019, at $45 apiece. The next day, CNBC featured the former venture capitalist Roger McNamee and the journalist Kara Swisher, who questioned whether Uber would ever turn a profit. The shares opened at $42 before slumping to $41.57 by the close of trading.

So as Slack neared its direct listing the following month, Gurley was watching closely.

The week before Slack's listing, cybersecurity firm CrowdStrike Holdings Inc. held a traditional IPO. Its shares nearly doubled in a day. The performance was enough to unleash a series of tweets from Gurley, who wasn't shy about sharing his opinions. A frequent guest on financial news networks including CNBC, since 1996 he'd maintained a widely followed blog, *Above the Crowd*, its title a nod to the fact that he was six foot nine. Gurley showed a talent for Twitter, too, easily touting his investments and debating financial theories in the clipped and symbol-heavy language of social media. The former basketball player also chimed in on NBA topics. Gurley had hundreds of thousands of Twitter followers who hung on his every word.

With the CrowdStrike IPO, Gurley now had reason to begin tweeting about the state of the IPO market. On June 12, he wrote, "One perspective— CrowdStrike (and other way underpriced deals) are the true definition of a 'broken' IPO." He calculated how much the company left on the table by selling at a lower price in its IPO.

"Imagine if a CFO/CEO gave away a half a billion dollars?" Gurley asked. "Or simply squandered it. How would that be viewed? This is similar, but it's institutionalized, and therefore everyone is numb to it. And the press views a 'pop' as success, which is just poor financial comprehension."

His final tweet of the thread referenced Slack's upcoming direct listing and the mechanism for setting its price. "There is no reason whatsoever [that] equities cannot be priced in a blind auction. Bonds have been priced/sold this way for decades. This is how 100% of IPOs should be done. And hopefully will one day."

The following day, two more IPOs—pet retailer Chewy Inc. and freelancing marketplace Fiverr International Ltd.—surged more than 50 percent when their shares started trading.

■ ■ ■

By the time Slack priced its direct listing, Gurley had laid the groundwork for his next Twitter thread. Little more than an hour after the close of the trading day, he placed his cursor into a blank space and typed out a message.

In this tweet, Gurley praised the lack of volatility in Slack's listing, which closed within 1 percent of its opening price, and name checked advisors Morgan Stanley and Citadel Securities, which handled the trading on the NYSE. And then he offered a full-throated endorsement.

"If your company is interested in a direct-listing, recommend you call Morgan Stanley," Gurley wrote. "Other banks want to position direct listings as 'exceptional' or 'rare.' MS believes they are 1) a better mousetrap, and 2) can be used broadly."

The message ping-ponged down the corridors of Silicon Valley and Wall Street almost as soon as he sent it. Goldman's head of technology banking, Nick Giovanni, wasn't happy. Giovanni, known for an intense and direct manner and a tendency to drive his people hard, headed a team that had led the IPO underwriter rankings for years. He could be difficult, but he was also talented and unavoidable if you wanted Goldman's expertise.

Giovanni called Gurley. Goldman had been the lead bank on the two direct listings so far—why was Gurley throwing his support behind the competitor? the banker wanted to know.

"Do you know how much business that tweet might cost us?" Giovanni snapped.

Gurley didn't want to hear it. "Nick, let me show you the Elastic math. You cost us sixty million. How much business do you have to lose before you and I are even?"

The two men spent another few minutes talking past each other until Giovanni suggested that Goldman and Benchmark should spend more time discussing Goldman's position on direct listings. Giovanni felt that because Goldman's take was more nuanced—it wanted what was best for the client, not a one-size-fits-all approach—it didn't fit into a clean narrative. He told

Gurley he would get back to him. Giovanni followed up with Gurley's Bench-mark colleagues. He didn't reconnect with Gurley, the venture capitalist said.

"One of the reasons why I was very supportive of Morgan Stanley was that they would at least come and sit down" and explain the reasons why a direct listing might be preferred, Gurley said. "I had a slide that [Grimes] had given me where he wrote down the six or seven things. I don't think that means the minute I leave the room, he's telling every customer that same thing, but I did appreciate the candor and the honesty from Michael. Whereas I would always hear, every time one of our companies would meet with Goldman, they'd try and talk them out of a DL, every time. It's just a little bit on the margin, but it was still something that seemed to matter, like anything that would help move us in the right direction."

■ ■ ■

If Gurley was the only one touting Morgan Stanley, that would have been one thing. But he wasn't. Two weeks after Slack went public, on July 2, Andrees-sen Horowitz partner Jamie McGurk published a blog post entitled "All about Direct Listings."

One of McGurk's roles was to work with portfolio companies in the pro-cess of going public, and he had worked on Slack's direct listing, getting under the hood of the direct listing process so the firm would know how to sell its shares in the listing.

The experience made McGurk into one of Silicon Valley's few experts in direct listings. He realized the rarity of his expertise at an event in Santa Bar-bara where he met a startup executive who strongly opposed direct listings. When McGurk pressed him, the executive cited premise after premise that was simply wrong. McGurk went to his hotel room almost immediately and wrote the broad outlines of the post.

The traditional IPO process was "ripe for innovation: The very first IPO technically happened over 400 years ago, and the rules for current IPOs were established nearly a century ago," McGurk wrote. "But technology has changed since." He cited Google's Dutch auction and the creation of the long-term stock exchange, the first exchange headquartered in Silicon Valley. Direct listings, he wrote, could become widespread by following the same trend.

Over nearly five thousand words, McGurk told readers about his behind-the-scenes role on the Slack direct listing, explained the differences between direct listings and IPOs, and dispelled six myths about both that he had identified:

> Price appreciation is the measure of a successful listing
> New listings need to price at a discount to attract new investors
> The IPO is a financing event
> Companies that need to raise capital can't do a Direct Listing
> Public Investors don't like Direct Listings
> Only "well-known" brands can pursue a Direct Listing

"One of the greatest myths of modern IPOs," McGurk wrote, which he said media coverage "aided and abetted," was the belief that a surging stock price is some measure of a successful offering. The first-day pops garner a lot of attention, he admitted, but all they do is show that the stock was mispriced. Instead, the success of direct listings can be judged, he said, on volume rather than price, because a high number of trades shows many buyers and sellers coming together to agree on a certain price.

McGurk said that for Spotify's direct listing, the stock opened on "thin volume" that led the price to drift down during the day. Slack's opening trade was more than 45 million shares, making it one of the largest listings in NYSE history.

McGurk also tried to dispel the notion that listings must price at a discount to the company's value to attract new investors. "IPOs currently rely on hand-picking investors," he wrote, whereas direct listings arrive at a market-clearing price that draws in those investors who are "most aligned" with the company. As a result, the direct listing, he wrote, is a "much more egalitarian process."

McGurk cited the conflicted position of investment banks by virtue of their role as intermediaries, which he argued had become less important over the last decade. In the past, companies needed investment banks to broker conversations with investors when mutual funds and hedge funds were "unapproachable and remote," he wrote. Now, many of those same investors were active in private markets and were meeting executives to discuss financing rounds years before it was time for startups to go public.

The preponderance of money available to private startups had also begun to remove the importance of the IPO as a financing event, McGurk wrote.

If a company needed money and wanted to do a direct listing, he suggested that it sell 2–3 percent of its capitalization in new shares in a private round to crossover investors. Those investors would remain through the listing and continue as investors in the public company. "By decoupling the [capital-raising] and the public listing, the company can better calibrate selling the right amount of shares—without discounting too much—and at the right market price."

Despite the problems McGurk identified in the traditional IPO, he stopped short of calling for investment banks to get cut out of the process completely. The banks, whose role changes from underwriter to advisor in a direct listing, offered "tremendous value" in Slack's listing. Morgan Stanley played a critical role in making the Slack transaction a success, McGurk wrote.

The post mentioned Morgan Stanley twice. Goldman's name didn't appear once.

Giovanni was once again unhappy, and he forced a colleague in charge of managing the Andreessen relationship to hastily convene a call with McGurk the following morning, July 3. Catching McGurk on vacation, Giovanni spent thirty minutes or so protesting the venture capitalist's decision to ignore Goldman's role leading the first two direct listings and make him look bad. Goldman was instrumental to the deal, Giovanni explained, offering as evidence the fact that Goldman made more in fees on the transaction than Morgan Stanley. The conversation was tense, and McGurk explained that he had not intended to make Goldman look bad. Morgan Stanley's inclusion reflected the fact that Morgan Stanley's bankers had reached out to Slack's shareholders much earlier than Goldman had to hash out the details of the transaction. Finally, Giovanni ran out of steam and the call ended, without a resolution.

While McGurk's post explained what many involved in the Spotify and Slack direct listings already knew, it was notable that Andreessen Horowitz, one of Silicon Valley's most powerful venture capitalists, was lending its name to support direct listings.

Around that time, Gurley reached out to Jeff Jordan, a partner at Andreessen to learn more about the Slack listing. The two financiers knew each other from OpenTable, where Jordan had been CEO while Gurley was on the board. Though partners at Benchmark and Andreessen harbored a rivalry that could be traced back to Marc Andreessen's grudge against Gurley over the latter's 1997 downgrade of Netscape, personal relationships could sometimes overcome the animosity.

Jordan directed Gurley to McGurk's blog post about direct listings and told him that he should talk to his partner. McGurk and Gurley met for lunch to discuss the listing.

Gurley was working on a plan for a daylong symposium that would educate startup executives and other venture capitalists about the direct listing process. Investment bankers weren't invited.

        ■ ■ ■

In early September, Slack disclosed its first quarterly results as a public company. Revenue had risen 58 percent, and the number of paying customers had increased 37 percent, to more than 100,000. Costs had risen quickly, too, jumping to ten times the amount registered in the previous year's quarter. This was due largely to $307 million in equity compensation costs and taxes related to the direct listing. The company continued to spend heavily on sales and marketing, suggesting that it felt the need to aggressively keep up with the competition. Slack said that it would likely suffer a bigger-than-expected third-quarter loss.

At the top of many investors' minds was the battle with Microsoft, and the company's press release didn't disappoint in terms of providing fodder. Butterfield intensified his fight with his largest rival, mentioning two Slack customers who also used the Microsoft 365 Office suite. One, he said, stuck with Slack because "only Slack was capable of meeting their needs."

Butterfield said on an earnings call that the next five years of Slack's life would be very different from the prior five, and that the company was increasingly focused on meeting the needs of large corporations. "The transition to being a public company is just one hallmark of what we see as the company entering a new phase," he said.

Investors didn't like what they heard. The company's stock price plunged about 15 percent in after-hours trading. Slack was facing tough questions about its ability to hold off Microsoft. The most obvious problem: Microsoft offered Teams for free to users of its other Office 365 products. The Teams platform now counted thirteen million daily active users, compared to Slack's ten million.

The following day, Credit Suisse and MKM Partners analysts cut their forecasts. Citigroup slashed its price target to $27 from $39. It didn't take long for the op-ed pages of the financial press to jump on, with both the *Financial Times* and the *Wall Street Journal* suggesting that Slack's stock slump still had room to run. The shares closed September 5 at $30.01. That put the stock price down almost 18 percent since its opening trade in June.

Spotify wasn't doing much better. Its stock closed the September 5 trading day at $135.68, down 18 percent from its opening price on the day of its direct listing. A few theories began to emerge. One was that the direct listing captured a broad swath of investor interest, because it was available to all investors at the same time. They could all participate in the direct listing, so there was no artificial demand created to buy the stock later in its life cycle. In that way, it succeeded in capturing a higher valuation than many IPOs, which only capture interest from a select group of institutional investors and, if all goes well, tend to rise in the months after the event.

Another theory was that investors had questions about companies' ability to execute on their business models as publicly traded entities. Still another suggested that investors were growing bearish on high-growth, and money-losing, technology companies.

The IPO market began to bear this out. On September 11, direct to consumer orthodontics startup SmileDirect broke issue when its JPMorgan-led IPO slumped 28 percent from the $23 IPO price to close below $17 on its first day of trading. It was the worst debut for a company valued at more than $1 billion that year.

Two weeks later, Peloton held its own IPO. The stock was priced above the range, at $29, and slumped 11 percent in its debut, making it the second-worst performance for a $1 billion company in 2019.

Four days after the Peloton slump, WeWork officially pulled its IPO.

■ ■ ■

By then, Unity Software, another software firm with roots in video games had begun its early steps toward listing its shares. Its headquarters was just a short walk up Market Street from Slack's San Francisco headquarters, in a wide box of a building that boasted exposed brick walls and timber beams.

Unity's engineers and executives developed software used by video game developers. They made the foundation of the game, known as the engine, that handled the physics, graphics, and light effects. With Unity providing that layer, which also included tools to make money with advertisements or in-game purchases, game developers could spend less time writing code and more time designing whatever it was that distinguished their products in the marketplace. Developers behind *Pokémon GO*, *Monument Valley*, and *Super Mario Run* used Unity's software.

Unity was founded in 2004 in Copenhagen as Over the Edge Entertainment to make a game for Apple computers called *GooBall*. When that didn't find commercial success, the founders—David Helgason, Nicholas Francis, and Joachim Ante—focused instead on developing the software tools they created and selling them to other developers.

Over the Edge enjoyed early acclaim, earning a second-place showing in the 2006 Apple Design Awards. When Apple introduced the iPhone in 2007 and the App Store in 2008, Over the Edge moved fast to give game developers the tools they needed to distribute their games on mobile devices.

The founders moved their headquarters to San Francisco in 2009, changed the company's name to Unity Software, and persuaded Sequoia Capital and partner Roelof Botha to lead a $5.5 million investment. With the backing of Sequoia, one of the world's most successful and powerful venture firms, Unity focused on growth.

Five years later, in October 2014, John Riccitiello, the former CEO of Electronic Arts, who had joined Unity's board the prior year, took over as CEO. He had a vision for how the company could support developers in augmented reality and virtual reality applications and a skill at selling investors on that vision. The company also worked with design and engineering clients looking to use 2D and 3D technology to produce renderings of large structures such as skyscrapers and interior spaces like offices or museums.

Under Riccitiello, Unity's valuation surged to $1.5 billion. In May 2017, Silver Lake's co-CEO Egon Durban led a $400 million round that valued the company at $2.8 billion and joined Unity's board.

As Slack prepared for its direct listing in early 2019, Riccitiello looked for a new finance chief. Former CFO Mike Foley had left in mid-2018. After an extensive search, Riccitiello hired Kim Jabal, Google's former investor relations chief. By the time she joined Unity, Jabal had held several startup finance roles. She'd left website creation tool Weebly, another company where Botha sat on the board, in late 2018.

Riccitiello talked up Jabal's experience in a press release announcing her hire. "Couple her finance experience with her deep roots in engineering and R&D, and it's no secret why she's a great fit." In the same statement, Jabal compared Unity to Google in its early days. "It reminds me a lot of when I started at Google, back when the company was a smaller, yet similarly positioned, and very technology-driven, company."

Jabal would wrestle Unity's technology systems and financial reporting functions into shape, much like McCarthy had done at Spotify to make the company ready for the public markets. And she would begin to think about how to get the company into the public markets.

CHAPTER 15

Unity, San Francisco, Summer 2019

Unity's listing gave Jabal a reason to reunite with her old Google colleague Lise Buyer, with whom she had stayed in touch over the years. The two women shared a common history around Google's offering and had crossed paths at various social events related to the Google alumni network.

They were also both navigating what was still a predominantly male industry. Over the years, Jabal had spoken up about the challenges of working in corporate environments that tended to disadvantage women. She remained close with Sheryl Sandberg, who had left Google for Facebook in 2008. Five years later, Sandberg wrote *Lean In*, a best seller that shed light on persistent gender imbalances in corporate America and encouraged women to take charge of their careers. In the book, Sandberg named Jabal as one of her "closest adulthood friends." Sandberg's openness in discussing the difficult issues that women faced in the workplace inspired Jabal to address even more openly the obstacles she faced.

In interviews, Jabal talked about balancing work and home life, and the need for fathers to play an equal role. She told one interviewer that, like many, she would work an eight-hour day, prepare dinner for her family, and then work for another three hours after her children were in bed. "It's not just the mom's job," she said. "It's the parents' job." Jabal had married a man she met at Harvard Business School, and the two of them worked for Google. By the time she landed at Unity, they had gotten divorced.

On April 16, Jabal sent an email to Buyer asking for a meeting. "Hi, just started working at Unity," Jabal wrote. "We're marching towards an IPO. I'd love your help. Let me know if you have time to meet sometime." She got a quick response, and the two women arranged to meet at Unity's offices in San

Francisco. Buyer had been through dozens of IPOs as a company advisor by then.

"Kim knew that I had worked on the auction, on the IPO, and she knew what I was doing now," Buyer said later. "We have mutual friends and acquaintances."

The timing seemed auspicious, with the IPO market beginning to heat up. During the first three months of 2019, the NASDAQ had shot up nearly 17 percent, leading to greater receptivity to technology IPOs. The favorable backdrop broke a logjam that had been building for years. Companies that could have gone public had chosen to stay private, content to raise money from venture capitalists and avoid the scrutiny that came with being publicly listed. Staying private, however, made it harder for investors and employees to cash out. As the NASDAQ rose, more and more startup entrepreneurs and their venture capitalist backers began to view the public markets as a viable alternative to staying private. For many in Silicon Valley, the boom was welcome.

On April 11, PagerDuty became what CNBC called "the first notable software company to go public this year." The shares rose nearly 60 percent when the company started trading. One week later, a day after Jabal emailed Buyer, Pinterest and Zoom listed their shares, the former at $19 apiece; by the close of trading the following day, they had risen a modest 28 percent. Zoom sold shares at $36, surging 72 percent in their market debut.

The first-day stock surges that bothered the likes of Gurley and McCarthy were once again taking place as the market moved higher.

■ ■ ■

On May 1, Buyer drove up to San Francisco from her home on the peninsula and navigated her way to Unity's offices. She didn't know what Jabal or Riccitiello had in mind, but she knew that direct listings were becoming the topic du jour among startups. Slack was gearing up for the second major direct listing, and newspapers and websites were full of analysis.

Once she had arrived and settled into a meeting room at Unity's headquarters, Buyer fielded a question from Jabal about how an IPO advisor like Buyer typically worked with companies. Buyer explained her business model, laying out how it differed from others around the IPO process. When a company hires underwriters, it pays them a gross spread of the IPO proceeds. A percentage, in other words, of the deal proceeds. Buyer, on the other hand, collected a flat fee regardless of the size of the transaction or its structure. The arrangement spared her the conflicts that peppered the underwriter-issuer relationship.

The two women also talked about Google. Jabal wanted to know why some things had gone right and others hadn't. She said that Unity was considering doing something other than a traditional IPO. Jabal's engineering background gave her a feeling that the data would show that there might be a better way to list the company's shares. She asked Buyer to pull some data and come back. "They had understandably bought into the rhetoric that maybe there were better ways to complete an IPO," Buyer said later. "There was a lot of noise at that time about direct listings, which were definitely the new shiny object in the spring of 2019."

When Slack started trading in June and Gurley took an increasingly public stand against the IPO process, Jabal turned her attention to ensuring that Unity's accounts would be in shape for its eventual public debut. This was one of her greatest strengths. An early career stop at Arthur Andersen gave her broad experience building technology systems.

The major task ahead was to figure out how to close Unity's books on time, a requirement if the company was going to comply with SEC regulations that governed the timeline of public companies' reporting of results to investors. A lot of private startups couldn't close their accounts on time. Private company valuations didn't usually change on a daily or monthly basis; as such, there was less need for a timely picture of financial performance. And while investors often required quarterly reports, they didn't dictate those reports' timing. Startups closed their books, made changes, and finally came to an accurate picture weeks or months after the quarter's end.

The SEC, on the other hand, required public companies to report earnings within forty-five days of the close of the quarter. Jabal needed her books closed soon after the end of the quarter if she was going to hit that deadline. The results also had to be correct. There would be no going back to make changes or update the numbers once Unity reported to public investors, who would be buying and selling the shares as soon as the results came in.

Unity was old for a startup, and its accounting, tax, and vendor management systems were a patchwork. Newer startups build that infrastructure on Day 1, but Jabal didn't have that luxury. She began to wrangle various systems into a new architecture that would deliver the data she needed. Only then could she make accurate projections, another thing she would need to do once Unity was public. Investors would expect her to be able to forecast revenue, earnings per share, the tax rate, and a count of diluted shares. Doing so meant being able to forecast many other numbers that went into those headline figures.

Jabal faced the same challenge that McCarthy had in his early days as Spotify's CFO, and she knew that she needed to hire more help to overcome it. She began to think about adding accountants, tax specialists, people with experience managing and investing a company's cash, and professionals who knew how to tell a company's story in a way that institutional investors understood. She also needed to know how the company was matching up to its key performance metrics.

■ ■ ■

Unity executives formalized their arrangement with Buyer in July, agreeing to give her a flat fee for advice on the company's upcoming public listing. On August 8, Riccitiello, Jabal, and Buyer met to begin talking about the structure of Unity's IPO. The company really liked the direct listing approach, which Riccitiello thought would also serve the interests of his employees. He was intent on ensuring that they get fair treatment in whatever Unity's listing became. "John was very clear, whatever structure they chose should be as beneficial as possible to all the employees," Buyer said. "That was a big part of their interest in the direct listing. It's a different kind of company that is really quite egalitarian."

That same month, Riccitiello spoke to Slack CFO Allen Shim about his company's direct listing. Unlike Unity's executives, Shim had experience with the traditional IPO process. He'd had a finance role at video ad-tech startup YuMe during its 2013 IPO, and as a result he could compare the two approaches. According to notes of the call, Shim told Riccitiello that the direct listing required a lot of work on the part of the management team because there were some things, such as educating investors, that the investment banks couldn't do in a direct listing that they could do in an IPO.

Riccitiello and Jabal had support from their board to think creatively about how they were going to list their shares. Sequoia's Botha had long thought that investment bankers didn't always have the best interests of the issuer in mind. As a former executive at PayPal and now a venture capitalist, he didn't like being subject to a 180-day lockup while other investors could sell at whim or being diluted when companies issued additional shares in an IPO. On August 18, Botha's colleague Michael Moritz, a former journalist and a Google board member when the company went public, wrote a scathing op-ed in the *Financial Times*, "Investment Banks Are Losing Their Grip on IPOs," to commemorate Google's IPO fifteen years earlier. It was a condemnation of what Moritz—like Botha—had long seen as a rigged system.

Moritz wrote that the time had come for investment banks to permanently "lose the gatekeeping position they have jealously protected." He acknowledged that Google's IPO had failed to "break the hammerlock that investment banks have always held on stock offerings," writing that "the banks closed ranks and succeeded, in a disinformation campaign worthy of the NRA gun lobby in the U.S., in portraying the IPO as a flop."

Companies had grown tired of being taken advantage of by investment banks and were open to alternative models like a direct listing, Moritz wrote. He called out the courage and "backbone" of McCarthy, and touted Hambrecht's earlier efforts before "his former competitors and collaborators made him a pariah in the manner that the mob treats a turncoat."

The op-ed was a shot across the bow of the investment banking industry from one of the most powerful venture capitalists in the world.

■   ■   ■

As Unity executives weighed their options for going public, they had a list of concerns. Jabal was wary of seeing the company's stock jump too much on its opening day of trading, which would tell her that she'd sold too cheaply and needlessly diluted existing shareholders. When CFOs sell stock at a certain price and then see it jump on the first day, it's hard for them not to think about how they could have raised the same amount of money by selling fewer shares at the higher price.

So direct listings looked attractive because more shares weren't being issued. But Unity wanted to raise more money, something that a direct listing wouldn't allow. "They had been acquisitive previously, and it never hurts to have money in the bank when there's things you want to buy," Buyer said later. "And two, nobody knows what the IPO runway is like at any one time, and it is always better to go public from a position of strength."

Unity began to consider a more complex series of transactions: a late-stage private round followed by a direct listing. Even there, Buyer had misgivings related to simple physics. A two-part transaction would mean at least twice the amount of work. It would also mean twice the fees to the bankers, potentially negating the money Unity would save.

Buyer also believed another private round would create the dilution that the direct listing avoided. Unity would simply issue new shares and dilute investors in the private round. "We looked at late-stage fundraising that happened just a small period of time before the direct listings and said, 'Wait a minute,' to point out that the dilution may not have been on the day of the deal," Buyer said.

Any discussion of a direct listing would also include an analysis of Spotify's and Slack's stock performance. Both stocks had fallen in the days after their listings. While it couldn't be ignored "that they did not leave money on the table that day," Buyer said, "you also had to showcase that they [both] had stock that went down."

This was one area where Buyer's and Wall Street's underwriters agreed. A flagging stock price in the days and months after a listing, whether it was a direct or a traditional offering, was widely believed to be bad for employee morale. Employees didn't appreciate seeing the shares or the options they had been paid as part of their compensation declining in value. They felt less wealthy.

Of course, in 2012, Facebook traded down in the months after its IPO. So it wasn't always a death knell for the company. Having gone through the fire of Google's auction, Buyer was a true believer in the power of the auction process. She advocated for including parts of it in Unity's structure early.

CHAPTER 16

Unity, San Francisco, October 2019

On October 1, Jabal made her way to the Palace, a San Francisco luxury hotel favored by the finance and tech crowd for conferences and other large events. With its marble columns and ornate chandeliers, the hundred-year-old hotel was an interesting location for a convergence of some of the world's most innovative companies. Jabal was one of more than a hundred startup executives and venture capitalists attending a half-day symposium about direct listings that Gurley, with help from Moritz, had organized.

Attendees received an agenda with the event's title laid out in blue ink: "Direct Listings: A Simpler and Superior Alternative to the IPO." Gurley had planned the event as a series of panels and question-and-answer sessions to educate the audience about his preferred way of entering the public markets. Moritz interviewed McCarthy and then Gurley followed, speaking for thirty minutes or so. A hoped-for video appearance from former Wall Street analyst Henry Blodget, a fervent critic of the entrenched IPO system, was beset by audiovisual issues.

Gurley had explicitly prevented investment bankers from attending his event. He clearly felt that they had too much control already, and he didn't want them advocating for the traditional IPO process or otherwise undermining his message. He made two exceptions.

One, Carl Chiou, was head of West Coast equity capital markets at boutique investment bank William Blair and a former Barclays PLC convertible bond expert. Convertibles required near-perfect pricing—and when Chiou started working on IPOs that Barclays underwrote, he couldn't understand why the process was so inefficient. He concluded that the problem was the conflicted position of the larger banks and their tendency to favor investor clients such as hedge funds over corporate clients. He soon left for Blair, where he was trying to build a franchise free of the conflicts that plagued his larger rivals.

Chiou had been putting out research reports that highlighted his analytical savvy, writing chops, and extreme "dad-ness." Both these—in which he occasionally referred to his two sons and their favorite topics, including the American Revolution and obscure *Star Wars* characters—and his Twitter feed had become required reading at Benchmark and Andreessen Horowitz.

Gurley had also invited a Citigroup banker named Doug Baird to the symposium. Baird's more than thirty years of experience included senior positions running IPOs in the 1990s at Alex. Brown & Sons. The balding Dartmouth grad had a self-deprecating sense of humor and an irreverent take on IPOs that kept him from getting hung up on historical precedent.

Importantly, neither had ever worked at Goldman Sachs or Morgan Stanley, the duopoly of investment banks that ran the most sought-after tech IPOs.

Baird and Chiou spent roughly half an hour offering a "Voice of Reason," as their panel was titled, explaining why they thought the traditional IPO was ripe for disruption. Wearing a dress shirt and slacks, Chiou encouraged the corporate executives in the audience to take ownership of their listing. He acknowledged that they might have come up believing that bankers and investors drove IPOs. But he reminded them that they were the ones who built the companies. They should feel empowered to shape the transaction for their purpose. Chiou implored them to understand the depth of their power and to use it to take more control of the most critical moments of the stock listing, when the shares got priced and allocated. He assured them that a direct listing was a viable alternative to the traditional IPO.

"You are the stars of the show," he told the audience. "Find people who are willing to show you transparency into how the process really works, and who are willing to work with you on a totally unconflicted basis where you are the only client."

Baird, the consummate investment banker in his suit, began his section of the presentation with a history of how IPOs had changed over the years. He discussed how a process that began as a way to determine the valuation of a non-public company had evolved into something resembling a transfer of value from companies to investors. In the early 1990s, bankers assigned stock prices in the low double digits and expected them to rise around 10 percent the following day, Baird explained. A series of events, including Broadcast .com's 1998 stock pop, Bear Stearns's lowered underwriting standards, and the internet boom, changed the equation. From then on, the idea that trading up on the first day was a sign of a good company.

Baird told the story of eBay, which went public on September 21, 1998. As one of the underwriters, Baird's firm got the list of the allocations. Securities filings showed the holdings of investors at the end of that month—nine days later. Fewer than five investors still held the stock, Baird said. Everyone else had quickly flipped it for a profit.

Baird wasn't done. He lampooned a metric that fellow bankers liked to cite—how many (and what percentage) of one-on-one meetings between a company and an investor led to an IPO order. On tech IPOs, he said, bankers liked to tout rates of higher than 90 percent. He cited a deal Citigroup had done for a private equity firm. The hit rate was more like 60 percent, he said. The stock rose 5 percent the next day, and the private equity company did a series of follow-on sales as the stock continued to rise over the next couple of years.

Once the bankers had finished their presentation, University of Florida professor Jay Ritter spoke to the audience about his decades of experience researching the IPO market. In Ritter's view, banks had an incentive to sell undervalued IPOs to investors because they received some portion of that value back in the form of trading commissions. Company executives didn't mind, Ritter theorized, because the absolute leap in their wealth numbed them to any worries about leaving some money on the table for their companies. Ritter and a coauthor, Tim Loughran, had likened the effect to prospect theory in a 2002 paper titled "Why Don't Issuers Get Upset About Leaving Money on the Table in IPOs?"

After an interview with Stacey Cunningham, who had become the NYSE president, and a short break, McGurk gave a presentation. By then a managing partner at Coatue Management, a hedge fund that made many investments in private technology startups, McGurk walked the audience through the nuts and bolts of the direct listing process.

Sessions on the designated market maker's role, a legal perspective, and panels with institutional investors and CEOs who had already gone through the IPO process followed. The conference broke for a cocktail hour sponsored by Latham & Watkins, after which the guests sat down for dinner and author Michael Lewis was interviewed onstage by Gurley.

Jabal tried to learn as much as she could. She left with two surprising realizations. Unity would still have to pay millions of dollars to investment banks, because direct listings were expensive. And they were also time-consuming.

■ ■ ■

Days later, Goldman Sachs hosted its annual Private Innovative Company Conference at the Wynn Las Vegas. The ninth such event, it gathered more than five hundred people from across the venture, private equity, and startup industries to connect and network with each other. Unlike Gurley's symposium, the event gave investment banks an opportunity to speak directly to their clients, many of whom were in various stages of considering life as a public company.

Riccitiello and Jabal had flown in from California. They were in the audience on Sunday, October 4, when Goldman hosted a panel on direct listings. McCarthy and Greg Rodgers sat onstage next to Goldman's head of equity capital markets for technology companies, Will Connolly, and Jake Siewert, head of Goldman's communications department. Siewert introduced the panelists and turned it over to Connolly to open the discussion.

Connolly was dressed casually for a banker, in a blazer, jeans, and loafers. His youthful face showed traces of stubble. After a brief joke about not starting at the invention of the mutual fund, he gave a short history of IPOs and attempted to show that Goldman was a creative investment bank open to recent changes. "We had the unique opportunity to work with both Spotify and Slack as the lead advisor on their direct listings over the course of the last couple of years," Connolly said. "And we're thrilled for their success, and Barry in particular, in really being the innovative force behind this new technology, if you will. And we're excited about the opportunity to continue to seek innovation on behalf of our clients."

When it came time for Siewert to ask questions, he repeatedly referred to the inherent riskiness of nontraditional IPOs. His questions reflected the risk-averse nature of the investment bank and the advice it typically gave clients. He started with a question for McCarthy, whom he referred to as a trailblazer.

"It was obviously risky to do it, but what gave you the confidence to know that it was the right thing to do for Spotify?"

McCarthy, wearing a dark designer t-shirt and white jeans, took a moment to thank the host while also deflecting some of the praise. "Before I answer that, let me just suck up to my host and say: no Goldman Sachs, no Spotify," McCarthy said. The comment served as a tip of the hat to Goldman's importance in Spotify's success, through the bank's help with both Spotify's private funding rounds and its public market debut. "And how much of an innovator was I? I just took an old, tired idea that had already existed in the public markets and recrafted it and applied it to a tech IPO."

According to McCarthy, Spotify was able to do a direct listing because it was so much bigger than Netflix was at that stage. "I realized that it was one of those 'Dorothy, we're not in Kansas anymore' moments," he ad-libbed. "And for a long time, I have watched the public market and thought that it was chronically broken. And I thought surely there must be a better way."

McCarthy made a comment about the direct listing allowing market-based pricing, leading Siewert to follow up with a question about companies handpicking their shareholders. "You talk about having the market decide the price and deciding who gets the shares. Most of the people in this room have had the ability so far to choose their shareholders and choose their prices. What's that transition like?"

"As a public company, you don't have any control over who your shareholders are," McCarthy answered. "If you think you're going to, you need to lie down till the thought passes, then get back up.

"The best you can hope to do is go spend time with people you think are really smart and convince them that they ought to own the stock, too," he said. "So you can encourage some people to buy it based on the way you allocate your time, but you can't prevent others from owning the stock once it becomes public."

Not only that, he said, but long-term shareholders like Fidelity and T. Rowe Price would have no influence on the stock price because they had theoretically put the stock on the shelf, he said. "No influence whatsoever."

Over his Netflix career, McCarthy watched as the average size of trades became smaller and smaller even as volume increased. He learned that it was because high-frequency traders, guided by algorithms that initiated orders in fractions of a second, had become a larger part of the market. They set the stock prices, he told the audience.

"Go spend time with the big guys," McCarthy said, referring to large institutional investors like Fidelity or T. Rowe Price, and offering a couple of reasons for his recommendation. "One, they can buy a lot of stock, so you get a good return on your investment of time. Two, they're super-smart, they have great insights, so you'll learn a lot. Those will be more enjoyable meetings. But don't do it because you think it will help your stock price—it won't."

At that, Siewert directed his next question to Rodgers, the best turned-out of the panelists, with a red pocket square sticking out of his dark blazer. Siewert asked Rodgers to discuss how the SEC was thinking about the direct listing in relation to the traditional IPO.

"Spotify came around at exactly the right time in the sort of regulatory regime," Rodgers said. "Over on the SEC side, we got sort of lucky. The chairman of the SEC, Jay Clayton, is an ex–deal guy himself. The head of corporate finance is a guy named Bill Hinman, he's a deal guy from the Valley. So from a very top-down perspective, we got a lot of support for trying to do something new. That's sort of the good news."

The SEC was focused on protecting the small investor, so once Spotify got buy-in from the top, it took roughly a year to work through the agency's concerns, Rodgers said. The upside to all that work, Rodgers told the audience, was that one of the SEC's top officials that very day had referred to the way that Spotify and Slack did their transactions as "the old way." Two direct listings "is now a playbook we can follow, and as long as you know the secret sauce, you should be fine if you go that route," he said.

Siewert returned to focus on risk. Then he asked Connolly how he would rate the two direct listings from the perspective of institutional investors. Connolly said that both listings were "hands-down successful." For that reason, there would be more of them, he said. He called out a couple of places where he thought the investor community would adapt. One investor, he said, didn't understand Spotify's process but became one of the most active in Slack's listing. "That shows the market's learning, and the market's capable of learning," Connolly said, pinpointing ways in which he expected the direct listing to evolve, particularly in giving companies an option to raise capital.

Siewert pivoted to McCarthy, again speaking of risk and asking the CFO if he had any advice for the audience considering his approach.

"Looking back on your IPO ten years from now, you'll realize that not-withstanding all of the hoopla, it's just a financing event," McCarthy said. "So if your business needs cash, just think opportunistically about where your lowest cost of capital is, go get it when the window opens, and then if you have the luxury of being well-capitalized, you can think more creatively about your going-public event."

Connolly was asked about the evolving options for companies going pub-lic. "There's no cookie-cutter approach that should be employed for every company," Connolly said. "People are going to start saying: What am I trying to design? And it'll be more efficient than when Spotify did it, because they broke a lot of new ground." People, he said, "will feel greater license to modify things around their set of objectives."

McCarthy had one warning for startup executives regarding direct list-ings: communicate their financial results and the overall structure of their business model directly to investors. Companies can lean on investment banks to do that in a traditional IPO, but that's not the case in a direct listing. They must be willing to teach investors, issue guidance, and hold an investor day. "However little you know about your business, you know a lot more than they do," he said of investors. "If you're waiting for them to fill in the blanks, it's going to end badly for you."

A technology and health care portfolio manager in the audience, who had founded and sold startups earlier in his career, had grown frustrated with some of the narrative around direct listings. In his view, the context of Gur-ley's pronouncements hung over the Goldman panel. The portfolio manager felt that Gurley had oversold the notion that public-investment returns should be avoided by newly public companies at any cost and wondered if the ven-ture capitalist simply wanted the greater flexibility that direct listings offered around when he could sell his stakes in newly public startups.

After the panel ended, the portfolio manager sat next to the CFO of a company that had recently gone public. "I feel like I left so much money on the table," the CFO said. He showed the portfolio manager a chart of his company's stock price, which had continued to rise after its IPO.

"Are you kidding me?" the portfolio manager responded. Like other

CEOs and CFOs, this executive seemed to have come to accept Gurley's position without giving it a lot of thought. The portfolio manager explained that the rising stock price pleased the CFO's public market investors and his employees.

Company executives liked to see their stock prices rise steadily, contributing to employee morale and attracting a stable base of investors. Spotify and Slack shares had fallen in price after their direct listings.

"Look at Spotify's chart, look at Slack's chart," the portfolio manager said to the CFO. "Do you actually want your stock chart to look like that?"

"Oh my God," the CFO said. "You're so right."

As the conference wrapped up for the evening, and Jabal returned to San Francisco, she was no more in favor of direct listings than when she had arrived. There was still a lot of uncertainty.

McCarthy flew back to New York on a private jet with the leaders of Tiger Global.

Siewert had attempted to put a friendly face on Goldman Sachs's support of direct listings. But his questions about their heightened degree of risk showed an underlying skepticism that went all the way to the top of the Wall Street bank.

CHAPTER 17

Unity, San Francisco, February 2020

Roughly two weeks after Goldman convened its conference, the bank reported its financial results. It followed the release with a routine conference call, during which CEO David Solomon answered questions from Wall Street analysts. He used the forum to downplay the threat that direct listings posed to the company's IPO practice.

"Whether or not this is the best path or a path that could be open to lots of companies approaching the market is still something that's questionable," Solomon said. "The noise around this really disrupting the IPO market or potentially disrupting the economic opportunity for the leading banks like ourselves and a handful of others in the IPO market is overstated."

Solomon didn't mention that for years, there'd been concerns about the shrinking revenue in the firm's equity underwriting unit. And he didn't acknowledge the splash the direct listing had already made in the world of tech.

Back in San Francisco, Unity executives including Jabal brought what they had learned from the two conferences into serious discussions with their advisors. They were coming around to the idea that the direct listing would mean a lot of extra work at the executive level. Unity would have to couple it with a private fundraising, making twice the amount of work. That meant other options needed to be brought to the table.

Those options were at the top of the agenda for an October 16 meeting with Credit Suisse. It was not one of the top IPO underwriters, an honor that had belonged to Goldman Sachs and Morgan Stanley for years. But the firm's bankers liked to pitch themselves as creative thinkers who were flexible in how they designed transactions. They touted their role in the Google IPO as a display of willingness to think outside the box. And they were early believers in the usefulness of blank check firms, having helped Palihapitiya with his first offering.

Credit Suisse's Matthew Walsh, who led the firm's IPO and stock underwriting business on the West Coast, along with his colleagues Homan Milani, Kirk Kaludis, Scott Palkoski, and an associate, Danielle Zhang, met at Unity's offices for a critical meeting. The group had something to show Unity; it might come off as a gimmick, or it might just give them an inside track on getting a choice role on the IPO.

At its heart, investment banking is a commodity business. Goldman Sachs and Morgan Stanley enjoyed brand recognition, but most investment banks offer similar services. There's only so much space for creativity in capital markets. As a result, bankers often have the same ideas.

To stand out, they do things that, in the light of day or in the glare of the media spotlight, may look foolish in retrospect. Kwan's gift of a pair of sneakers to Ek in advance of Spotify's direct listing had landed without much embarrassment. More than one team of investment bankers tried to earn a place on Lululemon's 2007 IPO by wearing yoga pants to pitch meetings. Grimes drove as an Uber driver for years as Morgan Stanley angled for a lead position that it ultimately got on Uber's IPO.

This time, Credit Suisse created an entire presentation within Unity's software. They loaded it onto a hard drive and attached a screen, which they housed in a black box fastened to a cart of some sort.

Once inside and out of the elevator on an upper floor, the Credit Suisse bankers wheeled their cart into a conference room near Jabal's desk, plugged it in and pressed a button. The screen lifted out of the box. Palkoski had been working hard to create a virtual pitch and a demonstration of the bank's new corporate offices using Unity's game engine.

Once they had booted up the program, virtual city streets appeared on the screen. As one of the bankers navigated the program, the group watched as street-level billboards or signs expanded almost like a video to show a likeness of slides that were in the bank's hardcopy PowerPoint pitch deck. The bankers also showed a rendering of their redesigned 650 California Street offices, the blueprints for which they had loaded into the program ahead of time.

One person remembers Jabal laughing. The bank's pitch reminded her of a story from the 1990s when Quattrone, when he was running technology investment banking for Credit Suisse, used a farm animal in his pitch for investment banking business.

"This is even better than a goat," she told the bankers.

Jabal was misremembering. It was a mule. When Intraware Inc. CEO Peter Jackson was interviewing investment bankers for that company's IPO in late 1998, he complained that he would "feel like a mule" getting loaded up to go from city to city to meet with investors. The joke was a play on a company slogan that asked clients if they were "tired of dragging your ass?" to trade shows. The morning after he made the comment, Quattrone's group sent a mule to the company's offices, with a bottle of wine tied around its neck, and a message that suggested that if Jackson didn't want to drag his "ass" around the country, he should pick Credit Suisse. Intraware chose the bank as one of the lead managers of its offering.

Jabal may not have realized it, but one of the architects of that stunt was none other than the woman sitting near her in the room that day. Lise Buyer.

As the Credit Suisse bankers demonstrated the ease with which they could navigate the company's product, they extolled its virtues. And they explained how they planned to position the company and its stock to institutional investors. They knew that Jabal and Buyer were considering alternative approaches, but the team wasn't as enamored with the direct listing product as some Valley insiders were. They pitched a modified auction structure.

"It wasn't just we're doing a fancy light show, or a fancy video, or a fancy demo. It was, 'Here's the demo, here's what we built, here's what we understand about the product and how we plan to position it to Wall Street,'" Buyer recalled.

Most banks didn't let associates speak at pitch meetings, but Credit Suisse gave Zhang, the junior banker, a chance to say a few words. Jabal, the feminist, remembered her experience at Goldman Sachs and respected the gesture.

As the bankers walked out of that meeting, Jabal and Buyer were impressed. Credit Suisse hadn't been at the top of their list. It wasn't at the top of Riccitiello's, either. The CEO was inclined to choose Goldman Sachs and Morgan Stanley.

Jabal persuaded Riccitiello that he had to meet with the bankers. They had spent a lot of time and effort getting to know Unity's product, and they had good ideas about how to position the company's story with institutional investors, she told him.

William Blair's Carl Chiou was one of the next advisors to visit Unity's offices. Jabal had seen Chiou speak at the Palace Hotel in October and knew that he was an unorthodox banker who would bring a fresh perspective. Chiou had developed a strategy of using Blair's independence as a wedge to get into deals that would have otherwise gone to larger investment banks. Blair was a small, Chicago-based investment bank owned by its employees. Because Blair didn't rely so heavily on trading, Chiou held to a belief that there were better ways to structure IPOs.

His pitch was simple. Chiou told clients that there was an advantage to working with a research-driven firm like Blair, because it enabled Chiou to share data and opinions with company executives uninhibited by any conflicts of interest that larger banks might have. His involvement would also help clients evaluate the advice from the larger banks, which often persuaded inexperienced management teams to do IPOs in a certain way. In Chiou's experience, the benefits from larger banks' process didn't favor his corporate clients as much as it benefited the investors who were the larger banks' client base.

Chiou gave Jabal his frank assessment of the benefits and pitfalls of a direct listing. While Buyer was a bigger skeptic of the direct listing, Chiou evinced optimism. As he gained Jabal's trust, his advice would play a critical role in Unity's IPO.

■ ■ ■

Back in New York, executives at the NYSE considered changing the exchange's listing rules so companies could raise money at the same time they went public through a direct listing. If they could pull it off, exchange officials thought that the new listing might eventually replace the IPO. John Tuttle, an energetic NYSE executive whose Michigan upbringing led him to believe passionately in making finance available to individual investors, took to calling it the "People's IPO."

On November 26, 2019, NYSE officials filed their proposal with the SEC. The "primary direct floor listing," as the exchange called it, would allow companies to sell newly issued stock for the first time during the price auction that took place on the morning that shares started trading. As in a direct listing, the shares would be sold at whatever clearing price was determined by the market.

The exchange shared the news on Twitter, anticipating SEC concerns around competition and giving a nod to Commissioner Clayton's concerns about capital markets access. The proposal read: "The proposed amendments would not impose any burden on competition, but would rather increase competition by providing new pathways from companies to access the public markets."

The proposal would have to be fully vetted by the SEC, a process that would require the agency to approve the initial submission and open up a months-long comment period to solicit perspectives from the industry and members of the public. The SEC would then consider those comments over its own multi-month period of review. Only then would it render an opinion.

On December 6, the SEC rejected the proposal over small administrative concerns, leading the NYSE to resubmit its proposal several days later. The agency opened the comment period immediately and accepted the NYSE's submission later that month.

Though the rule change would directly benefit companies like Unity that wanted to do a direct listing but also needed to raise money, it was a direct threat to Wall Street underwriters and institutional investors. Two trade associations representing their interests moved quickly to oppose the measure. The American Securities Association, which describes itself as "the only trade association that exclusively represents the wealth management and capital markets interests of regional financial services firms," came out swinging in a letter by CEO Christopher Iacovella. According to Iacovella, "underwriters serve a critical function that protects investors and keeps our markets functioning in the most efficient and effective manner possible." He listed the critical services underwriters provided: they helped market a deal to investors, gauged investor demand, determined the clearing price, underwrote the offering, allocated shares, and, once the deal priced, lent explicit support by making a market in the shares, providing equity research, and conducting outreach to investors.

The trade association also took aim at the supporters of direct listings, painting them as conflicted players who overlooked the poor stock perfor-mance that Spotify and Slack had suffered since listing their shares. "The primary advocates of direct listings are private investors in highly valued 'uni-corns' that stand to benefit the most from selling their shares directly to the general public," the ASA wrote. "But two high-profile direct listings—Spotify and Slack—haven't worked out particularly well for retail investors. Spotify continues to trade at or below its April 2018 direct listing price, while Slack is down roughly 45% since its direct listing in June 2019. Given that many of America's retail investors ended up buying these stocks at high valuations from large institutional holders, the SEC must examine potential investor harm associated with direct listings."

The group asked the SEC to impose automatic liability under the new rule, just as underwriters have with traditional IPOs, holding banks accountable for "material misrepresentations or omissions" in the offering document for an IPO. The ASA acknowledged the SEC's underlying reason for encouraging innovation in the IPO process—to stem the decline of publicly listed compa-nies in the United States—but said that the benefit wasn't worth the cost.

"A rigorous underwriting process promotes accountability for all those involved with a public listing and it gives hardworking American retail inves-tors the confidence and trust to participate in our capital markets," the ASA said. "The SEC must proceed with caution if it intends to weaken investor protections through the expanded use of direct listings. Otherwise fallen uni-corns, like Theranos…would have been able to use this process to access pub-lic capital while massively defrauding America's retail investors."

On January 16, the Council of Institutional Investors submitted its letter, raising concerns that investors buying shares in direct listings might enjoy fewer legal protections than those engaged in IPOs. The trade association cited an ongoing legal case that it said was cause for worry. Slack's poor per-formance had led investors to sue, and the company defended itself in U.S. district court in California by claiming that buyers of its directly listed shares couldn't sue the company for omissions or material misstatements under the 1933 Securities Act.

"We have become more concerned that shareholder legal rights," wrote Jeff Mahoney, CII general counsel, "may be particularly vulnerable in the case of direct listings."

Slack argued that investors couldn't prove that they had bought shares covered by the registration statement it issued as part of its direct listing, because a mix of shares were sold. Some of those were covered by the offering documents, while others weren't. Slack also argued that investors couldn't pursue damages, because it hadn't put an offering price on the cover of the registration statement. Thus there was no way to determine how much the plaintiffs lost.

"If Slack and other public companies are successful in limiting their liability to investors for damages caused by untrue statements of fact or material omissions of fact within registration statements associated with direct listings," the CII wrote, "we cannot support direct listings as an alternative to IPOs."

In January, John Tuttle traveled to the SEC to talk about the proposal. One thing Tuttle learned was that the agency had concerns about some of the distribution requirements for companies that might go through the direct listing process. The NYSE official didn't want the proposal to fail because of red tape.

"I don't want to get hung up on this distribution criteria," Tuttle told his team once he'd returned to New York. He suggested removing that part of the proposal. "Let's file an amendment, pull it out of there, but let's also get much more specific in our filing about mechanics, based on their feedback, of how the primary direct listing would work, meaning one price, one time."

Over the following months, dozens of comment letters piled up at the SEC. Tuttle continued his dialogue with agency officials. Any verdict would come too late to influence Unity's transaction.

■ ■ ■

In January 2020, Unity executives met with Goldman Sachs to talk about direct listings and other structures the company could use to list. An advantage Goldman Sachs had over other banks was its long-term relationship with Riccitiello. Goldman didn't need to win over Unity so much as lay out a potential plan for them.

The bankers showed up with pitchbooks that looked the same as they had when Jabal was working for them in the early aughts. The CFO laughed, noting that they were still spiral-bound and only slightly larger. Some people in the room were struck by Goldman's lack of creativity. At least in that department, Credit Suisse left them in the dust. It appeared as if Goldman took it for granted that Unity would work with them. While the firm's investment bankers discussed various offering structures, it was clear to several people in attendance that Goldman favored a traditional IPO.

Interestingly, Goldman had been thinking about alternative approaches as far back as 2012. In a slide deck dated June 1 of that year, less than two weeks after the LinkedIn IPO, the firm's investment bankers presented other options for taking companies public. While they stopped short of advocating for one of the alternatives, the bankers spent three slides framing the potential alternatives and listing the merits and deficiencies of each.

The bankers acknowledged that "the volatility in outcomes in recent technology IPOs merits further discussion of the IPO execution process," noting that both investors and corporate issuers disliked the volatility. "There may be alternative execution strategies, although novel, that can improve pricing outcomes without negatively impacting the quality of the shareholder base."

A straight auction, "in theory, will reflect true demand for the stock," minimize the first-day price surge, and reduce "the opportunity to 'game' the process," the bankers wrote. On the other hand, an auction might discourage "thought-leading long-term investors" from getting involved because they wouldn't get an advantage.

They also listed a different process, one that required investors to submit orders with both size and price details but within the confines of the traditional, or "subjective," IPO process. A transaction with those qualities would provide a clearer picture of investor demand, increase confidence in setting the price when the orders were combined with "qualitative feedback," and better allocate stock to long-term investors at a higher price, the bankers wrote. Two potential downsides would be an increased ability to rig the system and the potential for overlooking smaller institutions.

The bankers also devoted some attention to setting price and allocation using an algorithm, but largely dismissed it because of the difficulty of calibrating the algorithm correctly and getting investors interested in an entirely new process. It would, however, likely "level the playing field" for smaller institutions.

None of the alternatives that the slide deck contemplated looked anything like a direct listing.

"It's been on the back of our minds for a while, really no one ever wanted to use it until John Riccitiello kind of had a very specific set of objectives for his IPO," David Ludwig, the Goldman Sachs banker, said later. "We effectively pulled it out of a box to kind of create the process that he wanted to create." Unity executives saw two benefits to doing something different. They assumed that a direct listing would create a fairer price for the company's stock. It would also give employees a way to cash in on the company's success quickly, rather than being forced to wait to sell until 180 days after the IPO.

But a direct listing wouldn't allow Unity to raise money, something the company foresaw being necessary soon. Unity would need to raise the money from private market investors. Doing so at the same time as a direct offering would create a crushing workload for executives.

At this point, Unity executives were leaning against a direct listing. Because direct listings were a new process, there was still a lot of uncertainty around the model. Could direct listings work for everyone? Or did Spotify and Slack simply have strong brand awareness? Unity's team met again with Credit Suisse on January 16 to discuss if they should go ahead with a direct listing or seriously consider alternative structures. On January 28, the bankers sent a follow-up email to discuss "public market alternatives" and attached a slide deck comparing the different paths to the public markets.

Before Unity's executives could make a final decision, they had a cocktail party to host.

Goldman was hosting another event, this time the Technology and Internet Conference, across San Francisco. Looking to piggyback on it, Unity executives invited several dozen institutional investors to an event at Unity's headquarters. It was an opportunity for company executives and investors to get to know one another informally. Since Unity had yet to file paperwork with regulators related to its future IPO, the party did not violate SEC rules governing how companies communicated with investors during an IPO process.

Nonetheless, it was part of a growing shift around how companies developed relationships with public equity investors. For decades, investment banks played matchmaker between hard-to-reach hedge funds and mutual fund managers and corporate executives who didn't know those investors.

The executives relied on bankers to identify the best investors and secure meetings in order to pitch their company IPO.

In the years after the 2008 financial crisis, however, many corporate executives began talking to investors much earlier in their companies' lives, when they were still private, as part of fundraising rounds that increasingly featured public market investors crossing over into private markets. The practice gave investors who had traditionally only invested in public equities a way to get an early foothold in promising companies and the potential for the higher returns that conveyed. It also put company managers in touch with powerful investors years before they would otherwise have had reason to talk.

Unity was no different. Riccitiello had been building direct relationships with institutional investors for years, a philosophy Jabal embraced when she joined the company. They'd grown enthusiastic about the investor meet-and-greet after enduring a series of meetings at Goldman's Las Vegas conference, where they held forth in a cubicle carved out of a larger room. It would be more enticing to invite investors to Unity's headquarters, where the company could show off its offices and demonstrate its technology on its own turf. Buyer recalled that Google opened its doors prior to its 2004 IPO. She fondly remembered that event and lent her support.

On February 11, dozens of money managers arrived at the Unity office, finding a restored warehouse building on the fringes of the South of Market neighborhood that was home to San Francisco's flashy tech scene. The invitees had been chosen carefully. They were on a curated guest list made up of those managers that Unity executives perceived to be the ideal buyers in its eventual IPO.

The reception area was dominated by a counter made of blocks of end-grain wood and, behind, a glass-and-steel staircase that led down into a high-ceilinged area framed by brick walls. The layout telegraphed that Unity was willing to use its money to create a hip space with appeal to Silicon Valley's most talented software engineers and its most discerning investors.

As cocktails and hors d'oeuvres were handed around, Riccitiello offered words of welcome and executives gave a short presentation. Senior Unity project managers mingled and gave product demonstrations, including one on virtual reality that took place in a darkened lounge, referred to as a cave.

This was a time not for hard pitches but friendly introductions that both sides hoped would be remembered when it came time for investors to stump up real money for the company's shares.

For Jabal, the event was something of a data-gathering exercise. She sized up the investors, judged their interest and knowledge of her company and its industry, and took notes. She looked forward to getting more data when Unity hosted another cocktail party the following month, set to coincide with Morgan Stanley's Tech, Media & Telecom conference, scheduled for March 2–4, 2020.

CHAPTER 18

Unity, San Francisco, May 2020

As the first week of March approached, investors watching the news began to cancel non-essential travel, and many made the choice not to attend Morgan Stanley's technology conference. A potential government shutdown of all travel was under discussion due to an emerging novel coronavirus, soon to be known as COVID-19. The early cancellations signaled that many of these investors would also not attend Unity's gathering. And as the cancellations poured in, Unity executives had a hard choice to make. Eventually they would cancel too.

On March 11, the World Health Organization (WHO) declared the COVID-19 outbreak a pandemic, sending stock markets tumbling and essentially shutting down the global economy. Corporate offices closed, and employees at all levels began working remotely. Far from derailing its IPO plans, the pandemic provided a tailwind for Unity. The customer base for video games expanded rapidly as consumers were either working from home, temporarily furloughed, or unemployed. With schools closed, all key demographic age ranges had more time for gaming. From March onward, Unity saw a significant increase in overall revenue.

While the decision to cancel the cocktail party would deprive Unity of another chance to meet investors, company executives hoped that they had done enough work to establish a strong base of public shareholders.

Despite the pandemic, Unity moved forward with its IPO and aimed for a September transaction. As they looked ahead, executives felt good about the timing. The onset of the pandemic had driven many other companies to the sidelines of the IPO market, potentially giving Unity a rare chance to capture investor attention that would otherwise have been divided among many candidates. Most companies wanted to avoid going public around an upcoming presidential election that many expected to be contentious. Unity's executives figured that theirs might be one of the few software companies to go public in 2020, giving it extra leverage with investors and its bankers.

In April, Unity officially hired Goldman Sachs and Credit Suisse. The choice of Goldman reflected the longstanding relationship the bank had with the company. Riccitiello wanted to reward their loyalty. Ryan Nolan, a managing director based in Goldman's San Francisco headquarters, managed the relationship.

Credit Suisse was a more unconventional choice. The splashiness of its October pitch had ensured its selection as the second bookrunner behind Goldman. It helped that in a deal involving two veterans of Google's 2004 IPO, Credit Suisse and its capital markets chief, a twenty-six-year veteran of the bank, David Hermer, had also worked on that IPO.

Credit Suisse was fully on board with Unity's vision for its IPO. Goldman, however, wasn't as keen on the disruptive elements that Unity was considering. Nolan was supportive, but some of his colleagues, among them David Ludwig, Goldman's senior equity capital markets banker, were more skeptical, according to people with knowledge of the relationship. While Nolan's job was to get close to the company and make sure it hired Goldman for its IPO, Ludwig was geared more toward executing the deal in the market. And he knew that his best clients, the institutional investors, didn't like new wrinkles.

Hiring bankers just six months before a public market debut ran counter to a typical year-plus engagement. Unity's executives kept their bankers off-balance by hiring them late and not giving them a direct mandate. This was a deliberate choice. The delaying tactic kept the banks in a position of needing to please Unity as a potential client. Investment banks typically offer certain services for free. Unity could leverage Goldman Sachs's and Credit Suisse's excitement over their potential offering to extract more advice before signing an agreement. Some on the Unity side felt that Goldman, in particular, would be more receptive to new ideas if they were still angling to land the contract.

The moment Unity signed up the banks, those banks could potentially become intransigent, fighting any alterations to their mandate to take the company public. Unity wanted to keep them on their toes.

. . .

As the discussion moved to structuring the IPO, Unity grappled with defining its key objectives and overarching strategy. Executives were seriously considering doing what they had started calling a UPO, a traditional IPO with some auction-like features. Google's IPO would again prove to be an inspiration, containing elements that Buyer and Jabal were eager to think about incorporating.

In 2004, Google required investors to submit both the number of shares they wanted to buy and the price they were willing to pay for different amounts of stock. Those orders are called limit orders, and they transmit valuable information to a company and its bankers, creating a record of demand at various price points that was known in the argot of the IPO market as a demand curve.

With more data at their fingertips, the company and its bankers would have a good idea at what price investor demand began to wane and could use that information to set the IPO at a higher price than they otherwise might. Was it worth it to price the deal at $50 if Fidelity, for example, was only willing to pay $49? They would also know if there was demand at prices above the IPO price to a degree that it could support the stock when it started trading. Google used this extra information to make informed decisions about its IPO process. Unity wished to emulate their strategy.

Large institutional investors much preferred submitting market orders, which did not contain information about specific prices, and often told bankers they wanted 10 percent of the deal at any price. Market orders allowed investors to disguise the true nature of their interest. They were concerned that information was being shopped to other prospective investors. Rumors about where large investors were looking to buy shares warped the market, especially because large institutional investors also tended to submit low orders, the Unity team believed.

In booming markets with hot deals, even large investors wouldn't get a full allocation of all the shares they wanted in an IPO. They thus would need to top off their position by buying shares in the open market, where the price would be higher. They bid low for the IPO in order to lower their average price on the position, knowing that even if they did so, their market power would grant them one last call from bankers. In that call, they could increase their bid. Behind every IPO is an elaborate cat-and-mouse game.

Unity wanted to reduce that jockeying as much as possible. They looked to design a system that kept that kind of information—a whisper network—from spreading among the banks' clients and unduly influencing the IPO price. They wanted investors to have to submit their orders in a way that kept them from other investors and from Wall Street salespeople.

As the company and its advisors evaluated the merits of emulating certain aspects of Google's IPO, particularly the bidding structure, discussions with Goldman Sachs and Credit Suisse revolved around meeting Unity's objectives to maximize IPO proceeds while not upending the norms adhered to by institutional investors.

■ ■ ■

Not everyone at Unity was on the same page. Jabal and Buyer were committed to the auction model. Their position was backed by Credit Suisse. Riccitiello also leaned strongly in this direction. But the CEO wasn't ready to fully commit.

"There wasn't a whole lot of data to look at, because there hadn't been a bunch of auctions," Buyer said later. "We just did as much of a deep dive as we possibly could, to be able to convince John. And what we ultimately convinced him of was that we could go down this road and jump off of it, right up to the last moment, if it looked like it was going to involve greater risk than reward."

The company's lawyers, both in-house and at Cooley LLP, also had some concerns. Although the process was beginning to look like an auction—Jabal, Buyer, and others had taken to calling it a "modified auction"—the lawyers worried that using the term would attract additional scrutiny from regulators. They worried that they would have to spell out the process in painful detail and precise language that would entail months of back-and-forth with the SEC.

Two of the Cooley attorneys were among those who had left Wilson Sonsini after Sanchez. One, Jon Avina, had worked on the Google IPO. That IPO had been an auction, and had required sometimes tense and sustained negotiations with the SEC. The lawyers weren't keen on going in that direction.

Referring to the transaction as an auction would send a signal to investors that Unity didn't want to send. Auctions often required bids to be binding, meaning that investors couldn't back out at the last minute. And their bids would be subject to a pro rata allocation, with everyone at or above the clearing price getting the same percentage of the total orders placed at that price.

Only when Unity's team agreed to make the process nonbinding, allowing investors to walk away from the allocation at the last minute, did the lawyers relent and sign off on the new approach. Nonetheless, executives wanted to make it clear to investors that they couldn't do an end run around the process—if investors thought it was for fun, they wouldn't play along with the company's requirement to submit bids with specific prices.

The company decided that if investors bid at or above the clearing price, they would get an allocation of shares. It stopped short of promising a pro rata allocation.

■   ■   ■

With the negotiations underway, Unity decided to bring a fresh voice into the conversation by hiring its first head of investor relations. The position would be a critical one, as it involved communicating with investors potentially interested in Unity's IPO and with the Wall Street research analysts who would cover the company once it became public.

Riccitiello and Jabal were having trouble finding a suitable pick after reviewing more than two dozen candidates. Then Riccitiello called up Richard Davis, a veteran research analyst with over thirty years' experience tracking and evaluating public and private companies in the enterprise software industry. Davis worked for Canaccord Genuity Group Inc., a Canadian investment bank. He and Riccitiello already knew each other through Davis's research efforts.

Davis wasn't looking to move, until Riccitiello sweetened the offer by promising him that he could run strategy. Reckoning that he had done everything there was to do in research, Davis made the leap. He was chatty and high-energy, a lover of corny analogies delivered so well that they left some colleagues in stitches. His voice would add firepower to the message already being spun by Riccitiello and Jabal about the promise of the company's business model and its potential for the kind of future growth that would excite potential investors.

At the top of his agenda was forging a more productive relationship with analysts. Unity's history as the seller of services to video game companies made it a logical choice for analysts covering the largest developers—Electronic Arts, Activision Blizzard Inc., and others. Those analysts knew the industry well and understood Unity's place in it. But Unity's executives felt that their business model potentially fit other industries—that the company did not have to be limited to any one industry. And they needed to convince investors of that fact if they were going to elicit a lofty valuation when it came time to sell shares.

So the new investor relations chief began to sound out his analyst friends at other investment banks covering enterprise software, a much larger industry wherein computer programs were sold to corporations. Unlike investment bankers, who tend to be hyper-competitive, research analysts are fairly collegial. As Davis pitched Unity over the course of many Zoom meetings from his home in the Boston suburbs, he found that the analysts he was contacting were open to his entreaties.

If he could convince some of them to see the company's potential beyond video games, it would lessen the influence of pure gaming analysts and prevent Unity from being pigeonholed. The company helped developers create and operate their games, collecting money from players who watched advertisements to defray their expenses or bought items inside the games. But it had also begun servicing the automotive, design, and engineering sectors, which used Unity's systems to create product renderings.

With Davis's outreach to analysts underway, Unity took the next step in its long-running IPO plan and prepared the ground for him to begin talking to investors. On May 20, the company secretly filed its first registration statement with the SEC. The document, later made public, said that executives saw an addressable market of at least $29 billion in gaming and other sectors. More than 1.5 million monthly active creators used the company's technology at the end of March, creating games that were downloaded over 3 billion times per month in 2019.

Though still confidential, Unity's submission was its first official declaration of its intention to go public.

. . .

Davis began hosting meetings with investors in a process known as "testing the waters." Typically conducted only after a company had filed its draft securities prospectus with the SEC, the meetings were another outgrowth of the 2012 JOBS Act intended to make it easier to navigate a public market launch. Under the cover of less formal meetings, executives could get a better understanding of how they should position their company in the market. These discussions with trusted investors helped ease any early jitters about the IPO process among Unity's management.

Unity had already been meeting with investors, thanks to the work that Riccitiello and Jabal had done to build relationships with them over the last several years. Now, with Davis's help, they kicked these meetings into overdrive.

Over several months, Davis arranged about a hundred videoconferences with a wide swath of investor types. On one end of the investment spectrum was Norges Bank Investment Management, manager of the Norwegian pension fund known for holding stock positions for decades. On the other were New York and Connecticut hedge funds known for trading in and out of stocks multiple times a day. By one estimate, more than half of the investors in these meetings attended the pre-pandemic February cocktail party. That was exactly what Unity executives wanted. Davis knew that institutional investors wanted to meet management teams at least two or three times before committing.

As Davis arranged these meetings for himself, Riccitiello, and Jabal, a familiar pattern emerged. Davis's gregariousness and his long-standing research relationships with investors overshadowed the first minutes these investors spent with Unity's CEO.

"Richard, dude," one person recalled a potential investor saying. "How are you doing? It's so great to see you."

"Hi, I'm the CEO of this company," Riccitiello interrupted. "Would you like to talk to me? Because I kind of run the place."

At first awkwardly and then more self-assuredly, Riccitiello used humor to deflect tension and break the ice with investors. Over time, such exchanges evolved into an inside joke between Riccitiello and Davis.

The meetings, however, were serious. As Jabal had done after the February cocktail party, Unity executives took notes after each investor meeting and entered it into a massive spreadsheet they had built. Each row listed individual investors. In one column running down the document, Unity's team wrote notes from the meetings and their initial impressions of the investors.

"Every time that we met with them, we went to the right side of the spreadsheet," Davis said later. "We would say, 'Oh, good meeting,' or 'They asked this question' or 'They were engaged' or 'Not engaged.' Those kinds of things. So that gave us a template."

The team fed these notes and impressions into a rapidly growing data pool. They sought out information about the investors' previous experience with companies in similar sectors, whether software firms or other gaming companies. One of the things they wanted to know was whether the investors had the kind of familiarity with the industry that would lead to a deep understanding of, and commitment to, Unity.

Davis filled the spreadsheet with data collected from the fund's public disclosures and other information sources: for instance, BD Corporate, an investor-relations vendor owned by IHS Markit. He and Jabal focused on portfolio turnover—a measure of the average length of time an investor holds a position. A portfolio turnover rate of more than 100 percent meant that an investor held its positions an average of less than one year. As the average amount of time lengthened, the rate declined. It was those funds with a turnover rate well below 100 percent that Unity courted. Executives wanted to attract potential shareholders who held stocks for years. Investors who stuck with a company long-term created a stable base of support that management could rely on when other, more skittish investors bailed at the first sign of financial distress.

The turnover data exposed some interesting trends, particularly around the holding patterns of the world's largest mutual fund companies. Long considered the prototype of investors who held stocks over several years, some mutual funds had in fact moved away from being simply buy-and-hold investors. The data showed that some of the largest institutional investors ended up selling shares quickly, particularly those they bought in an IPO if the price surged once it began trading. A lot of smaller funds with more concentrated holdings, on the other hand, tended to keep them much longer.

Not surprisingly, the ever-growing spreadsheet also showed that many hedge funds had turnover rates above 200 percent, meaning that they held shares only for six months on average. The company wanted to keep its allocations to those types of investors to a minimum.

Unity soon had a record that listed hundreds of rows it could parse for deep insights into which investors would make the best partners for its IPO.

CHAPTER 19

Unity, San Francisco, July–August 2020

For months, Chiou's importance to the transaction had been growing. With his help, executives had begun to formulate a theory that could inoculate them from some of the risk entailed in disrupting the traditional IPO process. They believed that they could reduce their reliance on the largest institutional investors by finding a meaningful number of smaller investors to hold Unity's shares for years.

The strategy was an outgrowth of a worry that Jabal and Buyer harbored, which was that some of the largest institutional investors might boycott the company's IPO if Unity introduced too many new elements into the process. Many investors had sat out Google's offering for similar reasons, and the lack of demand had contributed to the search giant's decision to lower its IPO price. Bankers often said that when investors argued for a lower IPO price or against the introduction of new features, it suggested that they might eventually refuse to participate altogether.

Chiou, however, believed that there was an untapped supply of investors that Unity could draw from to ensure a successful offering. There were dozens of smaller funds ready to buy in if only they could get an allocation. The largest underwriters often ignored smaller funds because they weren't big enough to buy millions of shares and weren't large payers of commissions to Wall Street trading desks.

More than one investor had chosen to spend less energy evaluating IPO investments because he couldn't get a big enough allocation through the investment banks to make it worth his time. Others joked ruefully that unless you were a client of Goldman Sachs or Morgan Stanley's hedge fund business, you weren't going to get a meaningful number of shares in any of their deals.

If only companies he worked with chose to allocate more shares to smaller investors, Chiou argued, they would have a loyal base of shareholders.

Chiou had built his franchise on getting to know those investors. The informal contract he struck was that he would advocate for them to get bigger allocations in IPOs, on one condition: that they act in the company's best interest. The moment the banker saw them shirking their duties as long-term shareholders, by flipping stock for a quick profit, Chiou would cease to put them forward to company management as loyal shareholders. In other words, the banker leveraged his investor contacts for the express benefit of the company.

If Unity's auction-like structure alienated a few of the largest mutual funds, like Fidelity or T. Rowe Price—something that Buyer and Jabal were concerned about—Chiou contended that smaller investors would fill the gap.

In early July 2020, the company officially hired Chiou, offering William Blair a bookrunner role, the second tier below Goldman Sachs and Credit Suisse and one higher than the co-manager title that the boutique tended to get on high-profile IPOs. The bookrunner role conveyed bigger fees and thus more credit in the fee rankings watched closely by bankers and their clients, as well as more influence over the details of the transaction.

"Their banker had done a really good job and stayed engaged for a long time and knew John and the rest of the management team," Davis recalled, referring to Chiou. "Here's the fascinating thing about the investment banking world. It's very much like a caste system. You're kind of born into that position." The only way to move up was by winning bigger mandates, one transaction at a time.

■ ■ ■

With his direct reports focused on the minutiae of the upcoming transaction, Riccitiello kept his mind on Unity's nearly four thousand employees. The CEO had been intent on using the IPO to reward their loyalty.

Riccitiello had a keen understanding of the Silicon Valley talent market. Unity was only as good as the engineers it could hire and retain. Due to the fact that Unity was founded in 2004, it was also relatively long in the tooth by Silicon Valley standards. Many employees had been with the company for years.

Riccitiello was obsessed with ensuring that they were able to cash in their shares at the moment the company entered the public markets, or soon after. It's why he and Jabal initially favored the direct listing, since it gave all shareholders the option to sell any time they wanted. Even though Unity was no longer pursuing a direct listing, he believed that its IPO should have this feature.

For decades, underwriters prevented management teams and employees from selling stock sooner than 180 days after an IPO. The lockup was intended to give the shares time to season in the market. It artificially constrained the supply of stock available to trade, providing something of a floor under the price. Too much supply, the theory went, could depress the stock price.

Viewed from another angle, the lockup gave an advantage to institutional investors over insiders such as venture capitalists, management, and employees. The hypothetical price floor meant that the IPO investors had some assurance, though certainly no guarantee, that they'd have a supportive market in those first six months to exit their position. It gave them a chance to book early gains, while preventing employees and early investors from selling until the lockup expired. It was this dynamic that Hambrecht had pointed out to Templeton all those years ago.

Riccitiello was loath to disadvantage the people who had built Unity into a successful company. This was why he pushed his bankers to come up with a solution that would allow employees to sell early.

During one meeting attended by its bankers at Goldman Sachs, Unity executives floated the idea of allowing employees to sell some portion of their holdings before the customary 180 days. David Ludwig, Goldman's equity capital markets banker, reluctantly agreed. He suggested lifting the lockup if Unity's stock price rose by a certain amount. Other companies had begun experimenting with this type of modified lockup, and Ludwig told the executives that he thought something similar could work.

Of course, such a lockup would still provide protection to the institutional investors who had bought into the IPO. They would have a guaranteed return before having to worry about additional supply pushing down the price of their investment.

That wasn't what Riccitiello had in mind. Was Ludwig suggesting that already well-heeled investors would get a chance to make even more money before his employees got a chance to cash out?

"Let me get this straight," Riccitiello boomed. "So people on the Upper West Side can buy a bigger house. I have people that are living in four hundred-square-foot apartments in Copenhagen. They would like to be able to buy a big house too."

The executives and Goldman's bankers went back and forth. The bankers finally conceded to the idea of some percentage of shares being sold on the first day of trading but pushed to make it small. The two sides finally agreed on 15 percent on the first day and then another 15 percent after Unity reported its first quarterly earnings as a public company. Some of the executives had pushed for a higher percentage, only to face strong resistance from Goldman's bankers. Riccitiello found 15 percent to be a reasonable compromise. Employees would be free to sell other holdings once 180 days had passed. The executives stopped short of allowing employees to sell in the actual IPO. Unity was aiming for a modest first-day gain and wanted employees to benefit from the higher price before they sold.

■ ■ ■

In August, Unity finally committed to doing its UPO: an IPO with auction-like properties. While Riccitiello had been on the fence about the modified structure, almost everyone agreed that the company should list the following month. The CEO was satisfied with what they had negotiated with their partners. And global markets had come roaring back from their initial pandemic dip. The timing seemed right to make a splash with an innovative IPO.

For months, Goldman's bankers had postponed meetings regarding the technical challenges Unity now faced in taking itself public. If investors were going to confidentially submit orders for specific amounts of stock at specific prices, the company needed a new, secure order-entry system. Much of the IPO process was still conducted by telephone. Salespeople at the investment banks called their investor clients to tell them that the company was going public and to learn if they were interested in buying shares. As salespeople learned about investor interest, they could often share that information with other investors, creating a negative feedback loop that artificially depressed the share price. To prevent this, Unity wanted to create a technological upgrade to the sales process. They asked their bankers to create an online order-entry system that investors would use directly without engaging in dialogue with potentially leaky salespeople. This would put an end to the game of telephone that Unity felt would skew their IPO price.

Under the existing system, when salespeople received orders from investor clients, they electronically entered them into something called Equity Bookbuild, or EBB, a product from Ipreo Holdings LLC. EBB acted as a central repository for all the orders banks collected from investors for a particular IPO.

Credit Suisse theorized that Unity could offer an order-entry system that gave investors direct access to EBB. Using a onetime tokenized login could allow investors to place bids without first transmitting them to salespeople, effectively cutting out the middleman. The bankers felt so strongly about this that they persuaded the Ipreo folks to pitch Unity on what their front-end solution would look like.

On Friday, August 14, representatives from Unity, Goldman, Credit Suisse, and Ipreo met to hear Ipreo's pitch for their product. As Buyer, Jabal, and Unity's bankers listened in on the phone, Riccitiello showed his surprise that Ipreo's solution was so rudimentary. He thought he could build a better product in-house, one that would reflect the company's values and attention to high-end software design.

Another participant put it more baldly. "This is a company that creates 3D software.... You can't have them throw up an ugly, kludgy-looking 1972 UI," or user interface.

Unity couldn't build the product themselves because of SEC regulations. But Riccitiello's point, that a system for taking orders would be relatively easy to design, stood. As callers peppered Ipreo employees with questions about the potential for other features, they learned that it could take weeks to make such changes.

Goldman had considered the design of a new order-entry system for several months but had waffled on committing to it until Unity's modified auction plan was settled. After the Ipreo call, Goldman engineers immediately sprang into action and put the finishing touches on what they had started.

On August 19, the Goldman bankers presented their solution. This order-entry system was built on top of a Goldman Sachs website that institutional investors used to access research reports and risk management services.

A landing page contained two simple boxes. One asked investors to enter the number of shares they wanted to buy. The other asked them to submit a price. If either box was left empty, the system wouldn't let investors submit their bids. Investors were encouraged to enter more than one indication at various price points.

Goldman's engineers also built a charting feature that populated a bar graph with the total number of shares demanded at each price. The tool allowed a user to move a slider up and down to see the resulting decrease or increase in total shares that would be purchased. In that way, it was possible to see how much demand there was, and which investors would be lost at each successively higher price.

"As Unity decided that this was definitively the path they wanted to go down," one participant in the process said, Goldman "accelerated the development to make sure it was all ready and appropriately tested and all that stuff ahead of its IPO."

· · ·

On Monday, August 24, Unity released its first public IPO prospectus. The cover page listed the multitude of banks who would be involved, with Goldman Sachs appearing in the coveted lead-left position, followed by Credit Suisse. The second line of underwriters, in smaller font on a black background, listed Bank of America, Barclays, and William Blair.

Bank of America's involvement was somewhat unexpected. For months, the firm's bankers hadn't been intimately involved in Unity's deliberations or done much to earn selection. But Johnny Williams, a senior technology banker and Bank of America vice chairman, was close to Unity board member Egon Durban. The two men vacationed with their families at summer homes near each other. Through emails and phone calls, Durban encouraged Unity to add Bank of America to the IPO group.

The document also disclosed Unity's largest shareholders for the first time. There was little industry surprise that three venture capitalists—Sequoia, Silver Lake, and DFJ Growth—owned roughly 50 percent of the company. A holding company affiliated with cofounder Joachim Ante, Unity's chief technology officer, owned 8.2 percent, while cofounder David Helgason owned 4.4 percent. Riccitiello came close behind, with his 8.3 million shares and options amounting to a 3.4 percent stake.

The document also showed the savvy of Unity's lawyers at Cooley. The prospectus didn't include any language directly pertaining to the company's modified auction procedure.

Unity's filing was quickly overshadowed that day by the public release of documents from four other high-profile software companies aiming to go public. Snowflake Inc., Sumo Logic Inc., and JFrog Ltd. disclosed their intention to sell shares in an IPO, while Asana Inc., a developer of project management software founded by Facebook cofounder Dustin Moskovitz, filed plans for a direct listing. Snowflake was a cloud-computing company, Sumo Logic was a software analytics firm, and JFrog made it easier to deploy software updates.

As if to add an exclamation point to the bevy of Monday's filings, surveillance software developer Palantir filed for a direct listing on Tuesday. The disclosure made the company the third to announce an intention to use Spotify's creation, following on the heels of Asana's listing the day before.

The flurry of filings surprised the Unity executives. Months earlier, they had thought that the company would be in a class by itself when it came time to sell shares to the public. Instead, September was shaping up to be one of the busiest months for software IPOs in recent memory. Each of the six firms—Unity, Snowflake, Sumo Logic, JFrog, Asana, and Palantir—competed to win the affection of institutional investors interested in owning software companies.

Snowflake soon attracted more attention than the others. The eight-year-old company operated in the red-hot cloud-computing sector, the business of renting out expensive data centers and their attendant processing power for a fraction of the cost of owning them. Over the past decade, the business had become a cash cow for Amazon, Google, and Microsoft as more and more companies and consumers moved their digital lives into the virtual world. Snowflake didn't compete with those giants as much as it complemented them, providing tools to companies to manage the data they may have stored across services or space provided by one or more of the other providers. In an industry dominated by an oligopoly of well-established players, Snowflake was a rare opportunity for investors to get in on the ground floor.

The company was run by Frank Slootman, a straight-talking CEO who was as close as the industry could get to an IPO expert. Slootman had already taken two companies public as a CEO—Data Domain Inc. in 2007 and ServiceNow in 2012—which put him in the rare breed of executives with repeat IPO experience. Riccitiello, by contrast, was on his second CEO stint at a public company but experiencing his first IPO with Unity.

Despite his previous experience, Slootman wasn't an advocate for tearing up the IPO process. He had briefly considered a direct listing and quickly scrapped it because it wouldn't have helped Snowflake raise the money it needed to fuel its growth plans. Slootman liked the traditional IPO process for the freedom it gave him to pick his shareholder base. Just as Riccitiello and Jabal had been curating a wish list of potential investors, Slootman had been lining up shareholders to buy into his vision for Snowflake's future.

Slootman was turned off by the prevailing argument then dominating the conversation about first-day stock pops and whether they were a sign of a broken IPO market. Bill Gurley and others calculated the damage of the first-day pop by comparing the IPO price to the first trading day's closing price. Gurley argued that the difference, multiplied by the number of shares sold in the IPO, was the money a company left on the table by underpricing its shares. Slootman thought that was a weak argument. In his opinion, the last trade represented a price that could be set by a single share trading hands, whereas the IPO involved millions of shares. Investors demanded a discount, reflected in the IPO price, for buying a large volume of shares, because the higher amount would be harder to sell. Slootman would later tell *Forbes* that the underpricing argument was "nonsense talk."

He also ignored Gurley's warnings by choosing Goldman Sachs and Morgan Stanley to lead a cohort of nearly two dozen investment banks underwriting the IPO. According to data compiled by the University of Florida's Jay Ritter, Goldman Sachs and Morgan Stanley were the two worst underwriters when it came to underpricing IPOs.

Media reports suggested that Snowflake would seek a valuation of $15 billion to $20 billion, making it one of the most valuable members of its IPO cohort.

But first the company and its peers would have to navigate choppy markets. By Friday, August 28, the NASDAQ had fallen more than 10 percent. It was the worst performance for the tech-heavy exchange since the week of March 20, when the pandemic and its impact on the business climate was still uncertain. Nonetheless, the flurry of August filings began to build enthusiasm for what many bankers, investors, and company executives expected would be a busy IPO calendar.

CHAPTER 20

Snowflake, San Mateo, September 2020

The IPO market gained a vote of confidence in the last days of summer when the highly respected venture capital firm Andreessen Horowitz published something of an update to McGurk's June 2019 direct listing primer. This time, though, McGurk's former colleagues offered a defense of the conditions that lead to an IPO pop.

Andreessen partners Alex Rampell and Scott Kupor spent 3,800 words and seven charts telling readers why they disagreed with the critics arguing that the IPO market was broken. "There's a popular narrative that evil investment bankers are intentionally underpricing traditional IPOs to steal from companies, lining banker pockets and those of their fatcat Wall Street clients," they wrote. "An IPO is far from perfect, but this narrative is almost completely false."

Technology stocks surged on their first day of trading because investor demand far outstripped the available supply of shares. Lockups and the fact that companies only sold a 10 to 15 percent stake in the IPO crimped the share count, they wrote, at the same time that a variety of investors with different goals clamored for shares. If critics wanted to improve the IPO process, they wrote, they needed to reconsider the traditional lockup structure, aggregate more of the demand into the actual IPO process, and be more creative in "blurring the lines" between public and private companies.

Like Slootman, the authors were also wary of Gurley's argument. They argued that comparing the IPO price to the trading price was akin to comparing apples to oranges. And they spent several paragraphs explaining the theory behind their belief.

The authors did give some ground, writing lower in the post that "without a doubt, free profits are stupidly being handed away to lucky IPO participants" who are chosen specifically with the expectation that they sell the shares the next day.

The post was quickly shared across Silicon Valley and Wall Street, becoming an often cited rejoinder to critics who argued that the IPO process should be changed. Among others, the VCs thanked Carl Chiou for reading drafts.

■ ■ ■

Over the following weeks, the IPO candidates ramped up their discussions with institutional investors.

On September 8, Snowflake disclosed that it had signed up two large buyers to act as anchor investors in its IPO. Salesforce Ventures LLC and Warren Buffett's Berkshire Hathaway Inc. agreed to buy $500 million in stock at the IPO price. Buffett hadn't invested in an IPO in any industry, CNBC noted, since he bought shares in Ford Motor Co. in 1956. The following day, a Reuters column said that Snowflake's IPO was "so hot it could melt," and that the backing of Salesforce and Berkshire could send "Snowflake's valuation even closer to the sun."

Riccitiello, Jabal, and Davis had been busy too. That day, Unity disclosed the first price range for its offering, updating its prospectus to say that it planned to sell 25 million shares in an abnormally wide range of $34 to $42 apiece. The range represented indications of interest the company and its bankers had been collecting from investors. At the high end of the range, the company would garner a valuation of $11.1 billion.

The week of September 14, 2020, began with at least a dozen firms scheduled to go public, which Reuters said was the most in a week since 2014. The nearly $7 billion the companies hoped to raise would be the most in a week since Uber went public in May 2019.

Snowflake increased its IPO range substantially early Monday, raising the price to $100 to $110 per share, a 31 percent increase over the midpoint of the previous range. The higher range reflected the orders that institutional investors were calling in to their Wall Street salespeople since Snowflake was using the traditional IPO playbook. Investors were now willing to pay so much for Snowflake's shares that the company's valuation had soared above $30 billion.

On Tuesday, September 15, the tech-heavy NASDAQ notched its second consecutive gain, rising 1.2 percent.

That evening, Slootman, members of his board, and Snowflake's bankers met to settle on a price and allocate the shares. Considering the strong demand from investors, the group felt comfortable increasing the price above the top end of the range. They settled on $120, a full 50 percent higher than the midpoint of the original range. Once the price was set and the shares were allocated to investors, Snowflake had raised $3.4 billion, making it the largest software IPO of all time and giving it a value of $33 billion.

As Slootman huddled with his bankers, a small drama unfolded at JFrog. Based in Israel and advised by Lise Buyer and Carl Chiou, JFrog's executives had come to understand that bankers tended to market IPOs with a low initial price range to attract as many investors as possible. Chiou believed that the practice anchored investors psychologically to a lower price, making them less willing to raise their bids. Securities rules also contributed to anchoring the price by requiring companies to file an amended prospectus when a new range exceeded the old one by 20 percent. Bankers didn't like to refile too many times, essentially capping increases.

JFrog had pushed its bankers at Morgan Stanley to increase the initial range, and even boosted it once to a high end of $41, but now that it was time to price the IPO, the bankers advised against raising the price much higher. Company executives texted with Buyer and Chiou that evening, gaining support as they debated the IPO price. JFrog finally sold shares for $44 apiece.

Both companies hoped that their lofty IPO prices would reduce some of the pop in the shares the next day.

■ ■ ■

Citadel Securities, the same trading firm that had handled the opening trades for Spotify's and Slack's direct listings, had been hired by Snowflake to perform the same duty. By then, the firm had become the largest market maker on the floor of the NYSE, with responsibility for opening thousands of stocks every day.

As orders began filling Citadel Securities' electronic systems that morning, Peter Giacchi soon realized that few of the investors who had received shares the night before were willing to sell them. At 10:23, Giacchi sent his first pre-trade indication. Snowflake shares might open between $155 and

$160. The higher price told the Wall Street traders watching for his signal that demand for the shares was outpacing the supply.

Over the next hour, Giacchi increased the price of Snowflake's shares with a goal of finding enough sellers to match buyers at an agreed-upon price. His indications said as much, climbing to as high as $240 for one share of Snowflake's stock. When Giacchi finally opened the stock, at 12:38 p.m., he did so at a price of $245. Snowflake had more than doubled the IPO price it had set the previous night.

CNBC broadcast the opening trade to millions of viewers. As the network's producers flashed a "Breaking News" chyron across their screens, an anchor, Scott Wapner, declared, "Snowflake is now open for business." Wapner quickly gave a rundown of the IPO's superlatives—the biggest of the year, the biggest of all time for a software company, the fifth-biggest of all time for a technology company.

The stock shot up to more than $254, an increase of 111 percent from its IPO price. Snowflake's IPO "is a raging success, to say the least," Wapner said. His comment showed that despite the protestations of IPO critics, the media was still conditioned to view a large first-day pop as a marker of an IPO's accomplishment.

All of a sudden, another CNBC colleague on an open mic blurted out, "Halted." An on-screen graphic showed that the stock's price had flatlined. In fact, Snowflake's shares had surged so much that it triggered a pause in trading known as a circuit breaker that was intended to provide relief from wildly swinging prices. Once the stock was allowed to start trading again, it surged as high as $319.

With the shares now trading, Slootman made the customary rounds for interviews with financial journalists. In a video interview with CNBC, he shrugged off a question about Snowflake's massive price surge. "This is just a hot deal, and we'll have to live with the consequences of it," he said.

Perhaps a company could sell shares at a higher price than it did at the IPO price, he told Reuters, but to suggest that the entire IPO amount could be sold at the price where the shares were trading in the market was disingenuous. "The idea that we could have sold all twenty-eight million shares at the highest price we've seen today is complete and utter nonsense. Markets don't work that way," Slootman said. "That's why this whole DL [direct listing] narrative and all the noise around it is incredibly misguided.... What an IPO process does, it discovers the price at which you can move your entire offering. And of course that's a much lower number than the number at which you can move a hundred shares."

When Slootman appeared on Bloomberg Television that afternoon, it didn't take anchor Emily Chang long to probe similar ground. "You left a lot of money on the table," said Chang, speaking in front of a small set that showed bookcases over one shoulder and the Bloomberg logo over the other. "Do you have any concerns that you have given the bankers a little too much here?"

"There are always investors that are willing to buy some number of shares at higher prices," said Slootman, in lightly accented English that gave away his Dutch roots. "As you know, the IPO is a price discovery process, and we were after a very specific set of institutional investors, people that can hold multibillion-dollar positions, that are willing to hold them for five to ten years, and also people that don't chase momentum, either up or down. So that's really how we landed at our price."

Slootman continued, the corners of his mouth occasionally turning upward into just the hint of a grin that suggested he found the debate humorous. "It's not unusual for prices to get chased up by momentum players, retail and so on, so there is a lot of noise to it," he said, beginning to laugh. "The idea that we could have sold the whole thing at the price we closed at I don't think is reasonable."

When the trading day ended, Snowflake's shares closed at $253.93, a 112 percent increase over the IPO price. Snowflake now had a market capitalization of $70.8 billion, more than double its value the previous night.

JFrog's shares, on the other hand, rose a more modest 47 percent.

■ ■ ■

Gurley's influence over the industry dialogue was evident in how the media handled its interviews with Slootman. For much of the day, the venture capitalist refrained from wading into the debate. Then, at 5:40 p.m. EST, Gurley fired off a salvo of Twitter messages.

"Some encouragement to comment on $SNOW IPO," Gurley began, using the company's stock ticker. "While it would be easy to do normal post [with regard to] mispricing, it is important to understand what is different here from other IPOs. The most important data is broad (40 years of under-pricing, 2020 worst year yet), vs. 1 company."

In other words, Snowflake was just the latest company to underprice its IPO. Jay Ritter, himself a critic of the first-day pop, found that the average first-day gain for the forty-four companies that went public between July 1 and September 16 was almost 58 percent, the most since 1999 if it was sus-tained for a full year. Whether it was overexuberance or underpricing, the market was as hot as it had been in two decades.

Gurley sent a second tweet praising Slootman and offering congratula-tions to a handful of the company's venture backers, whom he called out by their Twitter handles. And then he sent a third tweet.

"Outside of if the company/shareholders 'gave up' anything, the hand allocated investors received $4.3B is one day wealth transfer," he wrote. "That's an insane amount of REAL money. That, along with watching the theatre and drama today, it is HARD to say—this is exactly how it should work!"

Gurley wasn't done. "In many ways, $SNOW is the final proof of just how broken [the] process is," he tweeted. "Frank Slootman is a HIGHLY experi-enced IPO CEO. He knows the game, & pushed hard to make sure he wasn't short-changing the company. But it didn't matter, because the process is set up to deliver this silliness."

Months later, Gurley said that he had traded messages with Slootman and come to believe that the CEO's experience allowed him to drive the pro-cess more than most executives could when it was their first IPO. "I think he knows how it works," Gurley said, "and he is so fucking smart that he figured out a way to game their game."

CHAPTER 21

Unity, San Francisco, September 2020

With the Snowflake IPO out of the way, investors continued using Goldman Sachs's website to enter their bids for Unity shares. That Wednesday, Snowflake and JFrog shares traded higher and Unity increased its range to $44 to $48. This was a clear sign to investors: if they wanted an allocation of shares and were below the range with their first bid, they knew that they now needed to increase it. Many investors also received verbal feedback from Unity's bankers about the strong demand for the shares and the price that other investors were willing to pay.

Riccitiello had given Goldman permission to use Unity's increased range as an opportunity to provide selective feedback to investors. The bankers now told their colleagues in sales and trading that they could share information with their clients about how the transaction was going. That message: The bankers had many orders from good investors at the prices indicated by the new range. In some cases, orders were for prices even higher than $48. The company, they said, could reasonably price 20 percent above the new range.

Though Unity's transaction wasn't technically an auction, it was running something similar to what's known as a sealed-bid auction. Several investors worried that without knowing what other investors were bidding, they might end up paying the highest price. T. Rowe Price, one of the largest wealth managers in the world and an investor that often influenced IPO prices, decided it wasn't interested in participating in the company's auction. T. Rowe Price, an early investor in WeWork, had famously started stepping away from that company years before. "Some people didn't understand it," Davis said. "A couple people didn't like it."

Auctions tend to have two ways of paying off. There is the private value, which is that given to the asset by an investor regardless of what others are willing to pay, and the common value, or the market-determined price.

Unlike art or real estate, which have some value, or utility, to an owner that's separate from what the asset might fetch in a sale, the price of stocks is almost entirely a common value. Stocks can't be hung on a wall to be admired or be expected to keep the rain off an owner's head. An investor might think that Unity's shares were worth more or less than someone else, but that belief was largely worthless unless the market was willing to bear that price.

Investors feared that if they won a large allocation they might be saddled with "the winner's curse," meaning that they couldn't sell the shares at or above the price they'd bought them. The shares could decline, saddling them with losses. Nonetheless, Unity's blind process encouraged investors to do the hard work of finding a fundamental value for the company.

On Thursday, September 17, Unity's pricing committee joined a Zoom call after the close of trading to discuss where they should set the company's share price. Riccitiello, Jabal, and Davis were involved, as were members of the board, including Botha. Using Goldman's tool, which aggregated all the orders and showed them on a graphic, the Unity team saw strong demand at $52 going all the way up to around $55, before it dropped off at higher prices. Jabal and Botha pushed for a higher price than $52; Davis preferred $52.

Goldman Sachs told the team that if they priced the IPO too high, they might lose out on particular investors or risk running out of demand the next day. Jabal countered by reminding everyone of what was at stake. Unity was selling 25 million shares. Each dollar in share price meant another $25 million in proceeds for the company. Was having one or another particular investor in the company's IPO worth $25 million or $50 million or $75 million in lost proceeds?

Unity executives and board members also knew that employees would be able to sell the next day. They wanted to leave room for the stock to appreciate in order to deliver returns to employees. Some of them also didn't begrudge investors for wanting modest early returns.

In the end, Unity's pricing committee, which included Riccitiello but not Jabal, made the final decision. Unity would price its IPO at $52, an increase of just $4 from the top end of its already upsized offering. Unity sold 25 million shares and raised $1.3 billion, giving the company a market capitalization of $13.7 billion. Some who were involved in the decision, including Botha, figured that the company probably would have priced the shares below $50 if it hadn't been for the new order-entry system.

With the price set, it was time to allocate the shares to investors.

As they had done in IPOs hundreds of times in the past, Goldman bankers gave the executives a spreadsheet showing their suggested allocations to hundreds of investors. At the top, getting the most shares, were some of the largest mutual fund complexes in the world. Unity kept those allocations stable. It was the rows below the largest investors where they got creative.

Jabal, Davis, and others on the team turned to the spreadsheet they'd been carefully curating. It was filled with hundreds of investors, notes from their meetings with management, and the associated data on their holdings. By then, Unity's team had boiled their choices down to between thirty-five and fifty accounts that they'd identified as smart money managers and the kind of shareholders they wanted.

Two of the investors on the list were Artisan Partners and Gilder Gagnon Howe & Co. Artisan was a $100 billion investment manager based in Milwaukee that Unity, with Chiou's help, had targeted months before. Founded in 1994, it was a midsize fund known to the large investment banks like Goldman Sachs and Credit Suisse. But it often got ignored because it didn't pay a lot of trading commissions to Wall Street. It had developed a reputation with Unity as being made up of thoughtful, smart investors who were willing to chase growth stories at the right price.

Gilder was a New York–based wealth manager that got its start in 1968 when its founder, Richard Gilder, purchased a seat on the NYSE and began managing money for wealthy investors. By September 2020, the company was managing multiple billions of dollars, much of it focused on companies with high expected growth rates. (Twelve days after the IPO, they held 606,300 shares and 933,532 shares, respectively, according to securities filings.)

As Unity continued to allocate shares, it moved a large block of a million or more from a collection of hedge funds that Goldman had suggested would provide a liquid market for the stock on the first day of trading. Instead, Unity handed those shares to other investors the company considered good potential shareholders. "You can't do this," one of the Goldman bankers said. "This is going to be a mess. The stock's not going to have enough liquidity."

Ludwig, in particular, was adamant that Unity was making a huge mistake. Davis, who understood the world of investment banking, was able to push back on some of the claims. "We would do these meetings with the bankers that we actually got along really well [with], but sometimes they would say stuff and I'd be like, 'Kind of not thinking that's true,'" Davis recalled. "And they're like, 'Oh yeah, I guess you're right.'"

Such an exchange played out in the allocation meeting. "It was the whole thing like how much do we need to allocate to the flippers?" Davis said. "And I would say, 'I think we could do 10 percent.' And they're like, 'Oh no, we got to do more.'"

Eventually Jabal had to call Riccitiello to ask for his support in allocating a smaller than usual amount of stock to investors who would sell it quickly. There was some risk, but Jabal was confident that the transaction would be successful. Company executives had already won the battle over the lockup. Starting the next day, Unity's employees could sell as much as 15 percent of their holdings, though Unity didn't require it. The executives figured that in the absence of hedge funds selling the shares for a quick gain, the company could count on some employee selling to add liquidity to the shares.

"Normally in an IPO, about 20 percent of the IPO is given to the flippers, the fast money people," Davis said. "What the old system was, you kind of underprice the stock by a bit, assign 80 percent of the stock to normal institutions. Slightly underfund them or underfeed them. So then now there's demand from the 80 percent, and then that 20 percent flips the stock immediately. So they let the stock lift a little bit, flip it, and then feed the 80 percent. It's a great job if you're the dudes that just are down in the 20 percent—you don't do any research, you just buy everything and you make free money all day.

"What we did is we said, 'We still need some flippers because we're going to slightly underfeed some people for sure.' Can't give everyone everything. So what we ended up doing is shrink that to 10 percent."

Riccitiello agreed with Jabal. Unity allocated a smaller percentage to hedge funds. By the time the executives finished, it was late at night. They had something special planned for the next day.

■   ■   ■

On September 18, Unity's 3,700 employees, including many in San Francisco who woke up before sunrise for the occasion, logged onto a common platform within the company's systems to watch interviews that the marketing team had arranged with employees, customers, and founders. One side of the screen showed a chat box where employees could communicate with one another.

At 9:30, the thousands of employees were superimposed visually on a large screen above the NYSE trading floor, and they rang a virtual NYSE opening bell to start the day.

A short walk away at Goldman's 200 West Street headquarters, Benny Adler, the senior trader who had offered advice around Spotify's direct listing, was having trouble coming up with a price for the stock. Unity's decision not to allocate to hedge funds meant there were very few shares to buy. Investors were clamoring for those few shares that were available, driving the stock price higher than where Goldman thought it should be. Banker Ryan Nolan was nearly frantic at one point. "Oh my God, this is not going to work," he told the Unity executives. "You guys didn't allocate enough to the hedge funds."

Jabal asked Davis to check in with Adler. From what Davis could tell, everything was fine. Adler was cool and unperturbed, an air traffic controller in his element. He could tell that Unity employees hadn't lined up to sell in the opening trade; otherwise there would be more shares available to buy. But he expected employees to sell throughout the day.

That gave Adler an idea, one he'd used in the past to get stocks to open. He reached out to a few investors who'd received shares in the IPO the night before. Would they be willing to sell some shares in the opening trade? he asked. The extra supply would reduce the price to a more reasonable level, and investors would be no worse off because they would get a chance to top up their position later in the day. "I'm pretty sure that this employee stock is going to come for sale after the open," he told them. "You can buy it back."

After considering Adler's offer, a few investors took him up on it. With more shares available to buy, the pressure on Unity's stock lessened, and the price dropped to a more reasonable level.

As Unity employees watched from across the world, 3 million shares changed hands at an opening price of $75.

Riccitiello appeared on CNBC's *Power Lunch* by videoconference, wearing an open-necked black shirt in front of a virtual background with an image of Unity's banner hanging on the NYSE facade. Unity employees watched the interview.

When CNBC anchor Kelly Evans suggested that Goldman Sachs had helped Riccitiello wrest control of the IPO, his eyes flicked momentarily to something off-screen. He chuckled. Resting his right hand on his left shoulder, he explained for CNBC's viewers exactly what he had been trying to accomplish. He listed two key goals, using his hands occasionally to emphasize his point. Unity had designed an order-entry system to get better information about investor orders and had modified the lockup to give employees an opportunity to sell on the first day.

"Do you think this has gotten rid of the stigma around letting employees sell on Day 1?" Evans asked. "Do you regret not pricing higher, raising more money?"

"Look, I'm thrilled with what we have raised. I don't know about the stigma, but I didn't do this to set a precedent."

Riccitiello said that the purpose of listing Unity's stock wasn't to raise a large amount of money by pricing the shares at the highest possible level. The CEO thanked his bankers at Goldman Sachs and Credit Suisse for helping the company execute on something new. Riccitiello gave a series of interviews to other news outlets, telling Reuters that the company focused on data in everything it did. "The idea of working with an IPO system perfected in the 1920s just didn't appeal to us," he said.

Unity's stock price drifted down during the day, settling at $68.35 by the close of trading. The price represented a 31 percent first-day gain, right in the range of where the company wanted it to be.

Less than two weeks after Unity's IPO, Asana and Palantir held their direct listings on the same day. It was a busy few hours for Morgan Stanley, which advised Citadel Securities on the opening trade for both stocks. Morgan Stanley split its bankers and traders into two teams to handle the workload. Asana opened first, with a price of $27. Palantir opened later, at $10. Almost 41 million Asana shares traded that day, and the stock price only varied by 11 percent, according to data compiled by Ritter, the University of Florida professor. More than 338 million shares of Palantir traded, with a 24 percent change in price throughout the day.

Investors and bankers deemed both transactions a success, lending further support to the direct listing model.

In a late September *Wall Street Journal* piece headlined "The IPO Market Parties Like It's 1999," NYSE president Stacey Cunningham put the recent innovations in context. "There's been more innovation in the last two years than in the last two decades," she told the newspaper. "There is a renaissance in the IPO market."

■ ■ ■

In the days and weeks after Unity's IPO, institutional investors criticized the auction-like properties of Unity's offering. In one late September screed, Cathie Wood, the founder and chief investment officer of ARK Investment Management LLC, ripped off four tweets in the span of a minute to her hundreds of thousands of followers. With an empire of innovation-themed exchange traded funds, including one, ARK Innovation, that was on its way to placing in the top quartile of 2020 returns for similar funds rated by Morningstar, Wood commanded a massive following.

"Equity Dutch auctions were designed to democratize initial public offerings," Wood began. She continued, using the ticker symbols for Unity and Goldman Sachs, "Despite best intentions, this week $U went public in a Dutch auction sponsored by $GS that we believe missed the mark."

She added a second tweet to the thread. "Some of us who placed bids above the initial 40–44 indicated range, and then raised our bids above the revised 44–48 range, assuming that our bids would be filled, learned the hard way that we would receive nothing. Very few things surprise me in this business, but this one did."

Her third tweet attempted to add some explanation to her ire. "Apparently, $GS introduced a Dutch auction twist that did not require it to inform those who had committed to a price above the 'range' that the range had changed, unless the 'indicated price range' had increased by 20%+. Excuse me?"

It sounded to her as if Goldman was informing only its best clients. "I am sure that $GS disclosed this twist in many documents, but it never apprised us despite discussions with its sales traders of our clear desire to gain exposure to $U. Did $GS's highest revenue generating customers get the word? I don't want to be in that club. Just wondering."

Later that day, after speaking to Buyer, Wood updated her followers to the nuances of the auction that she now understood. "I stand corrected: $U did a Unified auction, not a Dutch auction, something completely new to me. With thanks both to my compliance team and to a longtime professional friend, Lise Buyer, Partner at Class V Group LLC, for steering me correctly."

She apologized to Goldman as well. "With my apology to $GS, which was not monitoring the order book before it filled. That said, I do believe that our $GS sales trading contact, with whom we interacted many times for updates, should have explained the difference between Dutch and Unified auctions. Lessons learned."

Wood wasn't alone in misunderstanding the process. Many hedge fund managers were angry as well. They assumed that if they were open and honest with Goldman, the bank would let them know if they were a dollar or two below the clearing price so that they could increase their bid. They were valuable clients, after all.

But Unity executives were so focused on the integrity of the process that they prohibited the bank from alerting its clients. As such, there were several investors excited about Unity's prospects who missed out on the company's IPO because they bid too low.

"You hear back-channel grumbling," Davis said. "No one picks up the phone and goes, 'Whoa, we're mad at you.' Because they wouldn't do that. But yeah, we heard a little grumbling of like, 'Wow, these guys really did a tight,' as they call it, 'tight book.' In other words, they really picked classic, whatever, long-only" investors, he said.

One hedge fund manager who didn't want to be identified said that Unity's process and the lack of a whisper network about order sizes and price would set up a perverse incentive for the next IPO that used the playbook. Having been "burned" on Unity's IPO, the investor would simply inflate his bid next time. If his analysis showed that a company was worth $50, he would simply bid a few dollars above that price to ensure that he received shares. If dozens or hundreds of investors did the same thing, the practice would contribute to the market froth that bothered so many people.

Unity's executives heard the complaints and brushed them off. The process worked exactly as they had expected. They didn't want investors who only thought a share was worth $50. Those investors wouldn't be long-term shareholders and couldn't be expected to buy more shares in the aftermarket to support a higher price. They were the very types of shareholders they expected to quickly flip shares. And Unity had no time for them.

"When Unity looked at it and looked at all the different creative ideas, kind of ranging from direct listing to IPO to all different types of things in between, they again felt confident in their position in the world," Goldman's Will Connolly said later. "They felt confident that the investors were going to be there behind them. They had team members who had been at Google and it had done things a different way. John had a clear set of objectives in mind and was able to find the structure that he felt best represented those. So, I think once we did Unity and people saw how it worked, both the combination of the kind of the IPO with price-specific limits from every investor, the blind book build, plus the employee liquidity on day one, people said, 'Oh, so there's more choices we can make.'"

Nonetheless, investors pressured the Wall Street underwriters to undermine Unity's order-entry system to reflect their criticisms. The underwriters' response to that pressure would set the stage for a massive IPO coming down the pipe: Airbnb.

CHAPTER 22

Airbnb, San Francico, November 2018

With the rush of September listings out of the way, all eyes turned to the upcoming multibillion-dollar public offering for Airbnb. Founded by Brian Chesky, Joe Gebbia, and Nathan Blecharczyk, the company had helped define the sharing economy and elicited intense interest from investors.

By some measures, the company was an unlikely participant in the going-public process. Airbnb had assiduously avoided the public markets, ignoring years of encouragement and rumors about its IPO plans. It had last completed a traditional Silicon Valley fundraising round in 2017, setting a valuation of $31 billion, which made it one of the world's largest technology startups. As it entered 2020, it seemed to have little need for capital that the public markets would offer.

The company's path to its IPO started five years earlier, in 2015, when Airbnb hired Blackstone CFO Laurence Tosi to run its finance operations. At Blackstone, one of the world's largest private equity firms and a publicly traded company, Tosi had helped more than triple the company's assets under management. (Tosi was one of several candidates Airbnb considered. Kim Jabal had also considered the job and even rented out her house on Airbnb to better get a sense of the company's model.)

Airbnb's hiring of Tosi, who went by "L.T.," led many journalists and financial prognosticators to gather that he would eventually lead Airbnb to the public markets. Over the next two-plus years, the CFO brought financial discipline to Airbnb's operations. The company trimmed its annual losses under his watch, reporting a loss of just $70 million in 2017. Tosi also raised new rounds of funding, including $1 billion in 2017, which gave Airbnb the $31 billion valuation.

Chesky, the CEO, didn't relish the thought of facing the scrutiny of public market investors or their demands for quarterly financial reports, which he felt took the focus away from building a company for the long term. Chesky worried about how quickly a company could change. In 2017, he witnessed Uber's board, including Bill Gurley, move to fire CEO Travis Kalanick after investor pressure and criticisms about Uber's toxic environment.

Chesky had enormous ambitions for Airbnb. He envisioned a company that would exist for a century or more. It was a perspective that made any decision to sell shares to the public in a particular year less pressing than it was to others around Airbnb, such as investors or employees who thought in months or years.

Chesky's foot-dragging caused tensions with Tosi, who had designs on taking Airbnb public, as well as members of the board, and employees who were compensated with options and restricted stock units (RSUs) that stood essentially worthless until the company went public.

Employees were concerned about a delay in Airbnb's public listing because the options also came with an expiration date, meaning that if Airbnb wasn't public by a certain moment in time they would expire. Chesky told employees and ex-employees, many of whom belonged to an active alumni group with its own Slack channel, that he would take care of them, but the CEO stopped short of making any promises. Options for the rank and file were limited—unlike Spotify, Airbnb didn't encourage an active secondary market for employees to sell shares.

Chesky commissioned a review of other large companies that had been able to sidestep the public markets, such as United Parcel Service. (UPS had a class of controlling shares that didn't trade publicly.) Then, by early 2018, he was ready to tell the world what he was thinking. On January 25 he published what was effectively a corporate mission statement. Titled "Open Letter to the Airbnb Community About Building a 21st Century Company," it indicated that Chesky did not endorse the short-term thinking favored by IPO investors. Instead of focusing simply on the needs of investors, Chesky wrote, he would be managing the company with all stakeholders in mind: investors, hosts, guests, employees, and the communities in which they operated. The idea was to run Airbnb on "an infinite time horizon."

Chesky also had more prosaic concerns. The company's technology systems were a patchwork built up over years of uneven investment. If Airbnb was going to exist for as long as Chesky hoped, it would need better and more robust technology. Old programs would need to be shut down or stitched together more seamlessly. It was the kind of project that cost so much money—perhaps as much as $1 billion—that public market investors would be expected to balk.

Other projects also needed time to bloom. As Airbnb's home-sharing business matured, Chesky had pushed into ancillary businesses. He launched an Experiences line, with Airbnb curating cooking classes, tours of local landmarks, and other activities that it could sell to customers already using its platform to find places to stay. He created a collection of projects aimed at well-heeled travelers wanting an upscale experience.

His vision didn't square with Tosi's outlook, and he didn't choose his CFO for a larger strategy role. Tosi soon left, and with him any hopes investors or employees may have had for a near-term IPO. Ironically, his success at funding Airbnb's operations relieved Airbnb of some significant pressure to go public.

■ ■ ■

It took almost a year for Airbnb to find another CFO. In November 2018, the company announced that it had finally hired one, having settled on Amazon executive David Stephenson. Stephenson was cut from decidedly different cloth than his predecessor. He was earnest, straightforward, and analytical, less brash than many Wall Street personalities, but very competent. Schooled at Montana State University, it was Stephenson's seventeen years at Amazon working under some of the best business minds in the world that brought him to Chesky's attention.

If Stephenson wasn't a logical choice for a company considering an eventual IPO, he was a good fit for a company that had sprinted for a decade and was now looking to set itself up for a long future as a public company. He brought an Amazon playbook that relied on data analytics to measure performance and improve efficiency. He planned to whip the finance department into shape.

San Francisco was cloudy and damp on the day Stephenson walked into Airbnb's 888 Brannan Street headquarters for the first time as the company's CFO, in January 2020. The large building anchored an entire block in the

South of Market neighborhood, down the street from the Rainbow Grocery co-op, a relic of when hippies roamed the city.

Though it was constructed in 1917 to house Eveready batteries, the building was now outfitted to the specs of the Airbnb cofounders' aesthetic, honed at the Rhode Island School of Design. An atrium lent a light and airy feeling, with desks arrayed on the floors arranged around it. A massive wall of plants provided a splash of green.

Once inside the building, Stephenson found an out-of-the-way office and a windowless conference room where he and his team could discreetly discuss matters. For years, Airbnb had relied on cloud-based enterprise management service Workday to run virtually all its operations. Stephenson found that the company's new scale and breadth required a more elaborate accounting system than Workday could provide. It needed to be auditable, and with operations in 220 countries and regions of the world and $40 billion in transaction value, Airbnb needed a strong system underpinning its numbers. The executives adopted Oracle.

Within days, Stephenson realized that the job of CFO would not be exactly what he had expected. Sometime in early 2021, a large number of options given to Airbnb employees would expire. Hundreds of employees would be left out in the cold: collateral damage from Chesky's reluctance or unwillingness to go public.

As Stephenson read up on the terms of the options, he realized that Airbnb would need to go public sometime around August 2020 if it wanted to avoid having to do something messy, like renegotiate them or hand out an equivalent amount of cash. That was sooner than Chesky had let on in the hiring process, or perhaps had even internalized himself.

In other words, it was time to start thinking about an IPO.

■　■　■

As Stephenson and other members of Airbnb's management team began to engage in preliminary discussions about what it would mean to be a public company, they responded to the early excitement around direct listings. Slack had already announced its intention. Venture capitalists and media reports touted the potential for more companies to follow the lead Spotify had set just twelve months before.

Sometime around April 2019, consensus inside Airbnb had begun to settle on pursuing a direct listing. The new process would accomplish much of what Airbnb needed from its public market listing. It would give employees and investors who had grown impatient with not being able to sell their shares instant liquidity, and it would give the company a currency it could use to make acquisitions. A direct listing wouldn't require Airbnb to issue shares. So existing investors, including the cofounders, who owned 30 percent of the company, wouldn't be diluted.

Apart from not needing money—it had more than enough cash and easy-to-sell securities on hand, somewhere around $3 billion—there was something else that Airbnb didn't need that a traditional IPO offered: a marketing event. Tens of thousands, if not millions, of people already knew the company's brand. They didn't need a splashy IPO or the media circus it brought.

As Chesky considered the direct listing, he reached out to his friend Daniel Ek. The two executives had become friendly in something of a Frat Pack of thirtysomething CEOs that also included Mark Zuckerberg. Among other places, they would meet up at the annual Allen & Co. conference and sing karaoke. Chesky would often promise to come and never show up, leading Zuckerberg to fashion a life-size cutout of him that he brought along with the group and propped up in an empty seat.

More than once, Chesky told Ek that he wanted to talk to McCarthy, but the Airbnb CEO and Spotify CFO never connected. McCarthy even introduced himself to Chesky at one conference, but the Airbnb CEO never sought out the Spotify executive for a longer conversation. Despite the growing enthusiasm for direct listings, Airbnb insiders had some concerns. Among them were worries about the kind of valuation Airbnb might attract in a direct listing. Having raised money at a $31 billion valuation in 2017, executives didn't want to go public at anything less. Doing so, Stephenson and others feared, would hurt employee morale and signal to other investors and competitors that Airbnb was having problems. It could snowball and harm the company's prospects.

Airbnb would soon set those worries aside as it began talking to its bankers at Morgan Stanley and Goldman Sachs, who told them that the company could go public at a valuation of at least $40 billion to $50 billion. That matched executives' own internal projections. The estimate had the advantage of leaving enough cushion so that if the bankers' prognostications proved too rosy, as they often did, there would still be enough cushion to be public above that $31 billion threshold.

Stephenson had been barraged by bankers wanting to meet with him almost since his first day at Airbnb. For much of his first few months, he kept them at bay, content to work through the early discussions internally. In April, he finally met with Morgan Stanley, whose bankers had been close to the company for years.

Veteran banker Michael Grimes and Kate Claassen, who had both worked on Facebook's IPO, led the team. Thin and wiry, Grimes knew seemingly everyone. Claassen, by now a rising star in the bank's Menlo Park offices, had blonde hair and a tight smile. She had gone to Stanford University before getting her MBA from Berkeley's Haas School of Business. She and Grimes had been close to Airbnb for years.

In one of the company's early years, Grimes invited Chesky up to his Lake Tahoe property, where the banker worked with a local property manager to rent out his vacation home. The duo flew up on a turboprop that was one of a line of Beechcraft King Airs, associated as much with ferrying cargo as future billionaires. The modest travel inside a nonpressurized cabin became an inside joke.

Claassen missed that trip because of her son's birthday, but it didn't hurt her relationship with the company. In the early years of courting Airbnb's business, she had hosted her home on the platform—as Kim Jabal later did— to gain a deeper understanding of how the company worked. In 2013 Claassen persuaded Morgan Stanley to give Airbnb a credit line of $80 million, and she was instrumental in the company's 2015 fundraising round, when investors including Baillie Gifford, Fidelity, Kleiner Perkins, Tiger Global, T. Rowe Price, and Temasek came on board. That early work earned her a reputation inside Airbnb as a banker who knew its business model better than most.

The Morgan Stanley bankers arrived at Airbnb for what would be the first official discussion of the future IPO. They made their way to Stephenson's small conference room, where he brought them up to date on the company's listing plans. It would be the first inkling Wall Street would get of it.

"I arrived and it felt like every bank was calling me every single week trying to get on our calendar," Stephenson said later. "But Morgan Stanley is one of our longest, deepest relationships, so that was our first big meeting."

Stephenson turned to other sources too. He asked a member of his team, Ellie Mertz, to broker a phone call with Barry McCarthy for advice about conducting a direct listing and managing the investment banks throughout the process. Mertz had worked for McCarthy at Netflix and had already spoken to him once about direct listings, sometime after Spotify completed its listing in 2018. Now she arranged a second call.

Mertz, who had served as interim CFO and been considered for the permanent role, had emerged as a key lieutenant for Stephenson. The three-time Stanford graduate—undergrad, a master's, and then business school—brought nearly fifteen years of experience inside Silicon Valley tech startups and a deep understanding of Airbnb to the IPO process.

By May 2019, Airbnb executives had reviewed the details of the Spotify transaction and concluded that it could work for them too.

With the broad outlines of a potential listing sketched out, Airbnb executives began to think through how they might involve hosts in the process. A direct listing would make it much harder to include hosts because of how it worked: the company would have no influence over which investors received shares in the listing. Executives tossed around ideas—a host endowment program, and other host equity programs that would give the company a mechanism by which to reward the hosts on its platform—but didn't settle on anything.

CHAPTER 23

Airbnb, San Francisco, June 2019

On June 19, Airbnb executives made their way to a French restaurant in the Hayes Valley neighborhood of San Francisco. Chesky, Stephenson, Mertz, and Belinda Johnson, the company's chief operating officer, had a dinner scheduled with Goldman Sachs at Absinthe Brasserie & Bar, a corner restaurant that suggested Paris in the early 1900s. Large letters spelled out its name in green neon script above the entrance.

Goldman Sachs had reserved Absinthe's private dining space, which would provide an intimate setting for a conversation about Airbnb's listing plans. Chesky had a soft spot for the French city—one of his favorite conference rooms at Airbnb's headquarters was fashioned after an Airbnb rental in Paris. This space also had the advantage of being discreet—it was separated from the rest of the restaurant by a curtain and had its own entrance off the street. Airbnb executives were worried about being seen with bankers and sparking a news story about its IPO plans.

The meeting was critical because it involved all of the Airbnb decision makers—it wasn't just the finance team and bankers. Chesky's presence was notable, as was Johnson's. The executive had been at the company since 2011 and was another key player in Airbnb's listing plans. She had initially joined Airbnb as general counsel and since then had grown into one of Chesky's most trusted advisors. Johnson also knew her way around IPOs. As general counsel at Broadcast.com in the late 1990s, she had witnessed the IPO pop that Citigroup's Doug Baird credited with sparking years of subsequent infatuation with stock pops.

Goldman Sachs's contingent was represented by George Lee, an affable Silicon Valley veteran who as the bank's co–chief information officer was the most senior banker in the room. For most of his career, Lee had been a banker in Goldman's technology, media and telecommunications practice, and he was well known throughout the startup world. Tech banking head Nick Giovanni, the lead banker in the Airbnb relationship, joined him, alongside internet coverage banker Jane Dunlevie, and Ludwig, the capital markets executive.

The Goldman Sachs bankers had brought printed materials to share with the Airbnb executives, and over the course of the evening they discussed Airbnb's various options for going public. And they offered their own ideas for how Airbnb could make their listing special.

Led by Giovanni, a hard charging but engaging banker good at forming tight relationships with clients, the Goldman Sachs representatives persistently probed the Airbnb executives' motivations and helped them think through a list of priorities that included providing liquidity to employees and setting a high valuation. A direct listing would provide instant liquidity to employees but might not help Airbnb reach the highest valuation. A traditional IPO, on the other hand, would likely deliver a higher valuation by artificially constraining supply. One topic that the group didn't discuss in depth: raising capital. Airbnb did not need the money. By the end of the evening Chesky was suitably impressed. Despite his long-standing relationship with Grimes and Claassen, Chesky began to think that perhaps Goldman should be the lead bookrunner for Airbnb's listing. Chesky began to form a close working relationship with Giovanni that persisted over something like two dozen meetings where Giovanni was the only banker in attendance. Giovanni was granted a pass to Airbnb's corporate headquarters so that he could come and go as he pleased, without having to stop at reception each time.

"It really, really resonated with Brian," another attendee said. "Morgan Stanley realized that they're maybe not in the lead anymore. So then there was this back-and-forth between who's going to be the lead bank."

By July, a small group of company executives had decided to suggest to the Airbnb board that Morgan Stanley and Goldman Sachs serve as equal partners on the forthcoming direct listing. The recommendation came chiefly from Chesky, Stephenson, Belinda Johnson, and Chesky's fellow cofounders Nathan Blecharczyk and Joe Gebbia. The Airbnb group felt that there were nuanced differences in how the banks positioned internet companies with the institutional investors that would be expected to buy Airbnb's public shares. They wanted the benefit of both banks' skill sets. Airbnb "didn't want to choose one and miss out on the expertise that the other could provide," according to a person involved in the process. Allen & Co. and Bank of America, the lead bank on a revolving credit line that was the successor to the $80 million line Morgan Stanley had arranged, which now stood at $1 billion, would round out the small group of banking institutions involved.

The next month, Airbnb's board came together to hear an update on the company's IPO plans. Board members including former Pixar CFO Ann Mather, Andreessen's Jeff Jordan, Sequoia's Alfred Lin, former Apple senior executive Angela Ahrendts, and former American Express chairman Ken Chenault were broadly in agreement that it was time for Airbnb to go public. For the details on how, and with what banks, they turned to Stephenson. The CFO gave his presentation, offering the recommendation that the larger group had settled on to make the two banks equal partners.

The idea was unconventional. Wall Street banks competed vigorously to be the lead bank on a deal. Banks may have shared equal duties and fees in the past, but common wisdom suggested that a company only wanted one bank to be in the driver's seat for a transaction—to cut down on potential communication breakdowns or interbank squabbling. The rivalry between Goldman Sachs and Morgan Stanley was well known throughout the industry, and some of the board members worried that the tension between the two banks would distract from the direct listing plans. The board wasn't thrilled with the idea of making them equal partners. Directors pushed the IPO group to choose one lead bank.

■ ■ ■

In September, Grimes, Claassen, and Vice Chairman Colin Stewart visited Airbnb's office to present to a small group of managers including Chesky, Stephenson, Johnson, and Mertz. They assembled in a conference room, off Airbnb's atrium, that had a symbolic past. It was one of Chesky's favorite rooms, where the Airbnb CEO huddled with bankers in 2015 to prepare for a fundraising meeting with investors. As he prepared to host investors at the time, the CEO and former design student fiddled with the lighting in the room. A series of hanging lights hung too low, the founder worried, and he asked his team to raise them.

Whether it was the lighting, Morgan Stanley's advice, or something else, Airbnb successfully raised $1.5 billion at a massively inflated valuation. The startup went from a previous valuation of $10 billion to more than $25 billion with investments from General Atlantic, Tiger Global, and Hillhouse Capital.

On this day in September 2019, the Morgan Stanley bankers spent more than ninety minutes explaining how they would position the company in the marketplace. The bankers told the Airbnb executives that they would position the firm as a one-of-a-kind, category-defying business.

Airbnb formally launched the project that month, giving it the code name "Project Constellation." On September 19, it took the unusual step of announcing its intentions. "Airbnb, Inc. announced today," the one-line statement said, "that it expects to become a publicly-traded company during 2020."

Less than two weeks later, Chesky once again grew anxious about the ouster of a startup executive, according to someone who was in contact with him at the time, when WeWork founder Adam Neumann was removed after the company's IPO process collapsed over questions about his partying and WeWork's financial position. Chesky confronted his bankers at Morgan Stanley and Goldman Sachs, trying to get answers about how WeWork's IPO had gone so wrong.

"He was fairly destabilized by it," the person said. "He was as shaken as any entrepreneur I saw, like, 'This is what's going to happen to a founder when they start an IPO process. Wait a minute. This guy went from on top of the world to losing his company.'"

■ ■ ■

Nonetheless, Airbnb pressed ahead with its listing plans throughout the fall.

With sign-off from the board, a small team gathered to write the securities prospectus. Morgan Stanley wrote a draft, unbidden, and offered it to Airbnb as a template, as did Airbnb's communications team. Ultimately the group chose to create a third document. An early drafting group included Grimes and Claassen; Giovanni and Dunlevie from Goldman Sachs, and Airbnb's Stephenson and Mertz. Chesky would occasionally join and offer feedback.

A feasible timeline began to emerge. If Airbnb could file its prospectus confidentially with the SEC before the end of the year and negotiations with the agency were relatively straightforward, Airbnb could release the document publicly in March. That would allow it to include a fully audited 2019 financial picture. A briefing day for Wall Street analysts could then take place around April 15, with Airbnb aiming to go public on or around May 14.

The timeline followed common IPO practice. The date of the IPO, in mid-May, was chosen specifically for the benefits it conferred to the company listing its shares. It was roughly halfway through the second quarter, giving Airbnb time to update investors about the previous quarter without having too much material nonpublic information about the current quarter. Too early and the company might struggle to present its numbers accurately. Much later and investors might grow wary that there was information about the company's performance they didn't know.

If Airbnb missed the May date, its management team could shoot for mid- to early August—again, roughly halfway through the quarter—and still go public before employee options expired.

Executives conducted an extensive request-for-proposal process with both the NYSE and NASDAQ around which exchange would best fit the company's listing. The NYSE was emerging as the market leader in direct listings, having already hosted Spotify's 2018 listing and Slack's June 2019 transaction. NASDAQ, on the other hand, was still looking to break in. It was the exchange of choice for some of the world's biggest tech companies, including Alphabet, Amazon, and Facebook, but McCarthy's choice of the NYSE had put the larger exchange in front. After conducting some research into the NASDAQ's ability to conduct a direct listing, Airbnb settled on NASDAQ as a better fit.

As the 2019 holidays approached, Airbnb wasn't quite ready to submit the prospectus that the executives had been writing. The executives didn't know how soon their plans would change.

■ ■ ■

Heading into 2020, Airbnb's future looked bright. Stephenson, his team, and the company's bankers were close to being able to officially kick off their IPO process with a confidential submission to the SEC. The company had billions of dollars in cash at hand, seemingly more than enough to fund its growth plans and withstand any market gyrations.

By February, Airbnb executives were two to three weeks away from having a prospectus they could file with the SEC when cancellations began to tick up in China—one of Airbnb's largest markets—as the spread of COVID-19 shut down travel. Elsewhere across the globe, Airbnb's platform showed that fewer travelers were taking to the company's platform to book trips. Those who had already booked Airbnbs began to cancel their reservations.

As February bled into March, Airbnb approached an existential crisis just as Unity received cancellations for its second investor cocktail event. In March, cancellations on Airbnb's website surged with the WHO's announcement that the outbreak would be classified as a pandemic.

Stephenson's finance team convened Zoom meetings to strategize about how the company could make it through the pandemic. The models showed a disturbing trend. Airbnb was still spending liberally to get tour guides and cooking classes to become a meaningful part of the company's growth story. Even grander ambitions, such as Studios, an effort to create original video programming centered around travel, and little-understood efforts to improve the experience of traveling to and from an Airbnb, also drained the company of cash. Cancellations were then high, and bookings were falling rapidly. Between those two factors and spending on other projects, Airbnb might go through $1 billion a quarter in cash. Finance executives debated possible outcomes.

During one meeting, Christopher Lehane, the head of Airbnb's global policy and public affairs department, was just perplexed. A veteran of the Clinton White House, Lehane had joined the company in 2015. He was one of Airbnb's longest-tenured senior executives, responsible for shaping the company's image with hosts, guests, and the media.

Lehane couldn't understand what Stephenson's team was trying to accomplish. Executives couldn't model a pandemic. Models are based on an empirical framework, but Airbnb hadn't ever experienced a pandemic before. How long would it last? What percentage of people would continue to travel? The answers to those questions would help the finance team understand what it needed to do to conserve Airbnb's cash. But the answers were unknowable.

After some urging, Chesky joined the call. As he listened to the finance executives debate the merits of the various options, he came to a decision. You can't model this kind of thing, Chesky said, according to the recollections of a person on the call. "We are not a tobacco company. We should do what is in the best interest of public health. Let's not put anyone in a position of choosing between travel and health—especially because it could lead to the spreading of the virus to communities. We will need to find a way to use our cash to try to help hosts."

Airbnb made the decision to provide guests who had booked stays before the WHO's declaration with full refunds if they wanted to cancel. The decision would negatively impact hosts who had come to count on the income their rentals brought in. Many had already collected down payments for future trips.

On March 11, Greg Greeley, then the president of Airbnb's Homes division, wrote a post on the company's website to explain how management was responding to the pandemic. In the sixth paragraph, Greeley attempted to sound an empathic note: "When a crisis like COVID-19 hits, we know that it doesn't just impact us as a company, but also the individual stakeholders within our community: the hosts who rely on their Airbnb income, and guests whose travel plans have been disrupted. We are committed to doing everything we can to fairly support both parties, consistent with how this two-sided marketplace works."

Two paragraphs down, Greeley said guests could invoke a little-used clause in their rental contracts called the "extenuating circumstances policy" to cancel their reservations and get a full refund. Greeley also told hosts that it wouldn't leave them out in the cold. "We know our hosts depend on the economics generated through the Airbnb platform," he said, though he stopped short of saying how the company might help them.

Despite the turmoil, Airbnb executives continued working on the company's listing. On March 13, Morgan Stanley bankers and Airbnb executives met to continue drafting the prospectus. But that weekend, the difficult decision was made to shelve the direct listing plans. Airbnb needed to focus on managing through the pandemic.

With reservations plummeting and the future uncertain, the company would need money. Its objectives for entering the public markets had dramatically changed. It would have to scrap the direct listing and rewrite its prospectus.

CHAPTER 24

Airbnb, San Francisco, March 2020

Over the following weeks, Airbnb's board started meeting more regularly, gathering on Sundays to prepare for the coming week. Directors including Lin, Jordan, and Chenault put the IPO plans aside and focused on helping the management team shore up the business. At the top of the list was raising more money.

The company wasn't yet in dire need of cash—it had the multiple billions it had entered the pandemic with, as well as the $1 billion line of credit. Stephenson's calculations suggested that Airbnb's rate of burning cash would put it dangerously short by the end of the year. The company was also set to lose something like $150 million from the cancellations it had allowed.

It still had to think about hosts. The company had acted quickly to offer guests penalty-free cancellations, and now it was time to consider the hosts, who were set to lose more than $1 billion. But how much should Airbnb raise? Stephenson and his team figured that the company probably needed an extra $1.5 billion to cross the chasm and live to see another day. The models put it right on the edge. No one wanted to be forced to go back to the market for more money at a later date, making $2 billion a conservative estimate.

On March 19, CNBC broke the news that Airbnb was fielding "significant" offers from investors including venture funds, private equity investors, and even sovereign wealth funds. Ron Conway, an early investor, and a frequent advisor to Chesky, spoke to the news network for its story. He confirmed that he had been referring them to Airbnb's management team.

"Those investors are calling me saying, I hope Airbnb is raising right now because if they are, I want a seat at the table," Conway told CNBC. "They're saying, Coming out of this downturn, it's going to be companies like Airbnb that will be huge, huge market performers."

Not surprisingly, Airbnb executives agreed with Conway's observation. By some of the investors' estimates, Airbnb was worth roughly two-thirds or less of what it had been valued at in 2017. The company's executive felt that at some point, a vaccine would be developed, and travel would rebound. Airbnb would be well placed to take advantage and shouldn't settle for overly onerous terms.

Board members were less sanguine. Some wanted the company to move faster to take advantage of the investor interest, which, though still in its early stages, appeared to the Airbnb representatives to be robust. Airbnb executives got helpful financial advice behind the scenes from Lin, who had been the CFO at the online shoe website Zappos before getting into venture capital. Lin felt good about Airbnb's prospects and urged the management team to bide their time. The board met that week to review its options.

The company was getting offers that ran the gamut from a straight equity infusion all the way to straight debt. In all, Airbnb fielded about thirty offers of one sort or another. One option was a convertible bond that used earlier convertible transactions for Spotify and Uber as a template. The debt would turn into equity at some discount to the IPO price. Many of the investors saw an opportunity to make an investment in the home-sharing site at fire-sale prices, figuring that Airbnb's need for cash would give them leverage.

Chesky was almost offended at some of the offers, according to a person who spoke with him around that time. The CEO viewed many of them as bets that Airbnb would struggle rather than as a show of support for the company's management team at a difficult time. Some investors even considered demanding a pledge from Chesky to add a member of the management team to help the first-time CEO navigate the pandemic. He was opposed.

Chesky was adamant that he didn't want to take a bad deal if he could help it. "In a great way, Brian's instinct was, 'I don't want to accept these terms,'" the person who spoke to him said.

By March 22, when Airbnb's board met again, directors and the company's management team agreed that it was time to move forward with some of the investors.

. . .

On Monday, March 23, the company proactively sought out deal partners. A person close to the board put a call in to Sixth Street, the credit-investing arm of TPG Capital. Sixth Street was among a growing class of investors who made their money in the private credit markets, using money raised from public pensions, sovereign wealth funds, and wealthy individuals to make risky business loans to companies that had once been made by banks. The industry had blossomed after rules passed in the wake of the financial crisis discouraged national banks from making similar loans.

Sixth Street was used to the rough-and-tumble world of corporate debt markets more than it was to the venture capital industry that prided itself on being loyal supporters of management teams.

But Sixth Street had billions of dollars it wanted to put to work, and Airbnb was on a list it had created of about fifty pandemic-era targets. Sixth Street had been trying to get through to the company but wasn't getting much traction. CEO Alan Waxman, a former Goldman Sachs partner who had gone to the University of Pennsylvania with Ludwig, put a call in to his old friend. When Sixth Street got the call from Airbnb, its executives sprang into action.

One of the first things Waxman did was call his colleagues at TPG. Sixth Street was in the process of separating from TPG, which was already an investor in Airbnb, and Waxman didn't want to anger his colleagues elsewhere at the firm. Sixth Street quickly heard back that it could move ahead.

Later that day or the next, Sixth Street executives contacted bankers at both Goldman Sachs and Morgan Stanley to let them know that they were working on a deal. Over the following days, Sixth Street shared an initial term sheet with Airbnb's bankers. Due in part to the close relationship between Waxman, Ludwig and other bankers at Goldman Sachs whom Waxman had worked with, Sixth Street focused its initial efforts on working through that investment bank.

After several days of going back and forth with Goldman bankers, Sixth Street had a more formalized term sheet. The investment firm proposed a $1 billion term loan and another $500 million of higher-interest debt with warrants. The warrants, a type of financial instrument that converts into stock at an agreed-upon price, would give Sixth Street a potential upside on the deal. It would also allow the lender to lower Airbnb's interest payments.

With a formal term sheet ironed out, Waxman brought in private equity firm Silver Lake Partners and co-CEO Egon Durban. Durban and Waxman, among other finance types, were waiting out the pandemic at their vacation homes in Hawaii, just down the road from each other near Kuki'o Beach on Hawaii's Big Island. After quarantining for two weeks, the two men and others in their industry had been socializing in person. Goldman Sachs banker Gregg Lemkau was there. Billionaire tech founder Michael Dell and Spotify CFO Barry McCarthy owned properties on the Big Island too.

Waxman reckoned that adding a partner like Durban, who brought his own industry contacts, could only increase the chances of Airbnb accepting his terms. Durban had already considered an investment in Airbnb. In mid-March, Goldman's Nick Giovanni had asked Lemkau, who had a close relationship with Durban, to call the Silver Lake executive to see if he would consider an investment in Airbnb. Both bankers had helped sell Skype to Silver Lake in 2009 and then assisted Durban in selling it two years later. They reunited in early 2020, when Silver Lake invested $1 billion into Twitter. When Lemkau called Durban and asked him to consider it, Durban started laughing. "We just had Investment Committee," Durban told Lemkau. "I just told my firm that's exactly the kind of thing we're not going to invest in. We're not going to invest in one of these money-losing or money-burning companies right in the middle of a pandemic."

"Look, I totally get it," Lemkau countered, "but I've known you long enough. And I know you love iconic founders. You backed Michael Dell. You backed Ari [Emanuel]. You backed Jack Dorsey at Twitter. Brian Chesky is that guy. You've got to at least think about it."

A few days later Durban called Lemkau back and told him he would consider it. Durban and his Silver Lake colleagues could see that there would be attractive investment opportunities in travel companies that would eventually bounce back after being pummeled by the pandemic.

Initially Durban and his Silver Lake colleagues considered a convertible debt deal that Goldman was putting together. The growth team led by David Trujillo at TPG, which already owned a small stake in Airbnb, and Dragoneer Investment Group had emerged as two among a small group of investors willing to pony up cash for a convertible bond. But by Friday, March 27, Silver Lake was leaning against it.

That day, Waxman called Durban about his deal. This one would be straight debt, secured by a promise from Airbnb to repay it at favorable terms, plus some warrants that would act as a bonus if Airbnb came back from the brink, Waxman explained. "Is this something you'd be interested in?" he asked Durban.

Later that day, Durban texted Waxman to tell him he was in. He had been convinced by the deal's lower risk parameters. It was much safer than Silver Lake's usual strategy of buying an equity stake, and even preferable to the convertible deal that others were putting together.

On Saturday, March 28, Goldman's bankers introduced the investor group to Krishna Rao, Airbnb's global head of corporate and business development. The parties got to work finalizing a term sheet. On Sunday, Sixth Street and Silver Lake signed a nondisclosure agreement and began what would have to be a quick due diligence process.

Stephenson had set a deadline of April 5, when the board would meet next, for best and final bids to be submitted.

■ ■ ■

As Airbnb fielded various offers, the company had split its bankers into two work streams. Goldman Sachs's bankers doubted that Airbnb could raise straight debt at attractive terms, especially with Bank of America's credit line, which limited the company's options. The bankers continued talking to TPG and Dragoneer about the convertible bond. Morgan Stanley, on the other hand, thought it could get a debt deal done. The firm's leveraged finance bankers had found success arranging bond deals for technology companies without any profits, like Airbnb, and thought they could raise money from the same institutional investors who would take a position in the company's stock. As stock investors, they were betting on growth and Airbnb's eventual profitability. Morgan Stanley thought it could persuade them to make a similar wager on debt.

If they could pull it off, the terms would be better than anything Goldman would be able to come up with. The Morgan Stanley bankers worked on various debt deals and stayed close to Chesky and his management team as they evaluated the offers.

Intent on making sure Goldman Sachs and Morgan Stanley didn't work at cross-purposes, Airbnb executives made it clear that if one of the structures was chosen, the other bank would still get paid.

Airbnb was already leaning against the convertible. From executives' point of view, the structure faced the same problem as a straight equity infusion—it would have forced them to reprice its equity at the bottom of the market. They wouldn't know how many shares they would have to issue when it came time for the conversion. If the pandemic extended and Airbnb had to go public at a $20 billion valuation, for example, the convertible might become equity at a $13 billion valuation, leading a large number of additional shares to be issued and diluting existing shareholders. TPG had also angered some at Airbnb in an earlier funding round when they added a provision at the last minute that was widely considered to be unfriendly to the company.

Giovanni encouraged the executives to take the convertible note deal. In his view, the company needed the money, and it was a decent deal. Goldman was "like, 'Go, Go, Go,'" one person recalled. Airbnb wanted to exhaust the debt talks first. The team slow-walked Goldman while Durban, Waxman, and Chesky got to know one another and worked through the deal's details.

Airbnb's executives were also dealing with operational issues. In late March, the company suspended marketing to save $800 million in costs. Chesky, Gebbia, and Blecharczyk, the three founders, agreed to take no salary for the next six months, while other senior executives took a 50 percent pay cut.

On March 30, Airbnb unveiled several initiatives, including a $250 million fund to compensate hosts who had lost out on rental income for visits scheduled on or before March 14, for stays through May 31. The company still hadn't lined up rescue financing.

■ ■ ■

At some point in the first days of April, Sixth Street and Silver Lake realized that they needed to be talking to Morgan Stanley, because its bankers were already working on other debt transactions. Morgan Stanley was trying to raise a less expensive debt deal with institutions like Fidelity, T. Rowe Price, BlackRock, and Pimco.

As luck would have it, Durban had spent his early career at Morgan Stanley and knew its bankers well. Durban reached out to Grimes, and Morgan Stanley began offering feedback on the term sheet.

The bankers liked what they saw in the Sixth Street/Silver Lake deal but foresaw a problem. The warrants that Waxman's team proposed would relegate the debt to a more junior position than the Bank of America–led credit line. If the credit line was outstanding, Bank of America wouldn't let Airbnb take on more risky debt. It was already threatening that it wouldn't give Airbnb an extension on the line without better pricing and tougher loan terms. The lender didn't know how long the pandemic might last, how deep the resulting economic slump might be, or how Airbnb would fare.

After some thought, the Morgan Stanley bankers came up with a creative idea. If they could close out the credit line, that would free up Airbnb to raise the debt from Sixth Street and Silver Lake. Once Airbnb raised that $1 billion, it would need to raise another $1 billion of more senior and safer debt from institutional investors. It would mean much cheaper financing for Airbnb, and Morgan Stanley's bankers thought that they could do it. If the company's business rebounded, it could pay off the debt a year or so later after only paying a small amount on the total loan.

Airbnb's executives felt it was too good to be true. Airbnb didn't want to give up the security of the credit line unless they could be sure of raising a total of $2 billion. They gave Morgan Stanley bankers an ultimatum.

"We're not going to say anything today," one executive told Grimes, "but you've got to get Silver Lake locked in, and Sixth Street for a billion, and you guys have to be damn confident you can get the next billion with no warrants from the institutional market."

Over the following few days, Stephenson met with Durban, who was now leading the talks on behalf of him and Waxman. The two men developed a good rapport. Stephenson's finance team crafted at least one presentation to give the investors an understanding of Airbnb's finances—the remaining cash on hand, the $1 billion credit line, and various revenue projections, depending on when the pandemic receded and global travel picked back up.

On April 3, Waxman, Durban, and Chesky met over Zoom to hammer out the details. Durban and Grimes negotiated an annual interest rate to Airbnb of more than 10 percent. The investors would also get warrants equal to about 1 percent of the company. The warrants would convert at an $18 billion valuation, a discount of more than 40 percent from the previous valuation set in 2017 and lower than Airbnb's internal estimates. The day before, Chesky told employees that the company's internal estimate was $26 billion.

The Sixth Street team strung together a bunch of all-nighters. Waxman often appeared on Zoom calls wearing a backward baseball cap. In one call, the Sixth Street CEO's daughter came into the picture and flashed bunny ears behind her father's head.

On Sunday, April 5, Airbnb's board held a call to evaluate the two competing investment options. Goldman presented the convertible bond deal it had worked out with TPG and Dragoneer. The bankers viewed the deal as an attractive option for Airbnb, because it would put money in the bank at a time when the pandemic was crushing travel companies. Airbnb needed the money. However, the convertible would have required Airbnb to sell a larger portion of the company for a lot less than many of the insiders thought it was worth. It meant serious dilution to Airbnb's existing investors, management, and employees.

Some board members expressed surprise that Goldman put it forward as a good deal. "Can I buy that deal?" one of the board members said. Others snickered.

The Morgan Stanley bankers presented their financing package, including the Sixth Street/Silver Lake deal, the closing of the credit line, and the raising of $1 billion in additional debt. It was an easy choice for the board to make. They would vote in favor of Morgan Stanley's transaction if the bank could close the credit line and raise the extra $1 billion over the next week.

The bank had pulled off something that Goldman Sachs and some Airbnb executives didn't think was possible just days earlier. "All three of those pieces had to come together to kill the bad convertible plan," one of the people involved in the negotiations said. "They had no choice. You'd have to do the diluted convertible if you had no other choice."

On Monday, April 6, less than a month since the official start of the pandemic, Airbnb announced that it had secured $1 billion in emergency funding. Chesky complimented Sixth Street and Silver Lake and thanked them for their support. Both Waxman and Durban offered statements in the same press release praising the Airbnb founders. Terms weren't disclosed. "Alan was great on the structuring thing, but Alan is not really a tech investor," one of the people involved in the deal later said. "Egon's a great CEO/founder whisperer. You needed both."

Throughout that week, Morgan Stanley's bankers raced to line up investors for the additional $1 billion in debt, ultimately pulling together a group of more than twenty that included BlackRock, Fidelity, T. Rowe Price, and Eaton Vance Corp. Silver Lake and Sixth Street also participated in the deal, with Sixth Street cutting a $250 million check for the right to receive payments ahead of its other investment.

Airbnb announced the completed deal on April 14, bringing an end to a month of uncertainty and countless discussions and evaluations about emergency funding. The company now had an extra $2 billion on hand and the confidence that went with it.

When Airbnb announced the transaction, Chesky offered a public statement that hinted at how he'd been talking about the pandemic internally. The CEO had been using nautical analogies in his weekly Zoom town halls with employees. The CEO likened Airbnb to a ship heading into a tempest—employees needed to do what they could to batten down the hatches. If they succeeded, the company would be able to weather the dark clouds and heavy winds and emerge into brilliant sunlight on the other side. "All of the actions we have taken over the last several weeks assure that Airbnb will emerge from the storm of the pandemic even stronger, regardless of how long the storm lasts," Chesky said.

Morgan Stanley's success raising the debt and the deepened relationship between Chesky and Grimes was enough to push Morgan Stanley ahead in the horse race over who would lead the company's eventual IPO. "It flipped," one of Airbnb's management team said. "We got this great deal and then actually Morgan Stanley comes back in, more in the lead, over Goldman as being our primary banker, or our most lead banker for the IPO."

Goldman Sachs's bankers were surprised that Morgan Stanley had been able to pull it off, and at least one grudgingly admitted that they might not have thought as creatively as they needed to about solving Airbnb's problems.

Chapter 25

Airbnb, San Francicso, August 2020

E ven with its $2 billion in additional cash, Airbnb was still vulnerable to the pandemic economy. Worldwide reservations had plunged. As April came to a close, results showed that in the last two months cancellations had outpaced new reservations. Chesky realized that the world wasn't going to return to the way it had been before the start of the pandemic. Airbnb would have to reduce or eliminate some of the side projects that weren't yet contributing meaningfully to the company's financial results. Chesky and others began to finalize a plan to focus on the core operations of home-sharing.

Rumors began to circulate on online message boards that the company was going to announce layoffs, perhaps as soon as Tuesday, May 5, when an all-hands meeting was scheduled. One poster who identified as an Airbnb employee on the website Blind asked the community on Monday evening how to go about informing their family about being laid off. When Chesky joined the meeting via Zoom the next day, he did announce layoffs. Nearly two thousand: 25 percent of the company.

The news came with an internal memo that the company later posted to its corporate website. Noting that it was the seventh time that he had addressed his employees from his home, Chesky showed more compassion and humanity than many corporate executives announcing layoffs. He used the word "love" several times to express his feelings for the people who were being laid off and did his best to explain how he'd come to his decision.

There were "two hard truths," he wrote. No one knew when travel would pick up again, and when it did, it was going to look different. To brace itself, the company needed to get more focused, jettison or pause pet projects, and get leaner in its core operations.

It halted projects in transportation and Studios, the programming project started the previous year. Investments would be paused in Hotels, a way to get hotel rooms onto its platform, and Luxe, travel packages that featured stays at top-tier properties and came with an around-the-clock concierge.

Chesky's memo talked about how the world needed connection more than ever. He expressed his thanks to all who worked at Airbnb and said, "I have a deep feeling of love for all of you." "To those who are leaving," he wrote, "I am truly sorry. Please know this is not your fault. The world will never stop seeking the qualities and talents that you brought to Airbnb...that helped make Airbnb. I want to thank you, from the bottom of my heart, for sharing them with us."

Airbnb agreed to pay health insurance for a full year for those who were getting fired. And it dedicated a part of its website to help employees find new jobs. If employees opted in, they could list their names and job functions on the website to potentially make it easier to be found by other companies looking to hire.

Chesky's memo also hinted at something that was just dawning on him. Despite the massive drop in reservations, he noticed a new trend in the searches customers were doing on Airbnb's website. Instead of looking at international or cross-country vacations, city dwellers were turning to the platform to find houses in rural locations that were a short drive away. And they were looking not for a weekend, or a week, but a month or more at a time.

Searches tended to show up as actual reservations a couple weeks later. If Airbnb could just harness the city-escaping trend and convert those searches into new reservations, it might be the pivot that could pull the company back from the abyss. Executives began to work on what they took to calling a Go Near campaign. They made changes in the search algorithms of the website to deliver more long-term and whole house rentals. Other employees worked to quickly line up partnerships with national parks and other outdoor destinations to reflect that COVID-fearing travelers wanted hikes, not museums.

Those plans were put on pause after May 25, when white Minneapolis police officer Derek Chauvin killed a Black man, George Floyd, by kneeling on his neck for over nine minutes. Floyd's death ignited protests across the United States. Like the rest of the country, Airbnb employees were upset. The company paused the Go Near plans and hosted a series of internal conversations for employees.

On June 11, Airbnb finally announced its Go Near campaign. By then, the number of people using its website had already begun to rebound. In North America, the number of users was back to levels last seen in 2019.

．　．　．

As Airbnb shifted its business focus, its bankers at Morgan Stanley watched the markets and thought once again about an IPO. The actions that the Federal Reserve had taken in March and April to buoy markets worked, providing a floor under the turmoil and setting the conditions for a remarkable bounce back.

President Donald Trump's government had sent out a first round of stimulus payments, and retail traders stuck at home were plowing the extra money, as well as income they weren't spending on going out or traveling, into anything that looked like it could be a good bet. The traders drove up the price of bitcoin in addition to turning their attention to the markets.

In early June, a series of IPOs told the bankers that the market was looking past the pandemic and that maybe, just maybe, Airbnb could debut by the end of the year. On June 3, Morgan Stanley bankers took Warner Music public at $25 a share in what was the biggest deal of the year. The IPO price settled at the higher end of a range that the company had disclosed in its securities offering. The stock rose 8 percent the following day, a modest gain but enough to signal that the market was open to buying IPOs again.

After Warner Music closed its first day of trading, JPMorgan and Goldman Sachs bankers priced the IPO for ZoomInfo Technologies, a cloud-based provider of marketing and sales leads that became the largest technology listing of the year when it sold more than 44 million shares at $21 apiece. The number was above the price range, itself already revised upward. The following day, ZoomInfo surged 62 percent on its first day of trading.

On Monday of the following week, bankers for online car buying website Vroom sold the company's shares for $22 apiece, more than the range of $18 to $20. When Vroom opened for trading the following day, the shares surged higher. They ended the day up more than 117 percent.

The Morgan Stanley bankers had seen enough to know that Airbnb could once again think about an IPO. Claassen sat down with Grimes to talk about how they could position Airbnb, a travel company, during a pandemic. The bankers leaned on their presentation from the previous year and channeled

Chesky's own thinking. He'd already begun to think about how inspiring it could be if a travel company like Airbnb went public in a pandemic.

In mid-June, Claassen and Grimes decided that Grimes should make the most of his relationship with Chesky and deliver the pitch in a one-on-one setting. This time they framed their pitch to appeal to Chesky's interest in the hero's journey. Earlier that month, the founder had spoken on a podcast about his interest in *The Hero with a Thousand Faces*, a 1949 book by Joseph Campbell. Campbell suggests that personal narratives involve a hero who must overcome a challenge. In the process of his rising above it, a part of the hero dies, and a new version of him arises. Chesky had often thought of travel in similar terms—travelers take a trip, move through a series of experiences, and return home changed—but now he was thinking in terms of the pandemic and his own hero's journey.

One evening, Grimes sent Chesky a link to his personal Zoom meeting room. The two men were soon plotting the best way to bring Airbnb back from the brink and into the public markets. The Morgan Stanley bankers had put together a short presentation that Grimes now used in his discussion with Chesky. Superimposed over photos of iconic Airbnb properties—one was an underground home carved out of the Swiss Alps—the bankers had written just a couple of sentences of text on each slide. On the left of the slide, white text described a common narrative about IPOs. On the right, set apart with words in red, the text showed how Airbnb was in a class by itself, or a Space of One.

One slide read:

Usual: Company goes public when short term results are strong
Space of One: 21st century Airbnb goes public during worst travel downturn in a century.

Another:

Usual: Success narrative based on price relative to last raised round
Space of One: Success narrative based on doing the impossible, IPO of a travel/shared experience company in a pandemic.

A third:

Usual: Focus on first four quarterly results attracts short term investors focused on IPO immediate returns
Space of One: Going public with uncertain short term can only attract long term investors by definition.

A fourth slide suggested that the company should "surprise the market with truly secret filing and fall unveiling shortly before launch, retake control of narrative."

The slides weren't fancy, but they delivered a clear message. The time for Airbnb to be bold had once again arrived, even in the middle of a pandemic. Chesky liked what he was hearing. He went back to talk with his team and came back to Grimes a few days later.

On June 14, Chesky sent Grimes some data indicating that travel was trending up again. Google Trends showed that people were searching for trips closer to home and seeking out Airbnbs along the way. The next day, Chesky and Grimes agreed that Airbnb should restart its IPO process. Over the next few weeks, Airbnb and Morgan Stanley worked on the IPO plans in secret.

When the company closed its books for the second quarter, the financial data showed that it had gone through $1.2 billion in cash over the previous year, depleting more than a third of the cash it had had on hand at the end of March 2019. The biggest portion of the drawdown was in the first quarter, when the pandemic took hold and the company had to reimburse travelers for canceled travel plans.

But the business had begun to rebound. On July 14, Airbnb announced on its website that on a single day in the previous week, guests booked "more than 1 million nights' worth of future stays at Airbnb listings around the world," the most since March. Fifty percent of those bookings were for destinations within three hundred miles of the home of the person doing the booking. But the news wasn't all good—slightly more than half of the nights were for stays costing less than $100.

"Because short-term rentals are typically entire homes, guests get more space for their money and more control over their environment, including

private entrances and amenities such as kitchens and swimming pools," the
company said in the post. "Combined with the availability of entire homes
within driving distance for travelers and the Airbnb Enhanced Clean proto-
col for ensuring clean, sanitized accommodations, Airbnb's short-term rentals
are recovering because consumers see them as a safe, healthy and responsible
way for guests to travel."

On July 15, Chesky announced the departure of Greg Greeley, the president of the Homes business, at an all-staff meeting. Greeley, who had joined
Airbnb from Amazon two years earlier, was replaced by Catherine Powell,
a Brit who had been head of the Experiences business. Powell would now
oversee the Hosting vertical, a newly created position overseeing Homes and
Experiences.

"If we're going to get back to our roots, we must get back to great hosting," Chesky said.

The same day, he announced the company's triumphal return to the
ranks of those companies considering an IPO before year-end. "When
the market is ready, we will be ready," he wrote in an internal memo. "We
were down, but we're not out." One week later, he spoke at a Reuters event
and said that the company was "looking at everything" for going public,
including a traditional IPO, a direct listing, and a special purpose acquisition
company.

■ ■ ■

As Airbnb executives thought once again about the public listing, they realized that the pandemic had put their plans in perspective. Gone were the
ambitions to become the first direct listing on the NASDAQ. Instead, the
company focused on surviving the pandemic and using the public markets to
raise money and give employees a way to cash in on their deferred pay.

"At some point, we had to have a breather and step back to what our priorities were," said Stephenson. "Our priorities were supporting our stakeholders, not a confetti cannon celebration of wealth, and not about IPO
invention. It got a little hard that people got wrapped around us inventing
the new IPO. I'm like, 'Well, that's just not the most important thing for me
to do.'" Stephenson was receiving texts from Bill Gurley asking to know if

Airbnb was still planning on a direct listing. Other people called to advocate for Airbnb doing something different than a traditional IPO.

At the end of July, Airbnb moved to ditch the direct listing. Having raised $2 billion in debt, the company would now need to raise equity to pay off that debt. Before Airbnb could move forward, it had to prepare the board for the change. Directors had already approved plans for a direct listing, so if they were going to switch, their fiduciary duty required them to give the new idea a proper review. Morgan Stanley bankers came in and gave a presentation showing the pros and cons of the direct listing and a traditional IPO.

As the board and senior executives deliberated, they coalesced around three strengths of a traditional IPO over a direct listing. One, an IPO would allow Airbnb to communicate more information to potential shareholders who may have had a good idea of Airbnb's growth prospects before the pandemic and now had little idea how to model an uncertain future. If it went the IPO route, Airbnb could share models and projections with its bankers, who would then inform the analysts about the company's prospects, who would inform investors. This was the "discount on discount" theater that so annoyed McCarthy, but Airbnb saw its benefits.

Two, the company could pick its investors in a traditional IPO. While a direct listing left the choosing of shareholders up to market dynamics—those who paid the most would get the shares—a traditional IPO would preserve Airbnb's ability to pick its shareholder base.

Three, Airbnb would be able to pick its price. Morgan Stanley provided data showing that stocks either pop, get momentum and rise quickly, or lose momentum and sink deeply. There was very little in the middle. Company executives knew that they wanted the shares to rise on the first day and figured that they might be willing to price them a few dollars cheaper. Doing so would reward their IPO investors and provide momentum to the stock by allowing shares to trade higher in the days after the IPO. Airbnb would forgo the direct listing.

Shortly thereafter, bankers for Morgan Stanley, Goldman Sachs, and Allen & Co. met on Zoom to once again kick off the company's IPO process. They started planning a day to brief Wall Street research analysts on Airbnb's numbers, and began to map the sequence of securities filings and investor meetings for a December listing. Over the next month, company executives and their bankers rewrote the IPO prospectus. While there was a mostly completed prospectus from before the pandemic, the experience of the past year had crystallized executives' understanding of Airbnb's core mission and had helped them understand what made the company different from other lodging companies. The text began to morph from what had been a document telling investors about the kind of company Airbnb would become to one more focused on what Airbnb already was.

Chesky took an increasingly hands-on role in drafting the document, viewing it as a way to communicate Airbnb's values and business philosophy to a broader audience. The Airbnb CEO created a special font to be used in the document, which he named Cereal, after the "Obama O's" and "Cap'n McCains" breakfast cereal gimmick that the company had used to get through a tough patch early in its life.

"In a three-hundred-page document, one hundred eighty pages of that are the guts of those details," one person said. "But how it gets wrapped and how it gets articulated, I think that is what got a little more solidified and clarified."

On August 19, Airbnb confirmed reports that it had filed confidentially with the Securities and Exchange Commission to sell its shares to the public. It had not yet decided how many shares it would sell, and added a boilerplate note of caution that its IPO would be dependent on the SEC's review of the submission.

While some commentators thought that the company had picked a "terrible time" to enter the public markets, NYU professor Aswath Damodaran, an expert on corporate valuation and a frequent commenter on initial public offerings, told Bloomberg the following day that the company had gotten "the timing right." The company was in a good place because the market was favoring companies like Airbnb with small demands for capital, he said, and the company's competitors in the hotel industry had been "handicapped" by the pandemic.

In late 2019, Airbnb had told the world it would go public in a year. It was on track to meet its deadline. But its decision now to confirm the confidential filing ran counter to one aspect of Morgan Stanley's Space of One pitch, which suggested that the company keep quiet about the filing until it was time to make it public later in the fall. Airbnb could control the narrative and provide protection against facing negative press reports if it couldn't get its IPO done before the end of the year, the bankers argued. Airbnb took control of the narrative anyway.

CHAPTER 26

Airbnb, San Francisco, December 2020

The filing put an end to early-stage talks Airbnb had held with Bill Ackman, a hedge fund manager who had raised $4 billion through a special purpose acquisition company.

Since Palihapitiya's initial attempts to buy Slack with his SPAC, blank check firms had surged in popularity. By late August, eighty-two blank check vehicles had raised more than $33 billion to use in buying private companies and taking them public, exceeding the entirety of 2019's volume, when just fifty-nine companies raised $13.6 billion. Helped in part by Palihapitiya's evangelism, the trend also betrayed a realization on the part of market participants that SPACs might play a role in the broadening disruption of the IPO process that had been ignited by Spotify's direct listing.

Even Bill Gurley had come around. He recognized that what had once been a vehicle for marginal companies to enter the public markets had become a viable option for popular venture-backed companies. On August 23, four days after Airbnb alerted the public to its IPO filing, Gurley published a post on *Above the Crowd*, his blog, "Going Public Circa 2020; Door #3: The SPAC," extolling the virtues of SPACs.

He set the stage with some context. "If you are looking past or through Covid—and why not, all of Wall Street is—the topic du jour in Silicon Valley is Special Purpose Acquisition Companies, or SPACs. SPACs are all the rage, and everybody and their brother have either raised one or are talking about raising one." The post came with a roundup of links.

"Historically they have been a kind of back-door way for a company to go public, and as a result have historically had a sub-standard reputation," Gurley wrote. "But in light of where we are in 2020, especially with regard to the

degrading efficiency and sky-rocketing cost of capital through the structur-
ally broken IPO process, SPACs may emerge as a legitimate third option for
helping Silicon Valley companies efficiently and cost-effectively transition
into the public markets."

Gurley was encouraged, he said, to see that the increased SPAC issuance
had led to greater competition among SPACs and better economic terms for
the companies they targeted. It was this rosier picture, an improvement on
the massive first-day pops again taking place, that made the vehicles an attractive option for companies looking to go public. Gurley couldn't resist reminding readers about the broken IPO promise, brandishing Ritter's data to show
that through the first half of 2020, IPOs had been underpriced by 31 percent,
leading to $7.8 billion in proceeds that he positioned as a transfer of wealth
from companies to investors. SPACs, on the other hand, had several things
going for them. They were quick, potentially cheaper than IPOs when the
underpricing was considered, allowed a company to raise primary capital, and
gave a company much more control over the price it received.

"The bottom line is that SPACs are a very [legitimate] path to the public
markets," Gurley wrote. "I fully expect to see high profile companies walk
through Door #3."

In early October, Reuters reported that Airbnb was considering selling
stock at a valuation north of $30 billion, suggesting that the company and its
bankers expected it to be able to garner a stock market listing price above its
2017 funding round. As the month progressed, markets rose and then fell,
testing their September lows. The IPO market quieted down, and investors
began to look toward the U.S. presidential election. In the last few days of
October, Airbnb announced a stock split, telling shareholders that they would
receive two shares for every share they held. The split—a procedural step and
page out of the IPO playbook that sought to make the shares more palatable
for retail investors—took the value of Airbnb's shares from $69.76 at the end
of September to $34.88.

Airbnb prepared to publicly release its securities prospectus as the election came into focus. When President Donald Trump refused to concede
in an election in which millions more citizens cast a vote for Joe Biden, the
company delayed. Only on November 16 was the document released publicly,
formally kicking off Airbnb's IPO process. The company could now begin

official conversations with investors. The investors, in turn, could begin to place orders with Airbnb's bankers.

Investors dug into the filing for the first glimpse of how the business had fared during the pandemic. Guests and customers booked 146.9 million nights and experiences in the first three quarters of 2020, down 41 percent from the same figures in 2019. Bookings slumped 67 percent in the second quarter. In all, Airbnb suffered a net loss of $697 million through the first nine months of 2020, more than twice its loss during the same period in 2019.

The prospectus also showed how successful the Go Near campaign had become, and the effect of the company's actions to cut its marketing budget and lay off staff. Airbnb turned a profit of $219 million in the third quarter of 2020.

The company planned to list on the NASDAQ, sticking with its direct-listing-inspired choice even after pivoting to the traditional IPO.

With Airbnb's results showing that the company had weathered its existential crisis and come out the other side, much of the drama was drained from the upcoming IPO. Morgan Stanley, fresh off its role advising on the $2 billion emergency fundraising, commanded the upper left-hand corner of the banking list. Goldman got second billing, ahead of nearly three dozen other underwriters.

In conversations with investors, the Morgan Stanley bankers explained that they would be requiring investors to input their orders into a recently developed order-entry system. The success of Unity's offering and Goldman's marketing had persuaded Morgan Stanley that it needed to have something similar. Over the course of several months, the bank designed a system it called Alps.

Hosted on the same platform where Morgan Stanley clients went to read research reports, the system acted much like Goldman's, except for one thing. Unlike Goldman's, which kept the orders contained to just a few key people inside the investment bank, Morgan Stanley's didn't attempt to keep the order book hidden from its salespeople or bankers.

It was a philosophical difference, and it meant that the Morgan Stanley salespeople would have more information to share with clients who had questions about what others were bidding. Whether that would have an impact on the IPO price remained to be seen. The firm's bankers argued that a closed system didn't work, and that investors needed to hear feedback. The choice also meant that Morgan Stanley wouldn't risk alienating investors with a system that kept information from them.

. . .

As Morgan Stanley introduced the company to investors, it was also in charge of handling Airbnb's directed share program, the stock that Airbnb set up for hosts to buy. Those who wanted to participate would have to set up a Morgan Stanley account and place their orders through the bank's system. Over less than two days, more than twenty thousand hosts placed orders to buy the stock before Morgan Stanley had to cut off participation. While the bank had done similar programs for Uber drivers and General Motors dealers, its systems couldn't handle the volume of the Airbnb orders. A reliance on call centers was one of the bottlenecks.

Morgan Stanley searched for other options, even reaching out to archrival Goldman Sachs. They also tried Fidelity, but ultimately came up short. The bank began a massive project to update its systems to handle millions of orders, betting that in an age of democratization, other companies would want the option to offer a slice of their IPOs to affinity groups or customers.

Airbnb heard from all manner of customers and investors who wanted to get in on the IPO, including Chesky's dentist. A carpenter in Maine said he wanted to participate because he fixed up three houses so they could be available for Airbnb. He figured something must be going on with this company.

On December 1, Airbnb amended its prospectus to say that it planned to sell 57 million shares at an initial range of $44 to $50. The midpoint of the range represented a 35 percent increase over the value of the shares from the end of September. Two or three days later, after several meetings over Zoom, Morgan Stanley received some helpful feedback. One investor who had met with Chesky passed on word that they were "starstruck" in the meeting. It was an early sign to the bankers that Airbnb's stock was likely to rocket higher.

On December 7, Airbnb updated its prospectus to show that it now expected to sell shares in the range of $56 to $60. The enthusiasm that Morgan Stanley bankers had detected a week or more ago was coming through in the orders investors were entering into the bank's order system. Two days later, on December 9, it came time for Airbnb to price its shares. DoorDash, an app allowing people to order takeout food for delivery that had just gone public and seen its stock pop 85 percent earlier that day, was fresh in the minds of executives and bankers.

Executives including Chesky and Stephenson gathered on Zoom with Morgan Stanley's bankers to talk through the pricing. Some of the bankers used virtual backgrounds with slides from the Space of One presentation. Morgan Stanley's Alps system showed order size and price for hundreds of investors who wanted in on Airbnb's IPO. Over the course of the roadshow, Airbnb had met with thirty to forty investors in one-on-one meetings, and about a thousand investors in total. The order book showed institutional investors willing to buy shares up in the $85 to $90 range.

But Airbnb wasn't dogmatic about the price, or taking every dollar off the table. After some back-and-forth, the group settled on an IPO price of $68. It was 45 percent higher than the midpoint of the initial range, which, depending on who was talking, showed either that the initial range was too low or that the company was aggressively pushing the price higher. Everyone agreed that having data about price and size allowed the company to move the IPO price a few dollars higher.

At some point, someone made the call: "Look, this is actually high enough."

The next day, Morgan Stanley opened a Zoom call for Airbnb executives and employees who had worked on the IPO as John Paci, the bank's IPO trader, worked with the computers at NASDAQ to open the stock. At 10:10 a.m., the NASDAQ put out a trade indication showing that Airbnb might open at $139, already double the IPO price. Shortly after, Chesky appeared on Bloomberg Television. Anchor Emily Chang asked him what he made of that early price indication. "We just got an indication on your opening price. Shares indicated to open right now at one hundred thirty-nine dollars a share, which is more than double what you priced at," Chang said.

At the mention of the stock price, Chesky's eyebrows quickly shot up and his eyes got round.

"Are you at all concerned about froth? What do you think about that number and the potential that you're leaving billions of dollars on the table?" Chang continued.

"That's the first time I've heard that number," he said. "That is...that's... you know, when we..." He gave a quick chuckle. The CEO was almost speechless. "In April, we raised money, it was a debt financing, that price would have priced us around thirty bucks. So, I don't know what else to say...it's...that's, that's a very...that is...I'm very humbled by it."

He quickly gained control and continued. "We know that we are on a very long journey. We're going to be very, very focused, obviously today is a very special day for everyone, but the higher the stock price, the higher the expectations, the harder we will be working, obviously."

By 1:02 p.m., the stock looked likely to open at $157. Then the price dropped. During this time, Airbnb executives watched Paci juggling orders and phone calls with various investors. The frenetic scene—with Paci cradling multiple phones to his ear—reminded at least one Airbnb executive of an earlier era of Wall Street.

"What you think a guy like that looks like and how they act, and he's still got the four phones on his shoulders, and it felt like you had walked back like twenty, thirty, forty years, right?" one of the people who had watched Paci said. "All this stuff is high-tech, and still here's a guy on the floor with the phones and he has to release the stock, and it's held. It held multiple hours because there's such a disproportionate buy side versus sell side, so we had an enormous number. The retail interest was enormous."

At 1:38, Airbnb shares finally opened at $146, a 115 percent increase over the IPO price.

Airbnb's Lehane raised his hands in the air.

By the time Airbnb was done trading that day, the shares were at $144.71. The price valued Airbnb at over $100 billion.

CHAPTER 27

DoorDash, San Francisco, December 8, 2020

If the pandemic undercut Airbnb's plans to pursue a nontraditional listing, it added fuel to those of DoorDash, another company in the gig economy that was pursuing its IPO in parallel.

Unlike Airbnb, DoorDash was perfectly positioned to seize on the surge in orders from diners too fearful of infection to venture to local grocery stores or restaurants, or prevented from doing so by local ordinances. Diners provided a tailwind to the company's growth prospects. DoorDash would have to convince investors that the growth rates it exhibited during the pandemic months would persist even after the widespread adoption of vaccines made it safe again to dine at restaurants.

Founded in 2013 by Stanford University students Tony Xu, Stanley Tang, Andy Fang, and Evan Moore to deliver restaurant food around Palo Alto, before the pandemic, DoorDash got locked in a fierce battle with competitors like Grubhub, Postmates, and Uber Eats in what was a capital-intensive business.

DoorDash had found a key advantage: the U.S. suburbs, where higher growth markets sat untapped and competition was less intense. The strategy was initially lampooned because urban markets were thought to offer an easier path to profitability due to greater density in both customers and drivers, which the company called "Dashers." Xu disregarded common wisdom and went ahead with his own idiosyncratic plan, signing exclusive deals with national chains, and pushing through an effort to broaden its reach in second- and third-tier cities across America and Canada. Even before the pandemic, DoorDash's growth had surged.

With growth came an almost insatiable demand for cash. Over one mind-bending stretch from March 2018 through November 2019, DoorDash raised almost $2 billion from venture capitalists and other crossover investors who dabbled in both public and private markets. Its valuation soared during that period from $1.4 billion to $13 billion.

The man responsible for that fundraising and the design of the company's upcoming IPO was DoorDash's CFO, Prabir Adarkar. Adarkar had an engineering degree from the prestigious Indian Institute of Technology system, and an impressive résumé. He was a former McKinsey & Co. project manager, Goldman Sachs TMT banker, and senior finance executive at Uber, one of the world's largest consumers of corporate capital. Adarkar left Uber after three years to join DoorDash in 2018. In a July announcement that year, Xu offered a sharp assessment of his latest hire. "Having spent over 40 hours in the past two months with Prabir, I can tell you that he's got a sharp mind, possesses an owner's mentality, and leads from the front."

Adarkar had a keen interest in the design of DoorDash's public listing, and his engineer's mind liked to deconstruct the process. Like Airbnb, DoorDash considered a direct listing. It quickly ran into the key shortcoming of the direct listing: that it couldn't help a company raise capital. Food delivery was capital-intensive, and executives knew that if growth continued, they would need more money.

That could be done within the confines of the direct listing process if DoorDash wanted to wait. The SEC needed to approve the NYSE's rule change allowing a capital raise concurrent with a direct listing. Then the company would have to haggle over any remaining details. DoorDash executives held talks with their bankers at Goldman Sachs and JPMorgan, coming to realize that it would likely take another eighteen to twenty-four months if they wanted to go that route.

That was too long. Adarkar didn't want to waste the opportunity to go public in what looked at the end of 2019 to be a robust market for IPOs. Who knew what the markets would look like in two years' time? Put simply, the risk/reward calculus ruled out a direct listing. One person close to the process summed it up as a "science experiment" that departed too far from the company's primary goal, which was to raise money. Nonetheless, Adarkar and Xu were interested in exploring alternatives to the traditional offering and had the support of a board that included Alfred Lin and John Doerr. On February 13, 2020, DoorDash filed documents confidentially with the SEC. Disclosed later, the prospectus showed Goldman Sachs in the lead-left position, followed by JPMorgan. A week later, the company raised $340 million in convertible debt. And on February 27, DoorDash issued a press release stating that it had filed its draft prospectus.

The WHO's pandemic declaration would come less than two weeks later. DoorDash set aside its IPO plans to focus on doing what it could to keep its restaurant partners open for business and its drivers safe.

■　■　■

In the first few months of the pandemic, DoorDash's IPO plans remained on the back burner as executives concentrated on meeting the orders surging into its app and doing whatever it could to help its restaurant clients meet the uptick in delivery orders. In April, as the full impact of the pandemic had begun to sink in, DoorDash accounted for 45 percent of all third-party delivery orders in the United States, according to Edison Trends, a market research firm that analyzes anonymous e-receipts from consumers. That was up from 28 percent in March 2019, when the company took the lead from Grubhub.

In June, the company used that momentum to raise $400 million, turning to investors including Durable Capital Partners, run by former T. Rowe Price portfolio manager Henry Ellenbogen; Fidelity; and T. Rowe Price. The investors purchased shares in DoorDash that valued it at $16 billion. The money helped DoorDash start a Storefront product to help restaurants create their own websites for taking delivery orders.

By July, DoorDash executives felt confident enough in the state of the business and its partners to dust off its IPO plans. It submitted a new draft registration statement to the SEC, responding to the questions the agency had outlined in a letter it sent to the company on March 12, one day after the WHO's declaration of a pandemic.

DoorDash's financial condition served as a strong foundation for a management team considered by at least one banker to be one of the smartest in Silicon Valley when it came to raising money and accessing the capital markets. The need for cash had driven the company through many rounds of fundraising, but Adarkar's analytical background and curiosity about market mechanics kept the company focused on designing a bespoke IPO process.

On August 3, Adarkar moved to shore up his team, bringing in Andy

Hargreaves as head of investor relations. Hargreaves had known Adarkar and Keith Yandell, DoorDash's chief business and legal officer, for several years. He was already in frequent contact with the company. Hargreaves was a long-time securities analyst and had recently been doing contract work for Sands Capital, a small investor in DoorDash.

Hargreaves immediately got to work fine-tuning the draft registration statement that would become the public prospectus shared with investors. He started working with Goldman Sachs and JPMorgan bankers to draft materials DoorDash would share with investors, making a list of which ones the company wanted to meet and how often.

This would be the first IPO process for Hargreaves, much as it was for Adarkar. Like Adarkar, Hargreaves favored an analytical approach to thinking through DoorDash's particular objectives. While the direct listing was off the table, the executives could still thank Spotify for showing that the time had come to question the status quo.

■ ■ ■

DoorDash executives weren't sure what to make of the system. They wanted to do whatever they could to maximize the proceeds of their IPO by selling shares for as high a price as they could persuade investors to pay. The company also wanted to be able to pick its shareholders—due to its fundraising activities, it already had relationships with some of the world's largest IPO investors. Management wanted to ensure it could allocate shares to those investors who had been along for the ride and continued to act as strong supporters.

But they also realized that there were parts of the process that didn't make sense in 2020, particularly around the greenshoe option, the lockup provisions that Unity had already challenged, and the common wisdom that shares should be priced at between $10 and $25. Airbnb had also briefly considered doing away with the greenshoe, but ultimately kept it.

As DoorDash's management team met with its bankers and its board, they spent hours evaluating the greenshoe. The option was a common part of the traditional underwriting agreement and something that other companies had simply taken for granted. Pioneered in 1963, when the Green Shoe Manufacturing Company held a secondary offering underwritten by Paine, Webber, Jackson & Curtis, the feature allowed underwriters to sell more shares, typically 15 percent more, than those the company planned to sell in the IPO. This could be done if demand from investors dramatically exceeded supply. The additional supply from the greenshoe could be used to dampen volatility.

It also acted as an insurance contract of sorts. By selling extra shares, the banks were effectively short the stock and needed to buy shares to balance the position. If the shares rose after the IPO, the banks typically had thirty days after the issue to purchase the additional shares from the company. But if the shares fell below the IPO price, the banks could buy the shares they needed in the secondary market, thereby providing demand that would serve to prop up the share price.

Critics liked to suggest that on popular IPOs the greenshoe was easy money for the banks. If the stock price surged in trading, the banks could buy the stock from the company at the IPO price and sell it at the much higher trading price, pocketing the difference in profit.

Jamie McGurk, who had left Andreessen for a senior position at Coatue Management and advised DoorDash when it was considering a direct listing, summed it up. "Investment banks make a lot of money on the greenshoe," McGurk said. "It's a very lucrative part of the IPO for them, and the reality is if you have a robust market and a well-priced and well-opened IPO, you don't need a greenshoe. Maybe on a particularly volatile day, or a set of circumstances where something's mispriced, it's a useful tool to have, but it's almost like when things didn't go well that's when the greenshoe is actually useful. Otherwise, it's kind of an extra incentive for the underwriter."

The board, including director Alfred Lin, had a dim view of the greenshoe. DoorDash executives examined the data and found that it seldom acted as the shock absorber its supporters suggested. In cases where the stock declined in price, their research found that the extra buying power it created often wasn't enough to prevent the shares from continuing to decline. On an average IPO, only 40 percent to 50 percent of the shares are available to trade on the first day. Buying an extra 15 percent was often not enough. And if things went well and the stock price increased, the banks would benefit at the expense of the company, which was contractually obligated to sell the shares cheap even though they were trading at higher prices in the market.

As Adarkar asked around, he found that many large investors didn't care about the greenshoe because they were reasonably confident that they would still get the allocations they wanted without it. In other words, the extra shares are typically shared with less important investors lower down in the order book.

While DoorDash executives spent a considerable amount of time understanding the greenshoe, they also considered eliminating or adapting the customary 180-day lockup. Many practitioners blamed it for artificially limiting the supply of shares in the market. The DoorDash executives wanted to explore ways to reduce those limitations.

In considering the lockup, the executives pulled data on average daily trading volume for shares of other recent IPOs. They considered the potential effects on stock price volatility and liquidity of unlocking some percentage of the shares at various points in time. They weighed those quantitative factors with more qualitative factors, such as considering the rights of old and new investors, the asymmetry of information possessed by both types of investors, and the traditional thinking that new investors should get two quarters of earnings results before old investors could cash out. The results of the analysis were far from conclusive.

When Adarkar sounded out investors about the lockup, he received a very different answer than the one he had received about the greenshoe. Investors enjoyed the lockup provision because it protected them from a surge in supply hitting the market and gave their investment time to find a stable trading price. They didn't want to see it eliminated.

DoorDash executives were more focused on the influence of a lockup on the first-day trading performance than they were on the aspect that Unity executives worried most about, the fact that it disadvantaged insiders. DoorDash executives knew that the relative lack of supply on the first day of trading was to blame for some of the first-day pop, as Andreessen partners Alex Rampell and Scott Kupor explained in their August blog post. The selling that accompanied the end of the lockup often led to volatile price swings and a depressed stock price. Some institutional investors had even discovered that on a popular transaction, they could ride the stock price higher, sell for a quick gain, and then buy back the shares after the lockup expiration pushed the price down.

In the end, DoorDash decided on a two-stage lockup provision, giving employees and early investors two chances to sell stock and relieving some of the pent-up supply pressures. They'd get the first chance at least 90 days after the IPO, as long as a list of other conditions had been met. The management team and directors could sell 20 percent, while all other equity holders could sell as much as 40 percent. And then everyone would get a chance to sell their remaining shares after the customary 180 days.

The executives also decided against splitting DoorDash's shares in a way that would have brought the IPO price into a range of $10 to $25. The bankers told the executives that lower prices tended to attract more retail interest than higher prices, but DoorDash also knew that retail investors brought volatility. The executives ultimately did split the shares. But, like Google sixteen years before, DoorDash decided against splitting the stock in a way that artificially courted retail investors with a lower price.

With those final details ironed out, DoorDash publicly filed its IPO prospectus on November 13. The document listed Goldman Sachs, JPMorgan, and ten other investment banks as co-managers or other members of the selling group. The bankers could now begin talking to investors and collecting orders for the upcoming IPO.

* * *

By this point, Adarkar had witnessed Unity's IPO and the stock's modest 30 percent gain on the first day of trading. Armed with that success, Goldman was touting its role in developing the new blind order-entry system and offering it to any client that wanted to use it.

Adarkar reached out to Unity CFO Kim Jabal to get a better understanding of the process. He learned that one of Unity's goals was to run a meritocratic and democratic process, an objective DoorDash executives weren't opposed to, but one that wasn't high on their list. They wanted to make sure they could sell the stock at a high price and avoid dilution.

As the company mulled Goldman's order-entry system, it began its roadshow. Just as Unity had done, DoorDash met with investors, examined their turnover data and other investments, and attempted to come up with a nuanced understanding of which of them could reasonably be expected to hold the shares over several years.

Members of DoorDash's finance team looked at the last hundred tech IPOs going back to 2015 or so and found that many investors sold sooner than expected. While the market shorthand was that mutual funds held while hedge funds flipped, DoorDash's analysis, much like Unity's, showed that the diversity of investors in the current market made that axiom obsolete.

That was in part because there were many buy-and-hold hedge funds focused on specific industries like tech. Large mutual fund complexes were so big that any allocation they got—even if it was among the biggest—got split among various funds. It was hardly material to their bottom line unless the portfolio manager could build it out in the aftermarket. Some managers didn't like to keep stocks unless they represented a meaningful holding.

As the company sought to understand what mutual funds might be committed long-term holders, they found that hedge funds had done some of the best analysis on the company. The fact that hedge funds could be more nimble or global in their investment choices than some mutual funds meant that they had a good understanding of the worldwide implications of the food delivery industry.

The order-entry system that Unity had developed, by requiring both order size and price, gave DoorDash executives better insight into which investors were likely to hold. If an investor showed interest at share prices well in excess of where the company eventually set them, DoorDash could reasonably assume a bullish outlook. Every investor will tell a management team that it will act as a long-term holder, but DoorDash hoped that by looking at the bids, they could come up with a more data-based metric.

On November 30, the company amended its prospectus to show that it planned to sell 33 million shares in an initial range of $75 to $85. The price would value the company at $32 billion, roughly double what it received in the June financing. The range was the subject of some significant debate between DoorDash and its bankers. It was higher than traditional IPOs and ran up against a preference among bankers to set the range low in order to attract as much interest as possible. The problem, Carl Chiou and others believed, is that the lower price gets anchored—the company has to amend the prospectus every time the price increases, or decreases, by 20 percent or more. But bankers and company executives didn't like to amend the prospectus more than a few times, because it's cumbersome and time consuming.

Adarkar and other members of DoorDash's management team pushed the bankers to increase the initial range. As a consumer-facing brand, DoorDash didn't feel like it needed help drumming up interest by keeping the range too low. In the end, Goldman's bankers talked the executives down and the two sides settled on $75 to $85.

Investors soon showed that they knew how the game was played and provided support for the behavioral finance theory that investors anchored to the initial range. When the bids came in, most of them were exactly 20 percent above the range. DoorDash had effectively wasted its first round of bids.

On December 5, DoorDash updated its prospectus to show the new range. Now the company said it planned to sell shares between $90 and $95, or 15.6 percent higher than the initial range. The IPO was just days away.

Chapter 28

NYSE, New York City, December 22, 2020

Around this time, the DoorDash team began to sour on one aspect of the Unity-designed order-entry system. They had come to believe that Unity's process, in the push to keep the system blind, had missed out on a key lever companies could use to push their IPO price higher: the use of bankers and salespeople to share market feedback or whisper campaigns.

DoorDash believed that selective feedback could be used to encourage investors worried about missing out on a transaction to increase their bid. The knowledge that other investors were submitting higher bids was often enough for an investor worried about losing an allocation or receiving a smaller one to place a higher bid. In other words, issuers could command a higher price if investors had a fear of missing out on the IPO.

The theory works the same in home buying. A smart broker selling an in-demand property will communicate with potential buyers as bids come in. He might give buyers he has developed a good relationship with the chance to increase their bid at the last minute to win the house—asking them, for instance, if they are willing to lose the house over $10,000. In this way, he can walk a selling price higher, to the benefit of his client. It's critical that the asset being sold, whether it's a house or an IPO, is popular with a certain group of buyers. It has to be a hot deal, in other words, for the feedback to work in this way.

Unity executives had worried that investors wouldn't share their true bids, and would bid lower, if they knew they would get a last-minute opportunity to increase their bid. On the other hand, many people believed that investors talked to each other regardless of whether they were hearing from a company or its bankers. They wanted to know what others were thinking about the stock, though they were always very careful not to give up too much information, for fear that other investors might get a better allocation. Investors benefit by working together and sharing their bids with each other, but in practice the competitive dynamics are too much to overcome. Nonetheless, the investors are often aligned in their interest in getting as many shares at as low a price as possible.

There was an array of competing forces working against a company looking to raise as much money as it could through an IPO. To at least one person involved in DoorDash's offering, the process felt adversarial, like it was the company against everyone else. To get through it, the person felt, each party to the process needed to understand how incentives affected the advice they were receiving from the others.

Faced with the uncertainty of where their bid compared to others', investors would submit artificially low prices, Adarkar came to believe. Investors feared having buyer's remorse if they later found that they were the highest bid. If that was the case, instead of keeping investors in the dark with a blind auction, companies and their bankers could use feedback to encourage them to increase their bid to get an allocation. Auction theory tends to agree. Research has shown that knowing what others are bidding—being furnished with more information—makes bidders bolder in the prices they are willing to pay.

The theory suggested that open auctions might be better for companies looking to get every last dollar. Unity's executives had resisted that because of their belief that if the largest institutional investors knew they were going to get a last-minute heads-up, they would submit artificially low prices and pollute the integrity of the auction. William Blair's Carl Chiou had argued in favor of designing an open system for Unity's IPO but ultimately had been overruled.

As DoorDash executives thought through the mechanics, they heard similar concerns from potential investors. They made it clear to Adarkar and others in his finance department that they didn't like the blind order-entry system. Some felt cut out of the process and worried that they wouldn't get enough shares in the IPO.

DoorDash also worried about losing valued shareholders if those shareholders bid too low. Several of the largest public market investors were already invested in private rounds. Xu and Adarkar knew them and wanted them in their IPO.

As investors input their final orders into Goldman's system, the Door-Dash executives made the difficult but ultimately correct choice, they felt, to selectively brief investors on where they should bid. As the IPO neared, Adarkar and his bankers called the top five or ten investors and told them the price at which they would probably need to bid to get a meaningful allocation. Other investors were kept mostly in the dark. Goldman's bankers weren't pleased about the change in plans. They asked the DoorDash executives to keep it quiet. If word got around that Goldman's so-called blind auction could be gamed by investors who would get a last look, it would train investors to wait to put in their best bids until they got a call. The moment the DoorDash executives allowed the bankers and salespeople to start providing feedback, in other words, the resulting communications would begin destroying the exact value of the system, which was to get a true understanding of investors' interest at various price points. It would render useless the system Goldman had built.

"The communication back is challenging from a longer-term perspective for the hybrid auction, because if people get the expectation that they're going to get the call, then it does change their strategy," said one of the people involved in the process. DoorDash "probably had the good fortune of being fairly early in this."

■ ■ ■

After the close of trading on December 8, DoorDash executives and their Goldman bankers, including Jane Dunlevie and Will Connolly, gathered over Zoom to decide on an IPO price and allocate shares. The executives were already satisfied. Investor bids were more than where the company felt like it needed to price its shares. From the updated range, the executives could see that investor demand extended well above $100.

And yet they wanted to be smart about the price they chose. While the pandemic had been a tailwind, they didn't know what the future might hold. As a result, they were wary of pricing the stock too high and effectively promising a higher rate of growth to investors who bought at the higher price. If they disappointed investors with their earnings, the stock would come crashing down, they feared, and hurt their credibility with investors.

In the end, the executives felt confident at a price of $102, a modest 10.3 percent increase over the midpoint of the upwardly revised range. DoorDash became just one of the few companies, including Snowflake, to price its IPO at $100 or more.

"When they get to a certain price and feel like they've achieved a fair valuation or a valuation that's consistent with their target valuation," Goldman's Connolly explained later, "some companies say, 'Well, okay, I've gotten to this point. I'm less worried about the efficiency point, and now I'm more focused on: Can I also have this shareholder or that shareholder that I really like?'"

At $102, DoorDash knew it would be able to allocate shares to some of its favored investors. If they moved the share price higher, they risked leaving some of them behind.

In a role reversal, Goldman's bankers worried that the company might be setting itself up for a large pop the following day, and they advocated for a higher price, according to one person involved in the discussion.

.   .   .

The next morning, as Goldman gathered orders to open DoorDash's stock for trading, the bank struggled to come up with enough supply to meet the demand.

At 10:19, market makers on the floor of the NYSE sent the first price indication, suggesting that shares might open between $125 and $130. Demand continued to outstrip supply over the next hour and a half. At 11:50, the shares were still rising, and it now looked like they might open at between $180 and $185.

It took nearly another hour for market makers to release the stock, at which point it opened for trading at $182. That was 78 percent higher than the IPO price.

At least two factors explained the surge: a lack of supply and retail interest. The company had only sold 33 million shares, less than 15 percent of the total outstanding. And in their diligence to allocate those shares to long-term investors, Adarkar and DoorDash's team hadn't left many with investors who were willing to sell. The lack of a greenshoe kept underwriters from selling additional shares.

Another explanation for the huge pop was the influence of retail traders who had become a much bigger part of the market. According to the estimates of bankers and trading personnel, retail trading may have accounted for about

20 percent of daily trading activity, double the typical 10 percent or so, at the end of 2020, fueled by government stimulus checks and the popularity of trading apps like Robinhood.

As the NYSE brought trading to a close that day and Airbnb executives gathered with their bankers to price their own IPO, DoorDash closed at $189.51, an 85 percent pop. The steps that DoorDash's executives had taken to dampen the share surge had not succeeded. Some of that was expected. They had chosen $102 knowing that investors had placed orders at much higher prices. And some of it was the influence of retail traders.

■ ■ ■

The IPO market would have one more news event before the end of the year. Less than two weeks after DoorDash's IPO, regulators at the SEC finally rendered a verdict on the NYSE's proposal for the creation of the primary direct floor listing, which would allow companies to raise capital alongside a direct listing. The agency had approved the proposal in August, only to issue a stay when the Council of Institutional Investors asked that the matter be put before a vote of the SEC's commissioners.

On December 22, the SEC ratified its decision from August to approve the NYSE's rule change. In its discussion, it said that it did not interpret the law as requiring an underwriter in a securities offering. The involvement of a financial advisor, such as in a direct listing, would be sufficient to provide investors protection under the law, the agency wrote.

The SEC spent several pages explaining why it did not view Slack's legal defense around the traceability of shares to be something special to direct listings or worrisome enough to keep it from approving the NYSE's rule change. The explanation addressed the concern that the Council of Institutional Investors had shared in an early comment letter. And then the SEC wrote about the benefits it saw in the direct listing, particularly around its ability to involve a broader swath of investors and set the price of shares in a much more transparent matching of supply and demand.

First, investors "who might not otherwise receive an initial allocation" in an IPO might "be able to purchase securities in a Primary Direct Floor Listing," the agency wrote. "The proposed rule change therefore has the potential to broaden the scope of investors that are able to purchase securities in an initial public offering, at the initial public offering price, rather than in after-market trading."

Second, "because the price of securities issued by the company in a Primary Direct Floor Listing will be determined based on market interest and the matching of buy and sell orders, Primary Direct Floor Listings will provide an alternative way to price securities offerings that may better reflect prices in the aftermarket, and thus may allow for efficiencies in IPO pricing and allocation."

Two of the five commissioners voted against the proposal. Commissioners Allison Herren Lee and Caroline Crenshaw, holding the two seats reserved for Democrats during a Republican presidency, issued a statement saying that "the lack of a traditional underwriter means investors will lose a key protection: a gatekeeper incented to ensure that the disclosures around an initial listing are accurate and not misleading."

Nonetheless, the decision brought an end to thirteen months of haggling and set the stage for a radical transformation of the IPO process. The NYSE was ecstatic. "This is a game changer for our capital markets, leveling the playing field for everyday investors and providing companies with another path to go public at a moment when they are seeking just this type of innovation," NYSE president Stacey Cunningham said in a statement. Appearing on CNBC that day, she said it was a welcome change to the process of going public, and likely to lower the cost of capital for companies entering the public markets.

"Just think about all those examples when we see an IPO pop on the first day, and there are shares allocated the night before and it gets priced at a certain level," she said. "Then the next day it's up 100 percent and people say, 'Well, that's a great IPO. Look how wonderful and exciting this company is.' It's not a great IPO if you were the one that sold shares the night before, because you could've gotten a much better price if everybody was participating in that offering."

It was here that John Tuttle, who had watched the innovation unfold since helping Farley with Spotify's early analysis, offered a broader take on the significance of the moment. "I call it the People's IPO," Tuttle said. "It's about the people. That's who markets serve. If you think about how much wealth creation has happened because of the capital market system, and the ability to empower entrepreneurs and allow investors to be part of that success, the more people we can bring to that dance, the better it is for the world."

Gurley, too, couldn't help but weigh in on what had been an eighteen-month campaign on his part to get direct listings taken seriously. Appearing on CNBC's *Closing Bell* later that day, Gurley said that the SEC's approval would eventually bring an end to traditional IPOs. "I can't imagine, in my mind, when you can do a primary offering through a direct listing, why any board or CEO or founder would choose to go through this archaic process that has resulted in massive one-day wealth transfers straight from founders, employees, and investors to the buy side." He added, "In the future you'll be able to go on Robinhood and if you want to participate in an IPO, you can." He had taken to the Robinhood app just months earlier to test his point, purchasing ten shares in Palantir's direct listing. "Let's not let these intermediaries and gatekeepers hand-allocate who gets this underpriced stock," the venture capitalist said.

In an email to a reporter who asked whether the narrative around IPOs had truly been altered, Gurley wrote just four words: "It just changed. Forever."

EPILOGUE

SPACs, Everywhere, 2021

Whether Gurley is right remains to be seen.

By November 2021, nearly a dozen direct listings had taken place since Spotify's transaction, including six in that year alone. Among those was gaming platform Roblox, cryptocurrency exchange Coinbase, and eyeglasses retailer Warby Parker.

Some portion of those set a high-water mark on the first day of trading, only to see the shares decline over the following days. Institutional investors began to wait out the listings in the hopes of getting a better deal. It was a sign the market was beginning to adapt to the new listing approach.

Most companies continued to choose the traditional IPO, in what Goldman Sachs called a "supercycle" for technology listings supported by rising stock markets. More than 120 companies raised $71 billion in proceeds in traditional U.S. IPOs through November 12, 2021, delivering more than $3 billion in fees to Wall Street underwriters. The figures roughly doubled 2020's count. By November 2021, not one company had publicly announced any intention to figure out how to raise capital alongside a direct listing. While the surging IPO market was credited with giving entrepreneurs the freedom and safety to try new things, it also exerted a countervailing force. Companies felt like they couldn't wait to go public and hash out the primary direct listing with regulators if it meant missing the IPO window.

Instead, innovation largely took hold within the traditional structure. The Unity–Goldman Sachs order-entry system, which Goldman branded after the fact as the "transparent IPO," or T-IPO, and Morgan Stanley's look-alike became standard. Many firms scrapped the traditional 180-day lockup, instead allowing a portion of sales on the first day or releasing insiders once the stock price rose a certain amount. Retail investors became a bigger part of the conversation, spurred by features on Robinhood and other trading apps that gave users a chance to buy into IPOs.

Changes made to the traditional IPO market have spread to other industries. In 2021, the SEC chose to make the testing-the-waters meetings enabled by the JOBS Act available to companies in every industry. In financial markets as well as product markets, technology companies were leading the way.

There was still much to resolve about the mechanics of raising money with a direct listing. The biggest hurdle was finding and adjusting the price range that the SEC required every company to have published on the cover of its registration statement. Unlike an IPO, where the price of the shares is set over days and weeks, the direct listing would price in an auction in the middle of the trading day. Lawyers expected the SEC to require an amended prospectus if the price settled outside of the range. That was a nonstarter—approval for an amended filing typically took a day, which would slow down the process and potentially discourage investors from participating.

Workarounds were proposed, like a standard that would have the SEC review and sign off on an updated range within an hour or two. But not one company took the lead in negotiating a path through the thicket. The talks were likely to take months, all while other companies were getting wealthy by selling into rising markets.

The boom in blank check companies sponsored by the likes of Bill Ackman and Chamath Palihapitiya gave companies yet another option. In 2020, 248 SPACs raised $83 billion, while more than 550 deals raised more than $150 billion in 2021. Whether technology companies would fully embrace the trend by selling to the blank check firms remains to be seen.

Nonetheless, the SEC's approval just before Christmas 2020 served as a fitting coda to a four-year period of rapid change in how companies exercised their fundamental need to raise capital from public market investors. Markets change and adapt, often slowly and then all at once. What took place in the months leading up to Spotify's direct listing and in the years after felt like a moment in time that venture capitalists, startup executives, and investment bankers will remember for years. Suddenly someone challenged the status quo, which had felt broken to so many for so long. McCarthy's simple act of asking questions was a reminder to entrepreneurs that the IPO process was designed for them. And that they should take on the mantle and make it work for them.

In every IPO, company executives try to solve for particular objectives. Many want to raise as much money as possible by selling shares at the highest price, while others are more concerned with allowing insiders an opportunity to sell stock immediately. Some simply want to pay as few fees as possible to their investment banks. Still others may prefer exploring features further down the auction spectrum, by making orders binding or subject to pro rata allocations.

For those who are asking the hard questions about the process, the goal becomes finding the best way to balance the competing forces of supply and demand to arrive at the preferred outcome.

"Three years ago, I don't think you could even have these discussions with the banks, because there was no choice," said one executive at a company that successfully questioned the status quo. Now companies had more leverage because they can go public through a direct listing or a blank check company. The investment banks "recognize that the product has to evolve," the executive said.

By 2021, the group of executives, investors, and bankers who had led the recent wave of innovation began to move on. McCarthy stepped down as Spotify's CFO in early 2020, handing the reins to Paul Vogel. A year later, McCarthy joined the board of a blank check company launched by former Goldman Sachs banker Gregg Lemkau, who had left during the pandemic for a job running Michael Dell's investment firm.

Jabal's time at Unity came to a surprising end. The company announced her departure in March 2021 and gave her a generous separation agreement when she left in May. Unlike her statement in the press release announcing her March 2019 hire, the press release announcing her departure didn't quote the CFO. It's unclear what led to her exit. Riccitiello continued on as CEO. Jabal and the company declined to comment.

Gurley stepped back from day-to-day investing at Benchmark, choosing not to invest money from the firm's tenth venture fund.

Lise Buyer and Carl Chiou continued advising companies looking to go public. In June, they restored the secrecy of the bids in the Unity-designed order-entry system to help Marqeta, a payment processing firm, go public. The stock rose just 13 percent in its first day of trading.

Executives at Airbnb and DoorDash continued to ride the wave of the pandemic economy. In November 2021, Airbnb reported quarterly revenue of $2.5 billion and earnings of $1.22 a share, defying expectations. By the end of October 2021, DoorDash's stock was hovering close to $200. More important to the company's management team, nine out of the ten most important shareholders receiving allocations in the IPO held on to the majority of their shares.

Most prognosticators agreed that it would likely take a new personality, an executive or a group of executives with smarts and an independent streak, to continue pushing for change. If the new innovators make more progress, they will have the early disruptors to thank for paving the way.

Acknowledgments

I t isn't long into writing a book when an author realizes that, while much of writing is solitary, getting the finished product out the door takes an entire village. Thankfully, I was surrounded by a cast of collaborators who were generous, friendly, and thoughtful throughout this process. Each of them contributed something meaningful that made this book better. I'm so grateful.

First I want to thank my parents, Barbara, Bob, Chris, and Eloise, for raising me right. Dad, you bought me my first laptop when I returned from abroad and said I wanted to be a writer. Mom and Bob, you gave me a love of language and an appreciation for critical thinking. To my siblings and in-laws, thank you for your love and support. I love you all very much.

This book wouldn't exist without my agent, Jud Laghi, who saw in a WeWork feature story the potential for a considerably longer behind-the-scenes treatment on IPOs. Jud has believed in me and the book every step of the way, patiently going back and forth over many months of drafting the initial proposal, lending an ear when I was at my most needy, and always offering a calm and principled voice.

I want to thank Sean Desmond, my editor and publisher, for his sponsorship of this book. Sean was a wonderful ally, particularly when he weighed in with a suggestion on structure that saved the book from a morass. As a first-time author, I couldn't have wished for a publisher with more patience or flexibility than Sean, who rolled with it as well as I could have expected when I broke my elbow just weeks from an important deadline or asked for more production time to add polish. Thank you.

Thanks also to Sean's excellent team at Twelve, including Megan

Perritt-Jacobson, Zohal Karimy, and Bob Castillo, the production chief, who kindly held my hand through an uncertain production process with a strange lexicon and graciously answered my many questions.

I want to thank all of my peers who have covered IPOs, written insightful profiles of this book's subjects, or otherwise taught me about the machinery of Wall Street or Silicon Valley. Many of you know who you are or will find your clips in the source notes. Thank you for being such professionals.

To my current colleagues at Insider, former colleagues at Bloomberg and the Bond Buyer, and other friends in the industry, thank you for helping me along the way. I wouldn't be where I am today without you. I want to give special thanks to Cardiff Garcia, Brad Keoun, and Donal Griffin, each of whom has served as a mentor, friend, and professional North Star, helping me to navigate the world of journalism with competence and integrity. Thank you.

Thank you to my bosses at Insider, who encouraged me to pursue book writing and made sure I had the time I needed to create this work of nonfiction. To Henry Blodget, Nich Carlson, Matt Turner, Olivia Oran, and Amanda Cantrell—as well as Alyson Shontell and Meredith Mazzilli, who have since moved on—I owe my thanks.

Every writer needs a reader who edits, and I was fortunate to have four. Thank you to Maggie Millner for tightening my proposal in a way that kept my voice but made the prose sparkle. Thank you to Michele Host for your careful reading of the text and your many helpful suggestions. To Alex Millner, thank you for your meticulous read of an early manuscript and a key suggestion that immensely improved the opening of the book. To Christopher Bussmann, thank you for lending a hand when I couldn't type and for smoothing out my sentences when they needed them most. Alex, Maggie, and Christopher, our talks about books, writing, and journalism have made me a better reporter and a better person.

To Janet Byrne, an author's copy editor, thank you for the innumerable improvements you made to the text. Your verb suggestions made my writing more lively, you caught many factual errors, and, perhaps most important, you made me believe in this project at a moment when I was losing faith. Thank you. I hope we have occasion to work together again.

To Sean Lavery, one of the world's best fact-checkers, thank you for your tireless efforts and for adopting this book and its facts as your own. I owe you one.

To Evelyn Duffy, thank you for coming along for so much of this ride. Your early suggestions helped this daily journalist get his head around writing a 100,000-word book, your organizational ability kept me sane, and your answers to my many moral questions helped guide this work.

To my young children, whose births completely changed my outlook on life, I'm sorry my writing kept me away from you as much as it did. I hope the act of watching your father undergo the highs and lows of writing a book will have some positive impact on your future lives.

And, saving the best for last, I want to thank my lovely and selfless wife, Steph. I am forever grateful to you for taking on the majority of the childcare responsibilities throughout 2021 when I was holed up in the library writing. This book simply would not exist without you. Thank you for giving me the opportunity. I love you.

Source Notes

I conducted more than 150 interviews for this book. Most sources were granted anonymity so that they could speak openly. About 30 of the 150 interviews were done on the record during the course of reporting, though not all of those conversations ended up in the book.

These are the books I relied upon:

The Apple Revolution: The Real Story of How Steve Jobs and the Crazy Ones Took Over the World, Luke Dormehl, 2012.

Blood on the Street: The Sensational Inside Story of How Wall Street Analysts Duped a Generation of Investors, Charles Gasparino, 2005.

Capital Markets Handbook, Sixth Edition, John C. Burch Jr. and Bruce S. Foerster, 2004.

The Code: Silicon Valley and the Remaking of America, Margaret O'Mara, 2019.

A Critical History of Financial Crises: Why Would Politicians and Regulators Spoil Financial Giants?, Haim Kedar-Levy, 2015.

eBoys: The First Inside Account of Venture Capitalists at Work, Randall E. Stross, 2000.

The Golden Voyage: The Life and Times of William Bingham, 1752–1804, Robert C. Alberts, 1969.

In the Plex: How Google Thinks, Works, and Shapes Our Lives, Steven Levy, 2011.

Money and Power: How Goldman Sachs Came to Rule the World, William D. Cohan, 2011.

Netflixed: The Epic Battle for America's Eyeballs, Gina Keating, 2012.

No Rules Rules: Netflix and the Culture of Reinvention, Reed Hastings and Erin Meyer, 2020.

The Partnership: The Making of Goldman Sachs, Charles D. Ellis, 2008.

The Prince of Silicon Valley: Frank Quattrone and the Dot-Com Bubble, Randall Smith, 2010.

The Spotify Play: How CEO and Founder Daniel Ek Beat Apple, Google, and Amazon in the Race for Audio Dominance, Sven Carlsson and Jonas Leijonhufvud, 2021.

Steve Jobs, Walter Isaacson, 2011.

Super Pumped: The Battle for Uber, Mike Isaac, 2019.

That Will Never Work: The Birth of Netflix and the Amazing Life of an Idea, Marc Randolph, 2019.

Wall Street: A History, Fourth Edition, Charles R. Geisst, 2018.

Prologue

1   **Jobs had been preparing**: Marilyn Chase, "Apple Computer Registers Its First Offer, of 4.5 Million Shares at $14 to $17 Apiece," *Wall Street Journal*, November 7, 1980.

3   **Apple's bankers finally decided**: Robert J. Cole, "An 'Orderly' Debut for Apple," *New York Times*, December 13, 1980.

3   **played up the offering's success**: Mike Johnson, "Wall St. Gets Bite of Apple: $22 to $28.75," *San Francisco Examiner*, December 12, 1980.

Chapter 1

7   **An energetic man**: Andrew Pollack, "Hambrecht & Quist Loses Its Edge," *New York Times*, March 31, 1985.

7   **started in a Palo Alto garage**: "A home for innovation" brochure, HP Corporate Archives, December 2012.

9   **soon raised $1 million**: Susie Gharib Nazem, "The Folks Who Brought You Apple," *Fortune*, January 1981.

12   **a friend to the Ford family**: "The Power of Relationships Fuels Historic Ford Motor Company IPO," goldmansachs.com.

12   **secured the lead**: Records held by author.

13   **"never before in the history"**: "Ford Stock Offering Price Set; Announcement Is Due at 9 A.M.," *New York Times*, January 17, 1956.

13   **markets had begun to change**: Ellen Terrell, "History of the American and NASDAQ Stock Exchanges," Library of Congress, October 2012.

14   **christened the region**: Don C. Hoeffler, "Silicon Valley U.S.A.," *Electronic News*, January 11, 1971.

Chapter 2

17   **wrap up the IPO**: Robert J. Cole, "Genentech, New Issue, Up Sharply," *New York Times*, October 15, 1980.

17   **shares quickly surged by**: Charles J. Elia, "Genentech's Final Prospectus Shows Revenue Comes Primarily from Health-Care-Firm Jobs," *Wall Street Journal*, October 16, 1980.

17   **"Not since Eve has an Apple"**: Marilyn Chase, "Apple Computer Registers Its First Offer, of 4.5 Million Shares at $14 to $17 Apiece," *Wall Street Journal*, November 7, 1980.

18   **three regional firms patterned**: Michael Blumstein, "New Issues: Market Slumps," *New York Times*, September 19, 1984.

18   **promoted to oversee a banking unit**: Leslie Picker, "Alibaba IPO Grew Out of '80s Chaos and Guy from Goldman," Bloomberg News, May 10, 2014.

21   **won the job of advising**: Goldman Sachs, "Goldman Sachs Advises the British Government in the Country's Largest Privatization Yet," GoldmanSachs.com.

Chapter 3

26   **guidelines that sought**: Telis Demos, "IPO Quiet Time: Banks Can't Let Go," *Wall Street Journal*, August 20, 2012.

29   **internet economy was just so new**: Molly Baker and Joan Rigdon, "Netscape's IPO Gets an Explosive Welcome: SMALL STOCK FOCUS," *Wall Street Journal*, August 9, 1995.

31   **More than one hundred thousand people**: Reed Abelson, "Boston Beer: The Sad Fall of an I.P.O. Open to All," *New York Times*, November 24, 1996.

Chapter 4

33   **team's depth came into question**: Tim Povtak, "Depth Problems May Sink Gators," *Orlando Sentinel*, March 17, 1988.

33   **followed his sister**: Barry Ritholz, "Masters in Business: Bill Gurley, Benchmark," Bloomberg Opinion podcast, March 20, 2021.

33   **In early 1997, he downgraded**: "Netscape Stock Falls Again," CNET, January 14, 1997.

34   **priced its shares at $18**: Ari Levy, "Even During Amazon's IPO Process 20 Years Ago, Jeff Bezos Was Obsessed with Details," CNBC.com, May 14, 2017.

36   **Bear Stearns was much more cavalier**: Matt Siegel, "How Did Bear Stearns Bag So Many Net IPOs," *Fortune*, May 10, 1999.

36   **put a $400 price target on**: "A $400 Target Gives Amazon an Even Bigger Push Skyward," *Wall Street Journal*, December 17, 1998.

38   **a technique called a Dutch auction**: Sally Smith Hughes, Interviews with William R. Hambrecht in 2010, 2011.

38   **the third such effort**: Edward Wyatt, "Goldman Sachs to Take Stake in Wit Capital," *New York Times*, March 30, 1999.

39   **sent out mailers intended to provoke**: Lisa Bransten and Nick Wingfield, "Hambrecht Serves Little Guy, Tweaks the Big Guy, Online," *Wall Street Journal*, February 8, 1999.

39   **disrupt Wall Street's allocation process**: Jack Reerink, "W.R. Hambrecht to start selling IPOs via Internet," Reuters, February 8, 1999.

39   **would get his first opportunity**: Lorna Sheridan, "'End of an Era': Sonoma's Ravenswood Tasting Room to Close," *Sonoma Index-Tribune*, April 25, 2019.

39   **charged the winery**: Jack Willoughby, "Offerings in the Offing: New Wine, New Bottle; The 'Net Widens IPO Access," *Barron's*, April 19, 1999.

40   **sell all one million shares**: Dana Nigro, "Ravenswood Raises $11 Million Through Public Offering," *Wine Spectator*, April 10, 1999.

Chapter 5

44   **partnership came to an end**: "In a Paradigm Shift, Goldman Sachs Decides to Go Public," https://www.goldmansachs.com/our-firm/history/moments/1999-ipo.html.

44   **Few bankers personified the excesses**: Randall Smith and Susan Pulliam, "How Quattrone's CSFB Unit Doled Out Shares of Hot IPOs," *Wall Street Journal*, September 23, 2002.

45   **Dechman sent an email to some colleagues**: Joe Nocera, "Rigging the I.P.O. Game," *New York Times*, March 9, 2013.

46   **take a "fresh look"**: Securities and Exchange Commission, "SEC vs. Jack Benjamin Grubman," April 28, 2003.

47   **a higher form of liability**: Raymond Hennessey and Phyllis Plitch, "In IPO Scandal, Issuers Are Held Solely to Account," *Wall Street Journal*, June 13, 2005.

47   **busy propping up**: Suzanne McGee, "Hambrecht Continues to Buy Stock of Ravenswood Well After the IPO," *Wall Street Journal*, November 9, 1999.

47   **burning through their cash reserves**: Jack Willoughby, "Burning Up," *Barron's*, March 20, 2000.

48   **reached a settlement**: "Terence Neilan and Kenneth N. Gilpin, "Merrill Lynch to Pay $100 Million to Settle Analyst Charges," *New York Times*, May 21, 2002.

48   **Quattrone's empire crumbled**: Anupreeta Das and Randall Smith, "Quattrone Revisits 'Friends,'" *Wall Street Journal*, September 12, 2011.

49   **A *Frontline* documentary**: Martin Smith and Saran Silver, "Dot Con," PBS *Frontline*, January 24, 2002.

50   **might be an answer to the excesses of the past**: Nick Wingfield, "Effort to Use Dutch Auctions to Distribute IPOs Struggles," *Wall Street Journal*, July 31, 2002.

Chapter 6

51   **wasn't the first search engine**: Kevin J. Delaney and Robin Sidel, "Google IPO Aims to Change the Rules," *Wall Street Journal*, April 30, 2004.

52   **Google's "official lug-nut checker"**: Adam Lashinsky, "Google Finds a Good Analyst," *Fortune*, May 12, 2003.

54   **brushed off IPO talk**: "Google CEO Has No Near Term Plans for IPO," Reuters, May 5, 2003.

54   **Brin told another conference**: "Google Co-Founder Sees 'Good Chance' of Future IPO," Reuters, August 20, 2003.

56   **capture the public's imagination**: Bret Swanson, "Our Savior?," *Wall Street Journal*, November 4, 2003.

65   **an updated prospectus showing**: Jed Horowitz and Raymond Hennessey, "Google's IPO Will Be Including 31 Underwriters," *Wall Street Journal*, May 24, 2004.

67   **lead underwriters also required**: "Google's IPO Hurdles," *Wall Street Journal*, August 18, 2004.

68   **Peter Thiel joined CNBC**: Larry Kudlow and Jim Cramer, "Interview: Peter Thiel Discusses the Upcoming Google IPO," *Kudlow & Cramer*, CNBC, July 27, 2004.

70   **visited New York's Waldorf Astoria**: Gregory Zuckerman and Robin Sidel, "Google's Roadshow Leaves Investors Searching for Data," *Wall Street Journal*, July 29, 2004.

72   **PR team received word**: Kevin J. Delaney, Gregory Zuckerman, and Robin Sidel, "Google Interview May Set Back IPO; Auction Starts Today," *Wall Street Journal*, August 13, 2004.

75   **felt the need to seek out**: Robin Sidel, "Google IPO Tests Theories on Auctions," *Wall Street Journal*, June 7, 2004.

76   **Google told shareholders**: "Google Update," *Wall Street Journal*, August 18, 2004.

78   **each received 5.3 million to allocate**: "Morgan Stanley, Credit Suisse Get Most Shares in Google IPO," *Wall Street Journal*, August 19, 2004.

79   **"feeling particularly lucky"**: Gregory Zuckerman, "Google Shares Prove Big Winners—For a Day," *Wall Street Journal*, August 20, 2004.

79   **a narrative began to take hold**: Kevin J. Delaney and Robin Sidel, "How Miscalculations and Hubris Hobbled Celebrated Google IPO," *Wall Street Journal*, August 19, 2004.

80   **moved all over the place**: Riva Richmond, "Google's Stock: Up, Down And All Around," Dow Jones Newswires, November 11, 2004.

80   **lack of projections**: Kevin J. Delaney, "Will Google Finally Reveal Itself?," *Wall Street Journal*, October 20, 2004.

81   **Reyes, Google's CFO, misspoke**: Kevin J. Delaney, "Google Warning on Growth Unnerves Investors," *Wall Street Journal*, March 1, 2006

Chapter 7

82   **"leave your friends in a knife fight"**: Greg Sandoval, "Why Netflix's CFO Decided to Go," CNET, December 9, 2010.

83   **ready for something else**: Greg Sandoval, "Netflix's Lost Year: The Inside Story of the Price-Hike Train Wreck," CNET, July 11, 2012.

84   **headline at *Business Insider* said it all**: Dan Frommer, "Netflix CFO Leaves Because He Can't Become CEO," *Business Insider*, December 7, 2010.

84   **inviting 350 contacts to set up profiles**: Colleen DeBaise, "Launching LinkedIn from a Living Room," *Wall Street Journal*, October 21, 2009.

85   **left many shaking their heads**: Henry Blodget, "Anyone Who Still Thinks LinkedIn's IPO Pop Was Good Should Look at Amazon," *Business Insider*, May 31, 2011.

85   **doubling the price**: Julianna Pepitone and David Goldman, "Pandora Stock Surges in IPO, Then Cools," CNN Money, June 15, 2011.

85   **a group of eighteen experts convened**: James Freeman, "Kate Mitchell: How Silicon Valley Won in Washington," *Wall Street Journal*, April 7, 2012.

86   **"whose input and expertise"**: IPO Task Force, "Rebuilding the IPO On-Ramp: Putting Emerging Companies and the Job Market Back on the Road to Growth," Presented to The U.S. Department of the Treasury, October 20, 2011, Appendix B, 35.

87   **"test the waters" conversations**: Emily Chasan, "JOBS Act Obscures IPO Pipeline," *Wall Street Journal*, November 7, 2012.

87   **well into its IPO process**: Shayndi Raice, "Facebook Targets Huge IPO," *Wall Street Journal*, November 29, 2011.

87   **a way to avoid tripping**: Steven Davidoff Solomon, "The Legal Issues in the Goldman-Facebook Deal," *New York Times DealBook*, January 10, 2011.

88   **threw a wrench into its offering**: Khadeeja Safdar, "Facebook, One Year Later: What Really Happened in the Biggest IPO Flop Ever," *The Atlantic*, May 10, 2013.

89   **took steps to spell out the implications**: Suzanne Craig and Ben Protess, "Massachusetts Fines Morgan Stanley Over Facebook I.P.O.," *New York Times DealBook*, December 17, 2012.

89   **rehearsed with a senior Morgan Stanley banker**: David Benoit, "Mass vs. Morgan Stanley: Highlights from the Facebook Consent Order," *Wall Street Journal*, December 17, 2012.

90   **media outlets widely reported**: Aaron Luchetti and Jean Eaglesham, "Morgan Stanley Gets Facebook Fine," *Wall Street Journal*, December 18, 2012.

90   **failed to trade thousands of orders**: Chris Welch, "Facebook IPO 'Was Not Our Finest Hour,' Says NASDAQ Chief," *The Verge*, May 20, 2012.

90   **$10 million fine for NASDAQ**: Nathaniel Popper, "Nasdaq Is Fined $10 Million Over Mishandled Facebook Public Offering," *New York Times DealBook*, May 29, 2013.

91   **an influx of cash**: Michael J. Mauboussin and Dan Callahan, CFA, "Public to Private Equity in the United States: A Long-Term Look," Morgan Stanley Investment Management, August 4, 2020.

Chapter 8

92   **social media company partnered**: Alex Pham, "Spotify Music Service Coming 'Soon' to U.S.," *Los Angeles Times*, July 7, 2011.

93   **In 2013, Technology Crossover Ventures**: John D. Stoll, Evelyn Rusli, and Sven Grundberg, "Spotify Hits a High Note: Valuation Tops $4 Billion," *Wall Street Journal*, November 21, 2013.

95   **Spotify announced McCarthy's appointment**: Pater Kafka, "Former Netflix CFO Barry McCarthy Joins Spotify Board," *Recode*, February 11, 2014.

95   **a rare blunder**: Alyson Shontell, "A SILICON VALLEY DISASTER: A 21-Year-Old Stanford Kid Got $30 Million, Then Everything Blew Up," *Business Insider*, April 14, 2014.

Chapter 9

97   **companies had been christened**: Aileen Lee, "Welcome to the Unicorn Club: Learning from Billion-Dollar Startups," *TechCrunch*, November 2, 2013.

99   **Spotify put up impressive growth**: Ben Sisario, "Spotify Says Its List of Subscribers Has Grown to 15 Million," *New York Times*, January 12, 2015.

100   **turned to Goldman Sachs**: Ben Sisario and Andrew Ross Sorkin, "Spotify Attracts Investments from Coca-Cola and Fidelity," *New York Times*, November 14, 2012.

100   **publicly removed her catalog**: Hannah Karp and Sven Grundberg, "Taylor Swift Pulls Her Music from Spotify," *Wall Street Journal*, November 4, 2015.

101   **reports surfaced**: Douglas MacMillan and Telis Demos, "Spotify Nears Deal to Raise $400 Million at $8.4 Billion Valuation," *Wall Street Journal*, April 10, 2015.

102 **hiring was a sign**: Douglas MacMillan, "Spotify Names Barry McCarthy Finance Chief," *Wall Street Journal*, June 17, 2015.

103 **remembered those early days**: Polina Marinova, "Spotify's First Investor On Why the Company's Unusual IPO Makes Sense," *Fortune*, March 21, 2018.

106 **news of the convertible bond**: Douglas MacMillan, Matt Jarzemsky, and Maureen Farrell, "Spotify Raises $1 Billion in Debt Financing," *Wall Street Journal*, March 29, 2015.

106 **explain senior management's thinking**: Record held by author.

Chapter 10

109 **Many in the industry agreed**: Joe Nocera, "Was LinkedIn Scammed?," *New York Times*, May 20, 2011.

111 **new general counsel**: Ina Fried, "Spotify Taps Top Microsoft Lawyer Horacio Gutierrez as General Counsel," *Recode*, March 14, 2016.

111 **decided against taking the position**: Lucas Shaw, "Spotify's Top Lawyer Has Spent Years Making Apple the Bad Guy," *Bloomberg Businessweek*, July 14, 2021.

112 **the fundraising environment**: Richard Waters and Leslie Hook, "Death of the Unicorn?," *Financial Times*, June 28, 2016.

116 **directly listed a division**: "VMware Shares Soar After IPO Prices at $29 a Share," Reuters, August 14, 2007.

118 **tech executives had soured on it**: Crystal Tse, Katie Roof, and Olivia Carville, "Airbnb Chooses IPO Venue in Big Win for Nasdaq Over NYSE," Bloomberg News, October 27, 2020.

119 **host of a star-studded summer conference**: Douglas MacMillan and Telis Demos, "Allen & Co. Flourishes as a Tech Deal Maker," *Wall Street Journal*, February 23, 2014.

Chapter 11

125 **first speech as SEC chair**: Jay Clayton speech, Economic Club of New York, YouTube, July 12, 2017.

127 **worked with the SEC**: Lucas Shaw, "SEC Is Studying Spotify's Plan to Bypass IPO in NYSE Listing," Bloomberg News, August 21, 2017.

128 **a strategy for expanding into China**: Wayne Ma, "Music-Streaming Giants Spotify and Tencent Music Swap Stakes," *Wall Street Journal*, December 13, 2017.

128 **arranging for a share swap**: "Taking the Lead in the Future of Music," goldmansachs.com.

129 **signed a lease**: Steve Cuozzo and Lois Weiss, "Spotify Signs Massive Lease at 4 World Trade Center," *New York Post*, February 15, 2017.

132 **something more than a typical**: Anita Balakrishnan, "Chicken Wraps, Cuff Links and Cloud: The Details from Snap's IPO Roadshow in NYC," CNBC.com, February 21, 2017.

132 **opened the event**: "Investor Day—March 2018," Spotify.com, March 15, 2018.

137 **brought a good luck charm**: Nicole Bullock, "Trader Who Has Waited His Entire Career for an Uber IPO," *Financial Times*, May 8, 2019.

138   **Paci was well suited**: Dakin Campbell, "A Morgan Stanley Trading Desk Headed Up by a Former NFL Quarterback Will Play a Central Role in Palantir's and Asana's Public Debuts. Here's an Inside Look at How It'll All Go Down," *Business Insider*, September 28, 2020.

139   **wasn't going to make a big deal**: Sean Czarnecki, "No Bell-Ringing, No Problem: A Look at Spotify's Unusually Transparent IPO," *PRWeek*, April 5, 2018.

140   **he hunched over**: Records held by author.

141   **drifted lower to close**: Theodore Schleifer and Rani Molla, "Spotify's First Day of Trading Ended Up Being Surprisingly Normal—And That's a Win for the Direct Listing," *Recode*, April 3, 2018.

Chapter 12

142   **he traveled to Sun Valley**: David Gura, "Here's a Peek Inside Sun Valley's 'Summer Camp for Billionaires,'" NPR, August 20, 2021.

142   **an exclusive ticket**: Carol J. Loomis and Patricia Neering, "Inside the Private World of Allen & Co. Putting a Premium on Personal Ties, This Family Firm Thrives in the Land of the Giants," *Fortune*, June 28, 2004.

142   **a one-sentence mention**: Michael J. de la Merced, "As Moguls Gather in Sun Valley, Here's Who Might Be in the Mood for Deals," *New York Times*, July 10, 2018.

143   **cut from a different cloth**: Adam Bryant, "Stewart Butterfield of Slack: Is Empathy on Your Résumé?," *New York Times*, July 11, 2015.

143   **an unusual perspective**: George Anders, "Revenge of the Philosophy Majors," *Forbes*, September 3, 2015.

144   **Slack had grown quickly**: Rachel Feintzeig, "A Company Without Email? Not So Fast," *New York Times*, June 17, 2014.

144   **doubled its number of users**: Farhad Manjoo, "Slack, the Office Messaging App That May Finally Sink Email," *New York Times*, March 11, 2015.

145   **"went into hyper-drive"**: Evelyn M. Rusli, "Startup Values Set Records," *Wall Street Journal*, December 29, 2014.

145   **doubled its valuation**: Deborah Gage, "Slack Investment and Valuation Gains Come Despite Private Company Jitters," *Wall Street Journal*, April 1, 2016; Farhad Manjoo, "Is Slack Really Worth $2.8 Billion? A Conversation with Stewart Butterfield," *New York Times*, April 16, 2015.

145   **raised another $200 million**: Mike Isaac, "Slack, a Leading Unicorn, Raises $200 Million in New Financing," *New York Times*, April 1, 2016.

145   **soon attracted competitors**: Salvador Rodriguez, "Slack Adds 1 Million Paying Users Amid Increasing Competition," Reuters, May 8, 2018.

145   **a broadside against Slack**: Salvador Rodriguez, "Microsoft Debuts Free Tier in Competitive Workplace Chat App Market," Reuters, July 12, 2018.

146   **told media outlets**: Alex Konrad, "Microsoft Doesn't Take Slack's Bait in Unveiling Rival 'Teams' Product—But Poses a Real Threat," *Forbes*, November 2, 2016.

146   **"paranoid about this"**: Rachel King, "Slack Girds for Battle with Messaging Rivals," *Wall Street Journal*, November 14, 2016.

147   **yet another fundraising**: Katie Roof, "Slack Nears Close of Financing Round at $7 Billion Valuation," *Wall Street Journal*, August 8, 2018.

148   **considering a stock market listing**: Maureen Farrell, "Slack Actively Preparing for Early 2019 IPO," *Wall Street Journal*, September 28, 2018.

148   **didn't need the money**: Eliot Brown, "Boss Talk: Slack's CEO Wants to Unshackle You from Email," *Wall Street Journal*, October 10, 2018.

Chapter 13

151   **filed paperwork with the SEC**: Greg Bensinger and Maureen Farrell, "Uber Joins Lyft in Race to Tap Investors," *Wall Street Journal*, December 7, 2018.

151   **thirty-eight tech companies**: Corrie Driebusch, "Tech Unicorns Are Going Public at Near-Record Pace," *Wall Street Journal*, December 18, 2018.

151   **put it colorfully**: John D. Stoll, "How to Govern the Unicorns," *Wall Street Journal*, December 21, 1980.

151   **among thousands of government employees**: Aaron Back, "Why the IPO Boom Will Continue," *Wall Street Journal*, May 19, 2019.

151   **suggested for the first time**: Maureen Farrell, "Slack Plans to Follow Spotify on Unconventional IPO Route," *Wall Street Journal*, January 11, 2019.

151   **back-of-the-envelope math**: Jennifer Saba, "Slack Is the Tech Everybody Likes but No One Needs," Reuters, January 17, 2019.

152   **ran with the headline**: Richard Waters, "Slack Faces Growing Challenge from Big Tech," *Financial Times*, January 26, 2019.

153   **started interviewing banks**: Maureen Farrell and Dana Mattioli, "Peloton Interviews Banks for IPO," *Wall Street Journal*, February 11, 2019.

154   **revenue in the twelve months through January**: "Slack Posts $140.7 Mln Loss in FY 2019 as It Prepares to Go Public," Reuters, April 26, 2019.

154   **calculations conducted by**: Chris Nuttall, "Uber Sets Price Range, Slack Goes Direct," *Financial Times*, April 26, 2019.

154   **two classes of stock**: Corrie Driebusch and Maureen Farrell, "Slack Chooses NYSE for Direct Listing," *Wall Street Journal*, April 1, 2019.

154   **streamed to the internet**: Laura Forman, "Will Slack Be Another Shocker?," *Wall Street Journal*, May 15, 2019.

155   **published its reference price**: Corrie Driebusch and Maureen Farrell, "Slack's Reference Price Set at $26 for Thursday Trading Debut in Direct Listing," *Wall Street Journal*, June 19, 2019.

155   **sat down for an interview**: Andrew Ross Sorkin, Interview with Stewart Butterfield, *Squawk Box*, CNBC, June 20, 2019.

157   **that afternoon they hit $42**: Richard Waters, "Slack Valued at More Than $20bn in Stock Market Debut," *Financial Times*, June 20, 2019.

Chapter 14

159   **priced its shares at $15**: Lauren Thomas and Lauren Hirsch, "Stitch Fix Shares Retreat After IPO Pop, Close at $15.15," CNBC.com, November 17, 2017.

159   **disappointing performance was captured**: Corrie Driebusch and Maureen Farrell, "Stitch Fix Prices Shares at $15 Apiece in IPO," *Wall Street Journal*, November 16, 2017.

160   **took responsibility**: Nick Bastone, "The Search Tech Company Powering Uber and Tinder Just Went Public—And It Popped Up 94% in Its First Day of Trading," *Business Insider*, October 5, 2018.

161   **stumbled out of the gate**: Joshua Franklin, Aparajita Saxena, and Heather Somerville, "Uber's Market Debut Sours Most Anticipated IPO Since Facebook," Reuters, May 10, 2019.

161   **whether Uber would ever turn a profit**: "Uber's Problem Is Whether It Can Be Profitable, Says *Recode*'s Kara Swisher," CNBC, May 10, 2019.

161   **Gurley now had reason**: @bgurley (Bill Gurley), "One perspective—CrowdStrike (and other way underpriced deals) are the true definition of a 'broken' IPO. The stock was grossly under-priced by over 80%. As there were 20.7mm shares sold, this delta represents $575mm (20.7*27.8) that is absent from the company's coffers," Twitter, June 12, 2019.

162   **laid the groundwork**: @bgurley (Bill Gurley), "If your company is interested in a direct-listing, recommend you call Morgan Stanley. Other banks want to position direct listings as 'exceptional' or 'rare.' MS believes they are 1) a better mousetrap, and 2) can be used broadly," Twitter, June 19, 2019.

162   **ping-ponged down the corridors**: Rebecca Ungarino, "One of the Most Influential VCs in Silicon Valley Told Startups to 'Call Morgan Stanley' After Slack's Successful Direct Listing," *Business Insider*, June 21, 2019.

163   **published a blog post**: Jamie McGurk, "All about Direct Listings," Andreessen Horowitz, July 2, 2019.

165   **harbored a rivalry**: Tad Friend, "Tomorrow's Advance Man," *The New Yorker*, May 11, 2015.

166   **plan for a daylong symposium**: Dan Primack, "VCs Plan Invite-Only Meeting to Promote Direct Listings," *Axios*, September 19, 2019.

166   **"only Slack was capable"**: "Slack Shares Tank After Dismal Forecast," Reuters, September 5, 2019.

167   **pages of the financial press**: "Slack: Sells Like Team Spirit," *Financial Times*, September 6, 2019; Dan Gallagher, "Slack's Stock Fall Might Not Be Finished," *Wall Street Journal*, September 6, 2019.

167   **broke issue when**: Lydia Ramsey Pflanzer and Dakin Campbell, "SmileDirectClub's IPO Was Such a Disaster That the CEO Called Up JPMorgan's Jamie Dimon to Ask What Went Wrong," *Business Insider*, September 20, 2019.

168   **also worked with design and engineering clients**: Stefanos Chen, "How Virtual Reality Is Augmenting Realty," *New York Times*, November 8, 2019.

Chapter 15

170   **Jabal had spoken up**: Laura Emily Dunn, "Women in Business Q&A: Kim Jabal, CFO, Weebly," *Huffington Post*, February 3, 2017.

170   **In the book, Sandberg named Jabal**: Sheryl Sandberg, *Lean In: Women, Work, and the Will to Lead* (New York: Knopf, 2013), 181.

170   **She told one interviewer**: James Kosur, "17 Highly Successful Executives Explain How They Balance Work and Life," *Business Insider*, November 20, 2015.

171   **shot up nearly 17 percent**: "First Quarter Review and Outlook," NASDAQ, April 2, 2019.

171   **"first notable software company"**: Lauren Feiner and Ari Levy, "PagerDuty Pops Nearly 60% in Debut as Tech IPO Market Heats Up," CNBC.com, April 11, 2019.

174   **wrote a scathing op-ed**: Michael Moritz, "Investment Banks Are Losing Their Grip on IPOs," *Financial Times*, August 18, 2019.

Chapter 16

176   **received an agenda**: @KatieS (Katie Jacobs Stanton), "Grateful for leaders like @bgurley leading the conversation about direct listings. And bonus to do it with great women in venture @janamal @ImChauncey," Twitter, October 1, 2019.

177   **occasionally referred to**: @chetanp (Chetan Puttagunta), "In this evening's notes from @TheRealCarlChi1; folks like Carl and others are working on studying the data around IPOs so that there is better information," Twitter, July 6, 2020.

178   **likened the effect to prospect theory**: Tim Loughran and Jay R. Ritter, "Why Don't Issuers Get Upset about Leaving Money on the Table in IPOs?," *The Review of Financial Studies* 15, no. 2 (2002): 413–43.

179   **sat onstage**: @GoldmanSachs (Goldman Sachs), "@Spotify's Barry McCarthy, @latham-watkins' Greg Rodgers & $GS' Will Connolly discuss the ins and outs of direct listings, plus other innovative paths to going public at #GSPICC," Twitter, October 4, 2019.

179   **Siewert introduced the panelists**: Exchanges at Goldman Sachs, "Episode 139: What's Next for Direct Listings and IPOs?," Goldmansachs.com, October 11, 2019.

Chapter 17

184   **"something that's questionable"**: "The Goldman Sachs Group Inc. (GS), CEO David Solomon on Q3 2019 Results—Earnings Call Transcript," Seeking Alpha, October 15, 2019.

185   **tried to earn a place**: Dana Mattioli, "Wall Street Types Don Yoga Pants and True Religion Jeans to Win Deals," *Wall Street Journal*, June 10, 2014.

185   **Grimes drove**: Maureen Farrell and Liz Hoffman, "Morgan Stanley Banker Is Also an Uber Driver," *Wall Street Journal*, October 18, 2018.

186   **The bank's pitch reminded her**: Randall Smith, "Quattrone, His Group Work Their Magic at First Boston," *Wall Street Journal*, September 24, 1999.

187   **filed their proposal**: New York Stock Exchange, "SR-NYSE-2019-67," November 26, 2019.

188   **shared the news**: @nyse (New York Stock Exchange), "We're taking the next step today in the evolution of the Direct Listing: This morning we filed a rule change with the SEC to allow companies to raise capital as part of a Direct Listing," Twitter, November 26, 2019.

188　　**"would not impose any burden"**: Ari Levy, "NYSE Proposes Allowing Companies to Raise Fresh Capital in direct Listings," CNBC.com, November 26, 2019.

188　　**rejected the proposal**: Alexander Osipovich, "SEC Rejects NYSE Plan to Expand Direct Listings," *Wall Street Journal*, December 6, 2019.

188　　**came out swinging**: Christopher A. Iacovella, "Re: Investor Protection Concerns Related to Direct Listings," American Securities Association letter to the Securities and Exchange Commission, December 12, 2019.

189　　**raising concerns that investors**: Jeffrey P. Mahoney, "Re: File Number SR-NYSE-2019-67," Council of Institutional Investors letter to the Securities and Exchange Commission, January 16, 2020.

190　　**traveled to the SEC**: Securities and Exchange Commission, Memorandums about meetings between NYSE officials and Commissioners Elad L. Roisman and Allison Herren Lee, respectively, on January 30, 2020, and January 31, 2020.

191　　**presented other options**: Records held by author.

Chapter 18

195　　**the World Health Organization (WHO) declared**: "WHO Director-General's Opening Remarks at the Media Briefing on COVID-19," World Health Organization, March 11, 2020.

195　　**customer base for video games**: Noah Smith, "The Giants of the Video Game Industry Have Thrived in the Pandemic. Can the Success Continue?," *Washington Post*, May 12, 2020.

197　　**Executives were seriously considering**: Dakin Campbell, "Inside a Failed Attempt to Reinvent the IPO Process with Airbnb and DoorDash," *Business Insider*, December 18, 2020.

199　　**decided to bring a fresh voice**: Ben Ashwell, "How Unity Used a Modified Auction to Go Public," *IR Magazine*, June 15, 2021.

200　　**secretly filed its first**: Unity Software Inc., Form S-1, Securities and Exchange Commission, May 20, 2020.

Chapter 19

204　　**begun to formulate a theory**: John Detrixhe, "The Bonkers IPO Market Has Obscured an Important Innovation for Listings," *Quartz*, December 23, 2020.

207　　**The two sides finally agreed**: Unity Software Inc., Form S-1, Securities and Exchange Commission, August 24, 2020.

209　　**little industry surprise**: Danny Crichton, "Sequoia Strikes Gold with Unity's IPO Filing," *TechCrunch*, August 24, 2020.

210　　**quickly overshadowed that day**: Richard Henderson and Richard Waters, "Tech Stock Charge Provides Impetus for Flurry of IPOs," *Financial Times*, August 24, 2020.

211　　**wasn't an advocate for tearing up**: @alexrkonrad (Alex Konrad), "Snowflake's Slootman agrees with @arampell and @skupor's essay on IPO demand curves. But the CEO also dismisses the notion that a high volume of first-day trading means hand-picked institutional investors won't stick around," Twitter, September 17, 2020.

211 **Slootman would later tell *Forbes***: Alex Konrad, "Snowflake CEO Frank Slootman Talks IPO Pop: Narrative of Lost Billions Is 'Nonsense Talk,'" *Forbes*, September 17, 2020.

212 **began to build enthusiasm**: Eric J. Savitz, "Get Ready for a Crazy Wave of IPOs. Here Are the Ones to Watch," *Barron's*, August 31, 2020.

Chapter 20

213 **gained a vote of confidence**: Alex Rampell and Scott Kupor, "In Defense of the IPO, and How to Improve It," Andreessen Horowitz, August 28, 2020.

214 **signed up two large buyers**: Snowflake Inc., Form S-1, Securities and Exchange Commission, September 8, 2020.

214 **hadn't invested in an IPO**: Yun Li and Maggie Fitzgerald, "Warren Buffett's Berkshire Hathaway Just Made a Fast $800 Million on Snowflake's Surging IPO," CNBC.com, September 16, 2020.

214 **"so hot it could melt"**: Robert Cyran, "Snowflake's $2.7 Bln IPO Is So Hot It Could Melt," *Breakingviews*, Reuters, September 9, 2020.

214 **first price range for its offering**: Unity Software Inc., Form S-1, Securities and Exchange Commission, September 9, 2020.

214 **the most in a week**: Antony Currie, "Snowflake-Led IPO Boomlet Puts Hope Over Profit," *Breakingviews*, Reuters, September 9, 2020.

214 **increased its IPO range substantially**: Lauren Feiner, "Snowflake Bumps Expected IPO Price by About 30%, Could Debut at More Than $30 Billion Valuation," CNBC.com, September 14, 2020.

215 **settled on $120**: Ari Levy and Leslie Picker, "Snowflake Prices IPO Above Increased Range, Implying Initial Market Cap of $33.3 Billion," CNBC.com, September 15, 2020.

215 **increase the initial range**: Alex Wilhelm, "JFrog and Snowflake's Aggressive IPO Pricing Point to Strong Demand for Cloud Shares," *TechCrunch*, September 16, 2020.

216 **finally opened the stock**: Danny Vena/Motley Fool, "Overwhelming Demand Made Warren Buffett-Backed Snowflake the Biggest Software IPO Ever," NASDAQ.com, September 16, 2020.

216 **broadcast the opening trade**: CNBC, "Snowflake Begins Trading in the Biggest Software IPO Ever," YouTube, September 16, 2020.

216 **shrugged off a question**: John Fortt, "Snowflake CEO on Record IPO: We're Not Focused on Growth at All Costs," CNBC, September 16, 2020.

216 **"complete and utter nonsense"**: "Buffett-Backed Snowflake's Value Doubles in Stock Market's Largest Software Debut," Reuters, September 16, 2020.

217 **"left a lot of money on the table"**: Emily Change, "Snowflake CEO 'Thrilled' with $73 Billion Valuation," Bloomberg Television, September 16, 2020.

217 **fired off a salvo**: @bgurley (Bill Gurley), "Some encouragement to comment on $SNOW IPO. While it would be easy to do normal post wrt mispricing, it is important

to understand what is different here from other IPOs. The most important data is broad (40 years of underpricing, 2020 worst year yet), vs. 1 company. [cont]," Twitter, September 16, 2020.

218   **he sent a third tweet**: @bgurley (Bill Gurley), "Outside of if the company/shareholders 'gave up' anything, the hand allocated investors received $4.3B is one day wealth transfer. That's an insane amount of REAL money. That, along with watching the theatre and drama today, it is HARD to say—this is exactly how it should work!," Twitter, September 16, 2020.

218   **Gurley wasn't done**: @bgurley (Bill Gurley), "In many ways, $SNOW is the final proof of just how broken process is. Frank Slootman is a HIGHLY experienced IPO CEO. He knows the game, & pushed hard to make sure he wasn't short-changing the company. But it didn't matter, because the process is set up to deliver this silliness," Twitter, September 16, 2020.

Chapter 21

221   **Twelve days after the IPO**: WhaleWisdom.com; Artisan Partners Limited Partnership, Form 13F, Securities and Exchange Commission, November 12, 2020; Gilder Gagnon Howe & Co. LLC, Form 13F, Securities and Exchange Commission, November 16, 2020.

222   **had something special planned**: Ryan Peterson, "Ringing the NYSE Bell Together: How Unity Put the 'U' in UPO," Unity, November 5, 2020.

224   **wearing an open-necked black shirt**: CNBC, "Unity CEO on IPO: We're Thrilled with the Money We've Raised," YouTube, September 18, 2020.

224   **stock price drifted down**: C Nivedita and Krystal Hu, "Unity Software Soars in Blockbuster NYSE Debut," Reuters, September 18, 2020.

225   **put the recent innovations in context**: Corrie Driebusch, "The IPO Market Parties Like It's 1999," *Wall Street Journal*, September 25, 2020.

225   **one late September screed**: @CathieDWood (Cathie Wood), "Equity Dutch auctions were designed to democratize initial public offerings. In 2014, I founded @ARKInvest to help democratize investing in the innovation space. Despite best intentions, this week $U went public in a Dutch auction sponsored by $GS that we believe missed the mark," Twitter, September 21, 2020.

225   **added a second tweet**: @CathieDWood (Cathie Wood), "Some of us who placed bids above the initial 40-44 indicated range, and then raised our bids above the revised 44-48 range, assuming that our bids would be filled, learned the hard way that we would receive nothing. Very few things surprise me in this business, but this one did," Twitter, September 21, 2020.

225   **Her third tweet**: @CathieDWood (Cathie Wood), "Apparently, $GS introduced a Dutch auction twist that did not require it to inform those who had committed to a price above the 'range' that the range had changed, unless the 'indicated price range' had increased by 20%+. Excuse me?," Twitter, September 21, 2020.

225   **It sounded to her**: @CathieDWood (Cathie Wood), "I am sure that $GS disclosed this twist in many documents, but it never apprised us despite discussions with its sales traders

of our clear desire to gain exposure to $U. Did $GS's highest revenue generating customers get the word? I don't want to be in that club. Just wondering," Twitter, September 21, 2020.

226   **Later that day**: @CathieDWood (Cathie Wood), "I stand corrected: $U did a Unified auction, not a Dutch auction, something completely new to me. With thanks both to my compliance team and to a long time professional friend, Lise Buyer, Partner at Class V Group LLC, for steering me correctly," Twitter, September 21, 2020.

226   **apologized to Goldman**: @CathieDWood (Cathie Wood), "With my apology to $GS, which was not monitoring the order book before it filled. That said, I do believe that our $GS sales trading contact, with whom we interacted many times for updates, should have explained the difference between Dutch and Unified auctions. Lessons learned," Twitter, September 21, 2020.

Chapter 22

228   **setting a valuation of $31 billion**: Greg Bensinger, "Airbnb Valued at $31 Billion After New Funding Round," *Wall Street Journal*, March 9, 2017.

228   **The company's path to its IPO**: Devin Banerjee, Eric Newcomer, and Leslie Picker, "Airbnb Said Close to Hiring Blackstone's Tosi for CFO Role," Bloomberg News, July 23, 2015.

229   **foot-dragging caused tensions**: Cory Weinberg, "At Airbnb, Tensions Bubble Between Chesky and Tosi," *The Information*, January 23, 2018.

229   **came with an expiration date**: Erin Griffith, "Inside Airbnb, Employees Eager for Big Payouts Pushed It to Go Public," *New York Times*, September 20, 2019.

229   **Chesky did not endorse**: Brian Chesky, "Open Letter to the Airbnb Community About Building a 21st Century Company," Airbnb, January 25, 2018.

230   **finally hired one**: Airbnb, "Dave Stephenson Joins Airbnb as Chief Financial Officer," November 26, 2018.

233   **she was instrumental**: Becky Peterson and Dakin Campbell, "Meet the Star Women Running Silicon Valley's Largest IPOs at Goldman Sachs, Morgan Stanley, and JPMorgan," *Business Insider*, September 6, 2019.

234   **involve hosts in the process**: Aisha Al-Muslim and Maureen Farrell, "Airbnb Proposes Giving Hosts a Stake in the Company," *Wall Street Journal*, September 21, 2018.

Chapter 23

238   **Airbnb successfully raised $1.5 billion**: Airbnb, Form D, Securities and Exchange Commission, December 4, 2015.

238   **massively inflated valuation**: Telis Demos, "Airbnb Raises $1.5 Billion in One of Largest Private Placements," *Wall Street Journal*, June 26, 2015.

238   **took the unusual step**: Airbnb, "Airbnb Announces Intention to Become a Publicly-Traded Company during 2020," September 19, 2019.

240   **COVID-19 shut down travel**: Leslie Josephs, "Airbnb Halts Beijing Bookings Until May Due to Coronavirus Outbreak," CNBC.com, February 13, 2020.

241   **how management was responding**: Greg Greeley, "A People-to-People Marketplace," Airbnb, March 11, 2020.

Chapter 24

242   **meeting more regularly**: John D. Stoll, "Airbnb Defied the Odds of Startup Success. How Will It Survive a Pandemic?," *Wall Street Journal*, April 17, 2020.

242   **"significant" offers from investors**: Deirdre Bosa and Lauren Feiner, "Airbnb Is Listening to Investment Pitches Despite a Large Cash Pile and Down Market," CNBC.com, March 19, 2020.

243   **Board members were less sanguine**: Olivia Carville, "Airbnb Board Meets to Consider Raising Funds or Buying Assets," Bloomberg News, March 20, 2020.

243   **considered demanding a pledge**: Jean Eaglesham and Kirsten Grind, "Airbnb Paying More Than 10% Interest on $1 Billion Financing Announced Monday," *Wall Street Journal*, April 7, 2020.

245   **Lemkau was there**: @grlemkau (Gregg Lemkau), "Week 2 of #WFH begins from Hawaii. Awesome in concept…unfortunately 'in concept' doesn't happen until the sun comes up 6 hours into the workday. Hope everyone staying safe and healthy," Twitter, March 23, 2020.

247   **dealing with operational issues**: Joshua Franklin and Munsif Vengattil, "Airbnb Suspends Marketing to Save $800 Million, Top Executives Take Pay Cut: Source," Reuters, March 27, 2020.

247   **unveiled several initiatives**: Airbnb, "$250M to Support Hosts Impacted by Cancellations," March 30, 2020.

249   **the company's internal estimate**: Dave Lee, "Airbnb Lowers Internal Valuation by 16% to $26bn," *Financial Times*, April 2, 2020.

249   **Airbnb announced that it had secured**: Airbnb, "Silver Lake, Sixth Street Partners Invest $1 Billion in Airbnb," April 6, 2020.

250   **the completed deal**: Airbnb, "Airbnb Announces $1 Billion Term Loan," April 14, 2020.

Chapter 25

251   **Rumors began to circulate**: Tyler Sonnemaker, "Airbnb Is Holding an All-Hands Meeting and Rumors Are Circulating Among Employees That Layoffs May Be on the Agenda," *Business Insider*, May 5, 2020.

251   **One poster who identified as an Airbnb employee**: sVLN24, "How do u break to ur family that you got laid off?" Teamblind.com, May 5, 2020.

251   **he did announce layoffs**: Airbnb, "A Message from Co-Founder and CEO Brian Chesky," May 5, 2020.

252   **finally announced**: Airbnb, "Airbnb launches Go Near, a New Campaign to Support Domestic Travel," June 11, 2020.

253   **ended the day up**: Jessica Bursztynsky, "Shares of Vroom More Than Double in Public Debut, CNBC.com, June 9, 2020.

254   *The Hero with a Thousand Faces*: Eric Ries, "Out of the Crisis #7, Brian Chesky Part 1: Running Airbnb in Crisis Mode, Being Multi-Stakeholder, and Re-Founding the Company," *Startup Lessons Learned* podcast, June 9, 2020.

254 **put together a short presentation**: Records held by author.

255 **closed its books for the second quarter**: Cory Weinberg, Air Efrati, and Zoe Bernard. "Airbnb Burned Through $1.2 Billion as IPO Loomed," *The Information*, October 7, 2020.

255 **a single day in the previous week**: Airbnb, "For the First Time Since March, Guests Book One Million Nights in One Day," July 14, 2020.

256 **"get back to great hosting"**: Dave Lee, "Airbnb Shakes Up Management and Revives IPO Plans," *Financial Times*, July 16, 2020.

258 **confirmed reports that it had**: "Airbnb Announces Confidential Submission of Draft Registration Statement," PR Newswire, August 19, 2020.

258 **a "terrible time" to enter**: Alix Steel, "Airbnb Timed IPO Right, NYU's Damodaran Says," Bloomberg Television, August 20, 2020.

Chapter 26

260 **The filing put an end**: Vonnie Quinn, "Ackman Thinks Airbnb's First Choice Is to Do an IPO," Bloomberg Television, September 3, 2020.

260 **eighty-two blank check vehicles**: "SPAC Statistics," SPACInsider.

260 **Even Bill Gurley had come around**: Bill Gurley, "Going Public Circa 2020; Door #3: The SPAC," *Above the Crowd*, August 23, 2020.

261 **a valuation north of $30 billion**: Anirban Sen and Joshua Franklin, "Airbnb Aims to Raise Roughly $3 Billion in IPO," Reuters, October 3, 2020.

261 **two shares for every share**: Katie Roof and Olivia Carille, "Airbnb Tells Shareholder Group Board Approves Share Split," Bloomberg News, October 25, 2020.

264 **virtual backgrounds with slides**: Images held by author.

265 **CEO was almost speechless**: Emily Chang, "Airbnb CEO 'Very Humbled' by Stock's Indicated Opening Price," Bloomberg Television, December 10, 2020.

265 **raised his hands in the air**: Image held by author.

Chapter 27

266 **DoorDash had found a key advantage**: Candy Cheng, "DoorDash Won Food Delivery by Seizing the Suburbs and $2 Billion," Bloomberg News, November 9, 2019.

267 **man responsible for that fundraising**: DoorDash, "Prabir Adarkar Joins DoorDash as Chief Financial Officer," July 19, 2018.

268 **a press release stating**: "DoorDash Announces Confidential Submission of Draft Registration Statement for Proposed Initial Public Offering," PR Newswire, February 27, 2020.

268 **DoorDash accounted for 45 percent**: Edison Trends, "2020 Edison Trends U.S. On-Demand Food Delivery Sales Report," May 19, 2020.

268 **up from 28 percent**: Edison Trends, "DoorDash Surpasses Grubhub in National Market Share of Total Consumer Spend with 28% to 27%, with Uber Eats taking 25%," March 11, 2019.

268   **used that momentum**: Dan Primack, "Exclusive: DoorDash Valued at $16 Billion After New Funding Round," *Axios*, June 18, 2020.

Chapter 28

279   **DoorDash closed at $189.51**: Jessica Bursztynsky, "DoorDash Skyrockets in Market Debut, Closes Up 85%," CNBC.com, December 9, 2020.

279   **SEC ratified its decision**: "Order Setting Aside Action by Delegated Authority and Approving a Proposed Rule Change, as Modified by Amendment No. 2, to Amend Chapter One of the Listed Company Manual to Modify the Provisions Relating to Direct Listings," Securities and Exchange Commission, December 22, 2020.

280   **issued a statement**: Allison Herren Lee and Caroline Crenshaw, "Statement on Primary Direct Listings," Securities and Exchange Commission, December 23, 2020.

280   **"game changer for our capital markets"**: Katanga Johnson, "U.S. Approves NYSE Listing Plan to Cut Out Wall Street Middlemen," Reuters, December 22, 2020.

280   **a welcome change to the process**: Sara Eisen, Interview with Stacey Cunningham, CNBC, December 22, 2020.

281   **eventually bring an end**: Kevin Stankiewicz, "Bill Gurley Says Direct Listing Rule Change Will End traditional IPOs," CNBC.com, December 22, 2020.

Epilogue

282   **a "supercycle" for technology listings**: Dakin Campbell, "A Wave of Innovation Is Transforming IPOs. 3 Insiders Lay Out What Changes Are Next—And What Could Bring It All Crashing Down," *Business Insider*, February 6, 2021.

282   **delivering more than $3 billion**: Dealogic data.

284   **handing the reins**: Spotify, "Welcoming Paul Vogel, Spotify's New Chief Financial Officer," January 16, 2020.

284   **board of a blank check company**: MSD Acquisition Corp., "MSD Acquisition Corp. Announces Closing of $575 Million Initial Public Offering of Securities and Full Exercise of Overallotment Option," PR Newswire, March 29, 2021.

284   **announced her departure**: Unity, "Unity Appoints Luis Felipe Visoso as Chief Financial Officer," March 17, 2021.

284   **Gurley stepped back from day-to-day**: Yuliya Chernova and Rolfe Winkler, "Venture Capitalist Bill Gurley Isn't Joining Benchmark's Next Fund," *Wall Street Journal*, April 22, 2020.

INDEX

ABOUT THE AUTHOR

Dakin Campbell writes about Wall Street for *Insider*, where he is the chief finance correspondent. He joined what was then *Business Insider* in 2018, after a decade writing for *Bloomberg News*. He lives near Chapel Hill with his family.